Henry Bascom Corey

Law Without Lawyers

A Compendium of Business And Domestic Law For Popular Use

Henry Bascom Corey

Law Without Lawyers
A Compendium of Business And Domestic Law For Popular Use

ISBN/EAN: 9783744734172

Printed in Europe, USA, Canada, Australia, Japan

Cover: Foto ©Suzi / pixelio.de

More available books at **www.hansebooks.com**

Law Without Lawyers

A COMPENDIUM OF

Business and Domestic Law,

FOR POPULAR USE.

CONTAINING CONDENSED AND CONCISE EXPLANATIONS OF THE GEN-
ERAL LAWS AND THE LAWS OF THE SEVERAL STATES RELATING
TO THE RIGHTS OF PROPERTY, CONTRACTS, DEBTS, PARTNER-
SHIPS, BANKRUPTCY, INSURANCE, CORPORATIONS, MAR-
RIAGE, DIVORCE, ETC., ETC. WITH WHICH ARE
INCLUDED CORRECT COPIES OF ALL LEGAL IN-
STRUMENTS AND FORMS, SUCH AS NOTES,
DEEDS, MORTGAGES, LEASES,
ETC., ETC.

BY HENRY B. COREY, LL. B.,
Member of New York Bar.

NEW YORK:
A. L. BURT.

PREFACE.

THE title of this book indicates to some extent its nature and purpose, and it is hardly necessary to say very much in further explanation. The author has endeavored to meet the wants of large numbers of business men, farmers, and others, and to supply them with information on ordinary business matters in a shape which is at once simple, available, and inexpensive.

The book has been prepared with especial reference to those who have not enjoyed a legal education. It is not intended for the profession, though it is believed that even lawyers, particularly those whose libraries are not extensive, may find it useful for occasional reference. The style and general treatment throughout has been made as simple as the nature of the subject would admit. Technical law terms and legal phraseology have been either omitted, explained or translated into ordinary language. No pains have been spared to make the presentation of each topic clear, accurate and popular in the best sense of the word, a task, the difficulty of which will be appreciated by those who have experienced the strength of the temptation to fall into the use of technical language. Considerable thought and care have been expended upon the method of arrangement. The value of any work of this nature depends largely upon convenience and facility of reference. It is with this idea in view that each paragraph has its subject designated in heavy type, a system which permits the reader to ascertain the contents of a chapter with great ease, and to find the particular subject of which he may be in search without delay.

The author offers his book to the public trusting that it will be of service to those for whose benefit it was especially written.

H. B. C.

CONTENTS.

Business and Domestic Law.

CHAPTER I.

CONTRACTS.

Form of Contracts—Contracts in Writing—Who can Contract—Consideration—Implied when Seal Used—Subscription—Assent — Construction of Contracts — Performance—Time of Performance—Constitutional Provision—Damages—Specific Performance—Form of Builder's Contract.

A CONTRACT is an agreement between two or more persons to do or not to do a particular thing. It is essential to a contract that the parties assent to it, and that there be a consideration. A promise to do something gratuitously, or without consideration, is not a contract, and cannot be enforced.

Form of Contracts. Contracts may be made verbally, in writing, or in writing under seal. Most contracts are good without a writing ; some must be in writing; and others require a seal to make them valid. Contracts under seal are known as contracts of specialty. A separate contract or agreement in a sealed instrument is called a covenant. Deeds, mortgages.

leases—all instruments concerning real-estate, must be under seal.

Contracts in Writing. There are some contracts which are expressly required to be written, and which, if not, are absolutely void. These are: First, contracts for the sale of land; second, leases for more than one year; third, contracts in regard to marriage settlements; fourth, guaranties, or promises to pay the debt of another if he does not; fifth, contracts which require more than one year for their execution; sixth, contracts for the sale of goods of the value of fifty dollars or upward.

Many other contracts are frequently put in writing for the purpose of avoiding controversy.

Who can make Contracts? Infants or those under twenty-one years of age, cannot make contracts except for the necessaries of life. The contracts of any person of unsound mind are void. Married women were not formerly allowed to make contracts, but in almost all the States they now have power to contract so as to bind their own separate property. They cannot bind their husband by their contracts, except for necessaries.

Consideration. Every contract must have a consideration in order to make it valid. By the consideration is meant the promise in consideration of which the other promise is made. One party must promise to do something as an equivalent to the other's promise.

A *valuable* consideration consists of money or something having value.

A *good* consideration would be relationship or blood and affection.

Contracts founded on an illegal or impossible consideration, as where the promise is to do some illegal or impossible thing, are void.

The fact that the consideration is inadequate does not as a rule affect the validity of the contract. A party may sell his property, for instance, for as little as he pleases, but he cannot afterward rescind the contract on that ground.

Implied when Seal used. A consideration is always implied in a written contract under seal. If a consideration is acknowledged in such a contract, as the receipt of one dollar, the fact that there was a consideration cannot be denied by any party to the contract, even though the one dollar was never offered or received. The amount of the consideration, however, is always open to evidence.

Subscription. A subscription to a church or a charity is generally a promise without a consideration, and cannot be enforced against the subscriber if he declines to fulfill it. If, however, he has signed a subscription paper in which the subscription of each person is made the consideration of the others, the contract is valid and he may be compelled to pay, as in the case of any debt.

Assent. All the parties must assent to the contract. They must all understand its terms in the same sense. A mutual misunderstanding or mistake of fact under which the parties enter into a contract, is a ground for declaring it void, as not having the assent of all the parties.

By assent is meant the agreement or meeting of the minds.   If one man makes another an offer, he may withdraw it at any time before the other accepts, but if the acceptance takes place before the withdrawal there is a valid contract which is binding on both parties. But the acceptance must not change or vary from the offer.   There is then no assent and no contract unless the offerer agrees to accept the change.

The acceptance or assent of one person to the terms of a contract may be inferred from his profiting by it in cases where there was no express acceptance.

Construction of Contracts.   Contracts, written and oral, should be so construed as to carry out the original intention of the parties.   The intention must however be derived from the contract itself, and the parties cannot vary or explain it by verbal evidence. Words are taken in their ordinary sense and meaning. Technical terms will be construed in their technical signification.   Custom and usage will have some effect on the construction of many terms.

Performance.   The conditions or promises of the contract must be performed by the party in order to enable him to compel the payment of the money or other consideration.

Moreover, he must perform the contract in full before he can recover anything.   A part performance does not entitle him to a proportionate part of the compensation; he can recover nothing until all the work is done. When the failure to complete the work or perform the contract in full was not the fault of the party who had agreed to do it, he may then recover the value of what he has done. If he has been prevented wrongfully by the other party from completing the work, he is entitled not only to compensation for what he has done, but to damages for the breach of contract by the other party. Mere readiness to perform is always a sufficient ground of recovery where the other party breaks the contract by unwarranted refusal.

In many contracts, especially in building contracts, the consideration is usually payable in installments, a certain sum when a certain amount of work is done, and so on. When the work specified is completed, the installment is due, whether the entire contract is performed or not.

Time of Performance. The contract must be performed within the time specified, or within a reasonable time, if no time is mentioned in the contract. If the work is not completed or the contract performed within the time, there is no obligation on the other party to pay, provided the question of time is actually essential. If time is not especially important and essential, the obligation to pay will remain, although a deduction may be made for the delay.

Sickness or anything which renders performance an impossibility, is an excuse for non-performance or delay

Constitutional Provision. Under the Constitution of the United States no law can be passed impairing the obligation of a contract or affecting vested rights of property.

Damages. For the breach of a contract the remedy is generally an action at law for damages. The measure or amount of damages to be given is a fair compensation for the injury done. If no actual loss is incurred only nominal damages, as six cents, can be recovered. In some cases where the amount of damages may be uncertain, the parties often agree on a specified sum to be paid by one party to the other if the contract is broken. This is called "liquidated damages." If the amount of damage is certain, however, the parties cannot fix upon any sum in excess of the real damage as a penalty. The penalty will be reduced to the amount of the real damage.

Specific Performance. In most contracts a party cannot be be compelled to perform the contract against his will, but only damages can be recovered for his refusal. There are a few contracts, however, which will be enforced specifically if either party refuses to fulfill. In a contract for the sale of land, for instance, if the owner refuses to deliver the deed, he may be compelled to do so by law. In like manner the purchaser may be compelled to take the premises and pay the contract price. In both these cases the injured parties may, if they prefer, sue for damages. Either remedy is open for them.

The cases in which specific performance is decreed by a court of equity are those where there is no adequate remedy at law in money or damages.

FORM OF BUILDER'S CONTRACT.

ARTICLES OF AGREEMENT, made this ——— day of ——— 188—, between John Doe, of the city of ———, party of the first part, and Richard Roe, of the same place, party of the second part.

First. The said party of the second part doth hereby, for himself, his heirs, executors or administrators, covenant, promise and agree to and with the said party of the first part, his executors, administrators, or assigns, that he, the said party of the second part, his executors or administrators, shall and will, for the consideration hereafter mentioned, on or before the ——— day of ———, 188—, well and sufficiently erect and finish a building upon the lot (or field or farm) situated ——————— and known as ——————— agreeably to the drawings and specifications made by ——— ———, architect, and signed by the said parties and hereunto annexed, within the time aforesaid, in a good, workmanlike and substantial manner, to the satisfaction and under the direction of the said ——— ——— to be testified by writing or certificate under the hand of the said ——— ———, and also shall and will provide such good, proper and sufficient materials of all kinds whatsoever, as shall be proper and sufficient for the completing and finishing all the brick-work, mason-work and other works of the said building mentioned in the plans and specifications, for the sum of ——— ——— dollars.

And the said party of the first part doth hereby, for himself, his heirs, executors and administrators, covenant, promise and agree, to and with the said party of the second part, his executors and administrators, that he, the said party of the first part, his executors and administrators, shall and will, in consideration of the covenants and agreements being strictly performed and kept by the said party of the second part, as specified, well and truly pay or to cause to be paid unto the said party of the second part, his executors, administrators or assigns, the sum of ——— dollars, lawful money of the United States of America, in manner following; that is to say:

1. When (so much work, specifying what) is done ——— dollars

2. When ——— is done, ——— dollars.

3. When ——— is done, ——— dollars, etc., etc.

Lastly, when all the said work is entirely completed, according to the plans and specifications, ——— dollars.

Provided that in each of the said cases a certificate shall be obtained from and signed by the said architect.

And it is further agreed between the parties:

First. The contractor, at his own costs and charges, is to provide all manner of materials and labor, scaffolding, implements, molds, models and cartage of every description, for the due performance of the several erections.

Second. Should the owner, at any time during the progress of the work, request any alteration, deviations, additions, or omissions, from the said contract, he shall be at liberty to do so, and the same shall in no way effect or make void the contract, but will be added or deducted from the amount of the contract, as the case may be, by a fair and reasonable valuation.

Third. Should the contractor at any time during the progress of the work, refuse or neglect to supply a sufficiency of materials or workmen, the owner shall have the power to provide materials and workmen, after three days notice in writing being given, to finish the said works, and the expense shall be deducted from the amount of the contract.

Fourth. Should any dispute arise respecting the true construction or meaning of the drawings or specifications, the same shall be decided by the architect, and his decision shall be final and conclusive; but should any dispute arise respecting the true value of the extra work, or of the work omitted, the same shall be valued by two competent persons, one employed by the owner, and the other by the contractor, and those two shall have power to name an umpire whose decision shall be binding on all parties.

Fifth. The owner shall not in any manner be liable or account able for any loss or damage that shall or may happen to the said works, or any part or parts thereof respectively, or for any of the materials or other things used and employed in finishing and completing the same (loss or damage by fire excepted).

In witness whereof the said parties to these presents have hereunto set their hands and seals, the day and year above written.

        Signed,   (Name of owner.)   [Seal.]

                    (Name of contractor.)   [Seal.]

In presence of
(Name of witness.)

CHAPTER II.

ILLEGAL CONTRACTS.

What Are Illegal—Contracts in Restraint of Trade—
General Restraint — Contracts in Restraint of Mar-
riage—Restriction in Will—As to Widow—Marriage
Brokers — Gambling Contracts and Wagers — All
Securities Void — Sunday Laws — Hebrews — Closing
Stores — Liquor Saloons — Legal Papers — Usury—
Penalties of Usury—Form of Contract Immaterial—
Compound Interest not Usury—Notes—Difference in
Laws—Assignment of Salary by Public Officer—As-
signment of Pension—Bribery—Compounding a Felony
—Summary of Usury Laws.

THERE are certain contracts which are illegal and
void from the beginning, even though the parties expressly assented to the terms and the consideration
passed between them.   They are void for the reason
that it would be against public policy and the best
interests of society to allow them to be made or enforced in a court of law.

What are Illegal?   These illegal contracts are
those in restraint of trade or of marriage, contracts
to corrupt legislation, gambling contracts and wagers, contracts made on Sunday, contracts to pay
usurious interest, and, generally speaking, contracts

to do an illegal or immoral thing of any nature whatever.

Of course it is impossible to altogether prevent people from making such agreements. A party to an illegal contract may perform it if he sees fit. There is no criminal punishment in most of these cases. But he is not bound to do it. The law will not compel him to perform, even though the consideration money has been paid to him; and, generally, it would not compel him to pay it back.

Contracts in Restraint of Trade. It is for the interest of the public that trade and commerce should flourish, and that there should be competition between merchants, and an agreement by a man not to engage in a particular business, or to give it up entirely and never undertake it again, in order perhaps that the other party may have all the business to himself without a rival competitor, is a contract in restraint of trade, and void. In spite of his promise, he may go on just the same, notwithstanding that he may have received a large sum of money for his promise. And the other party cannot recover damages.

General Restraint. This rule is limited, however, to contracts which are in *general* restraint of trade. A broad agreement *never* to practice the profession or trade at any place, is always void. But a promise not to practice it in a particular town or county, if made for a valuable consideration, is binding on both parties. It is a contract only in partial restraint of trade, and such contracts are allowed. Yet, to be valid, it must be limited to one locality. A promise which takes in the whole State, such as an agreement not to run a steam-boat on any of the waters of California, cannot be enforced. But a contract by one physician with another not to practice medicine within twelve miles of a town, is valid. A merchant may sell out his business to another, and may lawfully promise the purchaser that he will not engage in the same business anywhere in the county. If he breaks this contract, he is liable for damages.

Contracts in Restraint of Marriage. Marriage, like trade, is regarded as for the welfare of society, and is encouraged by the law. Contracts, either by a man or a woman, not to marry, are void and of no effect. Neither party is bound. But a contract not to marry a particular person or class of persons, not being in general restraint of marriage, is good. A father, for instance, may deed property to his son on condition that he does not marry certain persons whom he names, and that if he does then the property shall go over to some one else. This is a valid contract.

Restriction in Will. This partial restriction may also be made by a will, and if the legatee marries the person named or referred to he loses the legacy. But even in a will this restriction must be only partial and not general. A condition that the testator's daughter shall *never* marry is void, and she may keep the legacy even if she does.

As to Widow.   An exception is made in regard to the widow.   A condition in the will of her husband that she shall never marry, and that, if she does, she is to lose the legacy, is valid.   A husband is regarded as having a special and peculiar right to make this restriction.

"Marriage Brokers."   There is a class of contracts more common in England than in America, known as "marriage brokerage contracts."   These are contracts where a person who wishes to marry a wealthy heiress for example, offers to pay another a sum of money on condition that the other will use his or her influence in pressing the suit.   The contract is void as against public policy, go-betweens and match-makers, especially the mercenary kind, being offensive to sound morals.   Even if the employe succeeds in effecting the marriage the other party to the contract can recover nothing.

Gambling Contracts and Wagers.   Wagers or bets depending on chance, as a race, a game, or a lottery, or any contingent event, are unlawful, and all contracts on account of money wagered are void.

This is generally the law throughout the United States, but the laws of the various States differ very much.   In Louisiana, lotteries are permitted and tickets may be freely bought and sold.   By the laws of Congress, however, it is unlawful to send such tickets through the mails, and persons doing so may be punished.

In most wagers the stakes are deposited with a

third person or stakeholder, to await the event. The stakeholder is liable if he pays over the money to the winner. The loser may, in some States, sue both the stakeholder and the winner for the amount he wagered. In New York the winner, if convicted of cheating, is guilty of a misdemeanor.

All Securities Void. All notes, checks, mortgages, or other securities, given to pay or secure a gambling debt, are absolutely void. Such notes or checks are void, even in the hands of *bona fide* holders who have bought them at their full value, in ignorance of the facts. This is an exception to the ordinary rules of negotiable paper.

Sunday Contracts. All contracts made on Sunday are void, except contracts which concern what are known as "works of charity and necessity."

It is perfectly lawful to sell food and medicine on Sunday, for these are necessities, but not other articles which may just as well be sold on other days. Contracts of sale of such articles are void, and if the purchaser refuse to pay for the goods he cannot be sued for the contract price, but only for the reasonable value which may be and often is much below the price.

Deeds and notes made on Sunday are void. This may sometimes be avoided by dating the document ahead as on Monday.

A will made on Sunday, if the testator is in fear of sudden death, is valid, but not if he is in robust health and could make it just as well some other day.

Under the influence of modern ideas in regard to the Sabbath, however, there is a tendency in the courts to hold a will made on Sunday valid in every case.

Hebrews. By the statutes of several States the Sunday laws do not apply to Hebrews who observe Saturday as their Sabbath.

Closing Stores. While contracts of sale on Sunday are void, there is now no compulsion by the State for merchants to close their stores. They may keep them open as on week days if they please, though they cannot compel their employes to work, as Sunday is a legal holiday. They cannot be indicted, or fined or punished in any way for so doing. The Sunday laws in their criminal phase are practically a thing of the past. They are no longer enforced by the courts with severity or strictness.

Liquor Saloons. Liquor saloons and bar-rooms, however, are very generally compelled to close on Sunday, but this is on the ground of public policy.

Legal Papers. Legal papers and process, such as a summons or subpœna, cannot be served on Sunday. If they are, the person on whom they are served may disregard them with impunity.

Usury. Usury is the taking of unlawful interest for the use of money. The legal rates of interest are fixed by the laws of the State. In the Eastern States the rate is usually six per cent., while in the West, where money is less plentiful, it runs up to eight or twelve.

The usury laws differ very much. Many States have have abolished them altogether and permit the parties to contract for any rate of interest they may agree upon. These States are Arkansas, Connecticut, Florida, Rhode Island and South Carolina.

Sometimes the law of the State establishes a certain rate as the lawful interest, but provides that the parties may agree *in writing* to a higher rate, which may be unlimited, as in California, Nevada and Massachusetts, or limited to a certain rate, as in most of the Western States.

Penalties of Usury. Other States, particularly New York and Virginia, provide severe penalties for usury. In New York, the contract, if tinged with usury in the slightest degree, is wholly void. The creditor cannot recover of the borrower either legal interest or even the principal. He loses the entire debt. Mortgages, notes and bills of exchange, if given under circumstances amounting to usury, are void, even if transferred to an innocent holder for value. The debtor cannot be compelled to repay a dollar of what he has borrowed, and can demand back his securities if he has given any. A call loan on collateral may, however, bear any rate of interest if the loan amounts to $5,000 or over.

Form of Contract Immaterial. The form that a usurious contract takes is immaterial, if there is an intention to evade the law and take more than the legal rate. One method is to make a contract for legal interest and then take a bonus or additional sum beside, or for the debtor, at the time of the loan, to pay back part of the money. Another method is for the creditor to sell the debtor worthless goods at an exorbitant price. Whether these contracts are usurious or not depends upon intention. A mere mistake, as by writing seven per cent. as interest on a note instead of six, if this was done innocently, under the impression that seven per cent. was the legal rate, is not usury and does not make the contract void.

Compound Interest not Usury. The taking of compound interest is not usury; neither is the discounting of notes by a bank, although the bank really gets more than legal interest, as it deducts the interest for the time the note has to run from the loan and yet receives full interest for that time from the maker of the note when it falls due.

Notes. If a note falls due and the holder agrees not to protest it or sue upon it for a certain time, and in consideration of this forbearance receives a sum of money, this sum must not be greater than the legal interest on the note for that time; otherwise this will be a usurious contract and void. Such an arrangement moreover has the effect of discharging the sureties and indorsers from liability.

It is not usurious to buy a note or a mortgage for less than its face value. The purchaser can enforce it against the maker or the mortgagor for the face value, however, without reference to the amount he paid for it.

Difference in Laws. Where the legal rates of interest in two States having usury laws differ, it is clear that a contract made in one State (the one having the higher rate) would be void if had been made in the other State. But a contract may be enforced anywhere without regard to where it was made, and if valid where it was made it is valid everywhere. Therefore a contract for ten per cent. interest made in Massachusetts would not be usurious or void in New York, although the rate there is only six per cent. The creditor can sue the debtor in the New York courts and recover the principal and the ten per cent. interest besides.

Assignment of Salary by Public Officers. There are certain contracts, which, although usually valid, are not allowed to be made by persons holding public or political offices. A Judge, or Governor, or Mayor, etc.. cannot assign his salary, which is to come due in the future, in payment of a debt, or as security for a loan to him. Notwithstanding the assignment, the officer may collect his salary, and the Comptroller or Treasurer of the State or the United States is obliged to pay it only to him and to no one else. The reason why the law refuses to permit this assignment is that the official, if deprived of his salary, might be tempted to relieve his necessities by peculation to the injury of the public. (He may, however, assign whatever of his salary is owing to him, but as yet unpaid.)

Assignment of Pensions. A pension granted to a soldier, or his widow, or children, or mother, cannot be assigned, for this would defeat the very object of the Pension Law, which is to provide a proper and continuous support for such persons. To allow it would be to open the door to the oppressing and defrauding of those who from poverty and other reasons are not perfectly able to take care of themselves. The law acts for them as a guardian.

Bribery. Any contract, which directly or indirectly tends to corrupt legislation, is absolutely void. A lobbyist, even if successful, cannot recover the promised reward from his employer, much less a Senator, or a member of Congress, or of a State Legislature, who is promised a money, or other valuable consideration, for his influence or vote. Such a contract, moreover, is a criminal offence for which a legislator may be impeached, and for which any person concerned may be indicted and punished.

Compounding a Felony. Any person who agrees to take money or value for refraining from exposing, accusing, or prosecuting another person who has committed a felony, such as murder, or theft, or seduction, is guilty of a crime. All such contracts are absolutely void.

The following is a summary of the usury laws of the several States:

ALABAMA.—The rate of interest is eight per cent. per annum. The principal only can be recovered by law on usurious contracts when usury is pleaded.

ARIZONA.—Rate of interest, ten per cent. But the parties may agree in writing for any rate.

ARKANSAS.—Rate of interest, six per cent. The parties may

contract for any rate not exceeding ten per cent.   Usurious contracts are void, both as to principal and interest.

CALIFORNIA.—Rate of interest, seven per cent.   The parties may agree in writing upon a different rate and for the payment of compound interest.

COLORADO.—Rate of interest, ten per cent.   No usury laws.

CONNECTICUT.—Rate of interest, six per cent.   No usury laws.

DAKOTA.—Rate of interest, seven per cent.   The parties may contract for a higher rate, not to exceed twelve per cent.   Penalty for usury is forfeiture of the entire interest.   Usury is also a misdemeanor, punishable with a fine of $500, or six months' imprisonment, or both.

DELAWARE.—Rate of interest, six per cent.   Penalty for usury is the forfeiture of a sum equal to the money lent.

DISTRICT OF COLUMBIA.—Rate of interest, six per cent.   The parties may stipulate in writing for ten per cent., or less.   Penalty for usury is the forfeiture of the whole interest.   If the interest is paid it may be recovered back by the borrower within one year after payment.

FLORIDA.—Rate of interest, eight per cent.   No usury laws.

GEORGIA.—Rate of interest, seven per cent.   The parties may agree in writing for any rate up to eight per cent.   Penalty for usury is the forfeiture of the excess of legal interest.

IDAHO.—Rate of interest, ten per cent.   The parties may agree in writing for any rate not exceeding one and a half per cent. a month.   Penalty for usury is three times the amount of usurious interest ; also a fine of $300, or six months' imprisonment, or both.

ILLINOIS.—Rate of interest, six per cent.   The parties may agree in writing for any rate up to eight per cent.   Penalty for usury is forfeiture of entire interest.

INDIANA.—Rate of interest, six per cent.   The parties may agree in writing up to eight per cent.   Penalty for usury is forfeiture of usurious excess.

IOWA.—Rate of interest, six per cent.   Parties may agree in writing for any rate up to ten per cent.   Penalty of usury is forfeiture of ten per cent. of the amount of the contract to the school fund.

KANSAS.—Rate of interest, seven per cent. May stipulate in writing for not more than twelve per cent. Creditor cannot recover usurious excess.

KENTUCKY.—Rate of interest, six per cent. Contracts for higher rate void only for excess.

LOUISIANA.—Rate of interest, five per cent. May stipulate for eight per cent.

MAINE.—Rate of interest, six per cent. Any other rate may be agreed on in writing. No usury laws.

MARYLAND.—Rate of interest, six per cent. Usurious excess is forfeited.

MASSACHUSETTS.—Rate of interest, six per cent. Any rate of interest may be contracted for in writing. No usury laws.

MICHIGAN.—Rate of interest, seven per cent. May contract in writing for any rate not exceeding ten per cent. Usurious excess cannot be recovered.

MINNESOTA.—Rate of interest, seven per cent. May agree in writing for as high as ten per cent. The penalty for usury is the forfeiture of the entire interest.

MISSISSIPPI.—Rate of interest, six per cent. The parties may contract for not more than ten. Excess cannot be recovered.

MISSOURI.—Rate of interest, six per cent. May agree in writing for any rate not exceeding ten. In case of usury, creditor forfeits ten per cent. to common schools.

MONTANA.—Rate of interest, ten per cent. Parties may stipulate for any amount. No usury laws.

NEBRASKA.—Rate of interest, seven per cent. May agree as high as ten per cent. The penalty for usury is the forfeiture of the entire interest.

NEVADA.—Rate of interest, ten per cent. Parties may contract for any rate.

NEW HAMPSHIRE.—Rate of interest, six per cent. Penalty for usury is three times tne amount of the usurious excess.

NEW JERSEY.—Rate of interest, six per cent. In case of usury all the interest is forfeited.

NEW MEXICO.—Rate of interest, six per cent. Parties may agree upon any rate, not exceeding twelve per cent.

NEW YORK.—Rate of interest, six per cent. In case of usury the creditor cannot recover either principal or interest. Call loans of $5,000 or more on collateral security may bear any rate.

NORTH CAROLINA.—Rate of interest, six per cent. Eight per cent may be stipulated for. Penalty for usury is forfeiture of entire interest.

OHIO.—Rate of interest, six per cent. Parties may contract in writing for eight per cent. In case of usury recovery is limited to principal and legal interest.

OREGON.—Rate of interest, eight per cent. May agree upon ten per cent. Punishment of usury is the forfeiture of original sum lent to the common school fund.

PENNSYLVANIA.—Rate of interest, six per cent. Usurious interest cannot be collected.

RHODE ISLAND.—Rate of interest, six per cent. Parties may stipulate for any rate.

SOUTH CAROLINA.—Rate of interest, seven per cent. May agree on any rate not exceeding ten per cent.

TENNESSEE.—Rate of interest, six per cent. Contracting for usury does not forfeit the actual debt.

TEXAS.—Rate of interest, eight per cent. Ten per cent. may be stipulated. Penalty for usury is forfeiture of all the interest.

UTAH.—Rate of interest, ten per cent. Parties may agree upon any rate. No usury laws.

VERMONT.—Rate of interest, six per cent. Usurious excess is forfeited.

VIRGINIA.—Rate of interest, six per cent. Lenders forfeit all interest in case of usury.

WASHINGTON TERRITORY.—Rate of interest, ten per cent. Any rate agreed upon in writing is valid.

WEST VIRGINIA.—Rate of interest, six per cent. Usurious excess cannot be recovered.

WISCONSIN.—Rate of interest, seven per cent. May contract in writing for ten per cent. Usury causes forfeiture of all the interest.

WYOMING.—Rate of interest, twelve per cent. Any rate may be stipulated in writing.

PROVINCE OF QUEBEC.—Rate of interest, six per cent.; but any rate may be agreed upon.

PROVINCE OF ONTARIO.—Rate of interest, six per cent. Parties may agree to pay any rate, but banks cannot recover more than seven per cent.

CHAPTER III.

DEBTS AND THEIR PAYMENT.

*What is a Debt—How Debts Must be Paid— What is Money
—Bank Bills Not Legal Tender—Effect of Tender—
What May be Tendered—Payment in Notes, Checks,
etc.— When Check to be Presented—Check Without
Any Deposit—Part Payment—Accord and Satisfac-
tion— Where, When and to Whom Payment to be
Made—To Creditor Personally—To Assignee of
Insolvent—No Right to Demand Receipt—Money in
Letters—Debt Recoverable Everywhere—Appropri-
ation of Payments—Debtor Has First Right, Then
Creditor—If Neither Makes it Law— When One
Debt is Secured—Interest—After Maturity—Rule as
to Partial Payments—Form of a Release of a Debt.*

THE word "debt" applies to every contract obligation to pay a sum of money.   A contract of
itself does not create a debt.   The obligation to pay,
which constitutes the debt, does not arise until the
work is performed, the goods sold, etc., in short,
not until everything has been done by the other
party which he was required to do.

Moreover, a debt refers only to money.   A contract of exchange or barter does not create a debt.
A debt, also, is something fixed and certain, or
capable of being made so, and would not include

an uncertain liability to pay damages for injuries caused by negligence or any other wrongful act. If a verdict is given and a judgment rendered for a certain sum, this would make the party a judgment debtor.

How Debts Must Be Paid. All debts must be paid in money. The debtor has no right to offer goods equivalent to or greater in value than the debt, and the creditor can refuse to accept them. If he does choose to take them in payment, however, the debt is paid.

What is Money? Money is anything which is provided by the laws of Congress to be "legal tender," this phrase meaning whatever may legally be tendered in payment of the debt. It includes gold and silver coin, and United States Treasury notes, and nothing else. Foreign coin and notes are not legal tender. Silver "trade dollars" are not legal tender.

Bank Bills Not. Bank bills, though they pass current as money, are not legal tender. They are not money in the strict sense of the word. A creditor has the right to refuse these bills and to demand either coin or Treasury notes.

Effect of Tender. The effect of tender by the debtor of legal tender money to the creditor and a refusal on his part to accept it, is to stop the running of interest on the debt, and if the creditor sues, he can, of course, recover the debt, but he must pay the costs of the action.

What May be Tendered. If, however, the debtor only tenders National Bank bills, or gold certificates, or silver certificates, and the creditor refuses to accept, interest continues to run on the debt until it is paid in legal tender, and if the creditor sues, the debtor must pay the debt, the interest. and the costs of the action.

Payments in Notes, Checks, Etc. A payment in counterfeit notes or coin is a nullity. Payment by the debtor's own promissory note or check does not of itself cancel the debt, unless expressly so agreed; and the creditor can sue either on the old debt, or the note or check, at his option.

When Check to be Presented. A check must be presented at the bank by the creditor who receives it, within a reasonable time, usually twenty-four hours. If he does not so present it, and the bank fails, the debtor is discharged.

Note or Check of Third Person. Payment by the note or check of a third person is, if accepted, a discharge of the debt, and the subsequent insolvency of that person will not revive the debt. The debtor will, of course, be liable, as indorser, if he receives proper notice of protest and non-payment. But if he indorses without recourse or simply transfers without indorsing he is not liable.

Check Without any Deposit. A man who buys goods, and at the time of purchasing, draws a check for the amount on a bank where he has no deposit, is guilty of fraud and felony, and is liable to indictment for the crime.

Part Payment. Payment in full, of course, extinguishes the debt. But a part payment, or a payment of less than the full amount, does not extinguish the debt, even if it is so expressly agreed. The creditor may take the money, promising to forgive the balance, and then, in spite of his promise, may sue the debtor and recover the remainder of the debt. There was no consideration for his promise, as he only received what he was before entitled to. The only method of making a part payment effectual in discharging the debt is for the creditor to execute a release under seal.

Accord and Satisfaction. If, however, in addition to the part payment, or without it, the debtor gives his creditor something to which he is not entitled, such as a watch or a book, no matter how slight its value, and the creditor receives it, in full payment, the debt is now entirely discharged. This is called an " accord and satisfaction."

When, Where and to Whom the Payment Must be Made. The payment must be made on the day when it falls due, and if any place has been specified, at that place. If no place was mentioned, it must be made at the creditor's office or residence, or wherever he is. It is the duty of the debtor to find his creditor, and not of the creditor to seek the debtor. If the creditor be in Europe or China, the debtor, legally, is bound to follow him thither, or else continue to pay the interest on the debt up to the time when the creditor returns, or the payment is finally made.

To Creditor Personally. The money must be paid to the creditor personally, or to his agent or attorney authorized to receive it. An attorney-at-law, however, has no general right to receive money for his client, except in connection with some suit or matter in which he is retained. If the debt is owing to a firm, the payment may be made to any of the partners. It may be made to a cashier or business manager, or any person who by the usage of the business is accustomed to receive it. It cannot ordinarily be made to the wife or son of the creditor, and if these persons receive it, and squander it, or refuse to deliver it up to the creditor, the latter may compel the debtor to pay it over again. A debtor is protected, however, when he pays the money to a person having the apparent authority to receive it, such as an intruder who might occupy the cashier's seat in the latter's absence.

To Assignee of Insolvent. When an individual or a firm has made an assignment for the benefit of creditors, debts due that individual or firm must now be paid only to the assignee. If a receiver has been appointed, they must be paid to the receiver. The debtor, however, must have notice of the assignment, which may be given him by mailing him a notice of the facts, or by publication in the newspapers. If he does not receive the notice, he is justified in paying the money to the partners or any of them. If he pays the money, after he receives the notice, to a partner, the assignee or receiver may compel him to pay it over again to him.

No Right to Demand Receipt. The debtor at the time of paying the debt is not entitled to demand a receipt. It is a mere matter of courtesy. If the creditor refuses the receipt, the only remedy for the debtor is to bring a witness with him.

Money in Letters. Money sent by letter is at the risk of the sender, unless the creditor requests or directs payment in that way.

Debt Recoverable Everywhere. A valid debt can be recovered anywhere in any country or State, no matter where it was contracted, if the courts of that country or State have jurisdiction of the persons of the creditor and debtor, or the property of debtor.

Appropriation of Payments. Where a debtor owes one person several distinct debts, and makes a payment of money not large enough in amount to day them all, it becomes a question as to which debt or debts it shall be applied or appropriated.

Debtor has First Right, then Creditor. The debtor has the right to pay any debt he pleases, and if he directs the creditor to cancel a particular debt, the creditor must do so. If the debtor makes no application of the payment, the creditor may appropriate it to any of the debts he pleases. This could be

shown by entries in his books, or by proof of a statement of his intention to the debtor. If one of the
debts is outlawed or barred by the statute of limitation, the creditor may nevertheless apply the payment to that debt, though he cannot regard it as a
part payment so as to revive the debt and give him a
right to sue for the balance.

If Neither Makes it, How ? If neither debtor or
creditor make any distinct appropriation of the payment, as evidenced by entries or statements made at
the time or contemporaneous with the payment, the
court of law in which the action is brought will determine the matter as justice would seem to require
under the circumstances.

When the amount paid satisfies just one debt and
no other it will be presumed that the intention was
to pay that debt. When the debts consist of the
items of an open account, it will be applied to the
earliest items. The interest will be extinguished
first, and then the principal.

When One Debt is Secured. When one debt is
secured by a mortgage or deposit of stocks, or bonds,
or any collateral security, and the others are not,
a general indefinite payment would be applied to the
oldest of the unsecured debts. Other creditors could
not insist on having it appropriated to the secured
debt, so as to increase the debtor's assets.

Interest. A debt does not bear interest until it is
due, unless so provided in the contract. A promissory note which makes no mention of interest carries

none. But if the note is not paid at maturity, interest is computed at the legal rate from the expiration of the three days of grace until the debt is paid.

After Maturity. If the note or debt bears a rate of interest less than the legal rate, as four per cent. when the legal rate is six, the interest after maturity is calculated at six per cent. and not at four.

Rule as to Partial Payments. When a partial payment is made on a debt bearing interest, the rule of business and of law is that the payment is not deducted from the debt so as to cause the interest to run only on the balance, unless the amount of the part payment equals or exceeds the amount of accrued interest up to the time of the payment

FORM OF GENERAL RELEASE.

To all to whom these presents shall come.

GREETING: Know ye, that I, John Doe, of the city of Chicago, State of Illinois, party of the first part, for and in consideration of the sum of one hundred dollars, lawful money of the United States of America, to me in hand paid by Richard Roe, party of the second part, the receipt whereof is hereby acknowledged, have remised, released, and forever discharged, and by these presents do for my heirs, excutors, and administrators, remise, release and forever discharge the said Richard Roe, his heirs, executors and administrators, of and from all, and all manner of action and actions, cause and causes of actions, suits, debts, dues, sums of money, accounts, reckonings, bonds, bills, specialties, covenants, contracts, controversies, agreements, promises, variances, trespasses, damages, judgments, extents, executions, claims and demands whatsoever in law or in equity, which against the said Richard Roe I ever had, now have, or which my heirs, executors or administrators, hereafter can, shall or may have for, upon, or by reason of any matter, cause or thing whatsoever from the beginning of the world to the date of these presents.

In witness whereof, I have hereunto set my hand and seal the first day of July, in the year of our Lord, one thousand eight hundred and eighty five.

Sealed and delivered }
in the presence of   }   JOHN DOE.   [Seal].
[Name of witness.]

CHAPTER IV.

STATUTE OF LIMITATIONS

Different Periods for Different Debts— When Period Be-gins—Open Accounts—Installments—Commencement of Action—A New Promise—Part Payment— When Creditor out of State— When Debtor out of State—Debts in Another State—Other Exceptions—Where Debtor Dies—Summary of the Laws of the Different States.

AFTER a certain number of years, debts and claims of every description can no longer be collected or re-covered. They are then said to be "outlawed." The period of time for which a debt remains good varies very much in the different States, depending on the provisions of the statutes of each State. These laws are called "statutes of limitation," because they limit the time within which an action must be brought to enforce the debt.

Different Periods for Different Debts. A debt which has been put into judgment is generally good for twenty years. Contracts under seal are usually good for a longer period than contracts not under seal. Thus in New York an ordinary promissory note is outlawed in six years; but if a seal was affix-ed to the note it would be good for twenty years. Such a note, however, is not negotiable.

Grounds of these Statutes. The ground on which these statutes is based is that the necessities of trade demand that the creditor should collect his debts speedily, and should not be allowed to carelessly wait many years; because the person sued as debtor may in the lapse of time have forgotten the circumstances, or lost his vouchers, or his witnesses may have died, or moved away into another State.

When Period Begins. The period of limitation begins to run when the debt becomes due; that is, whenever the creditor has a right to sue.

Open Accounts. In an ordinary open account the time is calculated from the date of entry of each item. If a balance is struck, and the account is rendered and accepted by the debtor, the period runs from such acceptance. If the accounts are mutual, as where both parties are merchants and each furnishes goods to the other and each makes entries against the other in his books, the time runs from the entry of the last item.

On a promissory note the time is calculated not from the date of the note, but from the date of the expiration of the three days of grace.

Installments. If money is payable in installments, the time runs against such installment from the day when it falls due. If there is a provision to the effect that if any installment is not paid, all the succeeding installments are to become due at once, then the whole debt commences to outlaw on the non-payment of that installment.

Commencement of Action. There are quite a number of exceptions enumerated in the statute. If an action is commenced, even on the last day of the period, all the rights of the creditor are saved. All that is necessary for the creditor to do, in order to prevent his debt from being outlawed, is to serve the debtor with a summons, signed by some attorney-at-law. The creditor can now recover his money, or at least a judgment, at any time he chooses to press the suit.

A New Promise. Any acknowledgment of the debt and a new promise to pay it, made either within the period or afterward, if in writing, as, for instance, in a letter to the creditor, revives the debt and makes it good again for the legal period, counted from the new promise.

Part Payment. A part payment by the debtor, whether of interest or principal, revives the debt from the time of the payment, and makes it good again, as in the case of a new promise.

Any partner may bind the firm to pay an outlawed debt, by a new promise or a part payment made before dissolution, but not after.

When Creditor out of State. If the creditor is not in the State when the debt comes due, the period of limitation does not run until he comes or returns into the State.

This applies both to residents temporarily absent, and to citizens of another State.

If the creditor never comes into the State, the debt is never outlawed.

If he does come, a subsequent re-departure will not stop the running of the period.

When Debtor out of State. If the debtor is out of the State, the period does not run until he enters it. It continues to run so long as he remains. If he departs again, the time he is absent is not counted, as it is in the case of the creditor. The debt is not outlawed until the sum of the various periods, during which the debtor has actually been in the State, amounts in all to the legal period.

Debts in Another State. The statute of one State may bar a debt contracted in another State, provided the parties have resided in the State long enough.

But the statute of one State has no force beyond the limits of the State, so that a debt outlawed in one State may be perfectly valid in another. If the creditor can serve the papers on the debtor in that other State, he can recover the debt, unless some law expressly forbids it, which is the case in New York.

Other Exceptions. If the creditor is an infant under twenty-one years of age, or a lunatic, or is imprisoned on a criminal charge for a term less than life, the period of limitation does not run until these disabilities are removed.

Where Debtor Dies. In case the debtor dies at any time during the period, the creditor will usually have eighteen months after his death in which to sue the executor or administrator, whether the period expires in eighteen months or less.

SUMMARY OF THE STATUTES OF LIMITATION OF THE SEVERAL STATES.

ALABAMA.—Judgments good for twenty years. Actions upon any judgment or decree of any court of the United States or of any State or Territory, must be brought within twenty years.

Within ten years; actions upon contract or writing under seal or for the recovery of lands.

Within six years; actions for trespass to real or personal property, or a promise in writing not under seal, or for the recovery of money upon a loan, upon a stated or liquidated account, or for unpaid rent, actions against attorneys for not paying over the money of their clients, or for neglect of duty, actions arising on simple contract.

Within three years; actions to recover on open and unliquidated accounts.

Within one year; for assault and battery, malicious prosecution, criminal conversation, seduction of a female, breach of promise of marriage, or for libel and slander.

ARIZONA.—Within five years; actions upon judgments rendered in the Territory.

Within four years; actions upon contracts in writing.

Within three years; actions for trespass on real estate, injuries or conversion of personal property, actions on the ground of fraud.

Within two years; actions on contracts not in writing, actions on judgments of courts of other States or Territories, on open accounts for goods sold and delivered.

ARKANSAS.—Within three years; actions on contracts not in writing, actions on accounts or for injuries to personal property.

Within five years; actions on promissory notes and other contracts in writing, not under seal.

Within ten years; actions on judgments, bonds and contracts under seal.

CALIFORNIA.—Within five years; actions to recover real estate, and on judgments.

Within four years; actions on contracts in writing.

Within three years; actions for trespass upon real property, injury or conversion of personal property, actions on the ground of fraud.

Within two years; actions on contracts not in writing, for damages for the death of a person caused by the negligence of another.

Within six months; actions to recover property seized wrongfully by a tax collector.

COLORADO.—Within six years; actions on contracts, judgments of inferior courts, for arrears of rent, for trespass upon land, for injury or conversion of personal property.

All other actions within three years.

CONNECTICUT.—Within seventeen years; actions upon contracts under seal or on promissory notes not negotiable.

Within six years; actions upon contracts in writing but not under seal.

Within three years; actions on express contracts not under seal, actions of trespass and slander.

Within one year; actions for damages for loss of life from negligence of another.

DAKOTA.—Within twenty years; actions to recover real estate upon a judgment or a sealed instrument.

Within six years; actions upon contracts, for trespass upon real property, or for injury or conversion of personal property, criminal conversion, actions on ground of fraud.

DELAWARE.—Within twenty years; actions to recover real estate.

Within six years; actions on promissory notes, bills of exchange and demands acknowledged under hand.

Within three years; ordinary debts.

DISTRICT OF COLUMBIA.—Within twelve years; actions on bonds, judgments, contracts under seal.

Within three years; actions upon simple contracts, including bills of exchange, promissory notes, book-debts, accounts and replevin.

FLORIDA.—Within twenty years; actions on judgments and contracts under seal.

Within five years; actions on contracts not under seal.

Within three years; actions for trespass upon real property, for injury or conversion of personal property, actions on the ground of fraud, actions on contracts not in writing.

Within two years; actions on open accounts for goods sold and delivered.

GEORGIA.—Within twenty years; actions on bonds and contracts or instruments under seal.

Within six years; actions on promissory notes and on all contracts in writing not under seal.

Within four years; open accounts and contracts not in writing.

IDAHO.—Within six years; actions upon judgment.

Within five years; actions upon contracts in writing.

Within four years; actions upon contracts not in writing.

Within one year; actions against a public officer, as the collector of taxes, to recover damages for wrongful seizure of property.

ILLINOIS.—Within twenty years ; recovery of real estate, and judgments.

Within ten years; bonds, notes, bills, written leases and written contracts.

Within five years; contracts not in writing, or to recover damages for injury to real or personal property.

Within one year; libel and slander.

INDIANA.—Within twenty years; judgments, the recovery of real estates and written contracts other than those for the payment of money.

Within ten years; promissory notes, bills of exchange, and other written contracts for the payment of money.

Within six years; accounts and contracts not in writing, for rent, for injuries to property, for relief against frauds, and for money collected by a public officer.

IOWA.—Within twenty years; judgments of courts of record.

Within ten years; actions on contracts in writing and judgments of courts not of record.

Within five years; contracts not in writing, for fraud, for injury to property.

KANSAS.—Within five years; contracts in writing.

Within three years; contracts not in writing.

KENTUCKY.—Within fifteen years; contracts in writing, judgments, actions for the recovery of real estate.

Within five years; contracts not in writing, bills of exchange, drafts, promissory notes placed on the footing of a bill of exchange, open accounts between merchants.

LOUISIANA.—Within ten years; stated accounts, judgments and mortgages.

Within five years; promissory notes and bills of exchange.

Within three years; open accounts.

MAINE.—Within twenty years; judgments.

Within six years; contracts not under seal, for rent, trespass and injuries to personal property.

MARYLAND.—Within twelve years; contracts under seal, bonds, and judgments.

Within three years; contracts not under seal, open accounts, arrears of rent, injuries to real or personal property.

MASSACHUSETTS.—Within twenty years; actions for the recovery of land and judgments.

Within six years; contracts not under seal, for arrears of rent, except upon leases under seal, injuries to personal property.

MICHIGAN.—Within ten years; judgments and contracts under seal.

Within six years; contracts not under seal.

MINNESOTA.—Within twenty years; recovery of real estate.

Within ten years; judgments and actions to foreclose a mortgage.

Within six years; actions on accounts, and ordinary contracts.

MISSISSIPPI.—Within seven years; judgments.

Within six years; notes, bills, contracts in writing, whether under seal or not.

Within three years; contracts not in writing.

MISSOURI.—Within twenty years; judgments.

Within ten years; contracts in writing.

Within five years; contracts not in writing, open accounts, for taking personal property, for damages, for injury to person or property, trespass on real estate.

MONTANA.—Within six years; judgments, contracts in writing.

Within three years; contracts not in writing.

NEBRASKA.—Within ten years; for recovery of real estate.

Within five years; contracts in writing and foreign judgments.

Within four years; contracts not in writing, trespass upon real or personal property, actions on ground of fraud.

NEVADA.—Within five years; recovery of real property, except mining claims, which are limited to two years, and judgments.

Within four years; contracts in writing.

Within two years; contracts not in writing, or an open account for goods and merchandize sold and delivered, action for any article charged in a store account.

NEW HAMPSHIRE.—Within twenty years; actions to foreclose mortgages, judgments, contracts under seal.

Within six years; all contracts not under seal.

NEW JERSEY.—Within twenty years; judgments.

Within sixteen years; contracts under seal.

Within six years; contracts not under seal.

NEW MEXICO.—Within fifteen years; judgments.

Within six years; actions on contracts in writing, bonds, notes, etc.

NEW YORK.—Within twenty years; actions to recover real property, judgments, and contracts under seal.

Within six years; contracts not under seal, whether in writing or not.

NORTH CAROLINA.—Within ten years; judgments, contracts under seal, actions to foreclose mortgages or deeds of trust.

Within three years; contracts not under seal.

OHIO.—Within fifteen years; contracts under seal or in writing.
Within six years; contracts not in writing.

OREGON.—Within ten years; actions to recover real property, judgments.

Within six years; contracts of all kinds, whether in writing or under seal, or verbal.

PENNSYLVANIA.—Within twenty years; the payments of judgments, mortgages, and all instruments under seal will be presumed after twenty years, but this presumption may be overcome by proof of non-payment.

Within six years; contracts not under seal.

RHODE ISLAND.—Within twenty years; contracts under seal.
Within six years; contracts not under seal.
Judgments are not a lien on real estate.

SOUTH CAROLINA.—Within twenty years; judgments, contracts under seal, except sealed notes and personal bonds for the payment of money only, and not secured by mortgage.

Within ten years; actions to recover real estate.

Within six years; all contracts not under seal.

TENNESSEE.—Within ten years; actions on judgments.

Within six years; contracts, including bonds, notes, bills of exchange, accounts, etc.

TEXAS.—Within ten years; judgments.

Within four years; contracts in writing, actions between partners and merchants on mutual current accounts.

Within two years; actions on open accounts.

UTAH.—Within seven years; to recover real property.

Within five years; judgments.

Within four years; contracts in writing.

Within two years; contracts not in writing; open accounts, etc.

VERMONT.—Within fifteen years; to recover real property.

Within eight years; judgments, contracts under seal.

Within six years; all contracts not under seal.

VIRGINIA.—Within twenty years; contracts under seal.

Within ten years; judgments.

Within five years; contracts not under seal, except action for an article in a store account which must be brought in two years.

WASHINGTON TERRITORY.—Within six years; judgments, and contracts in writing.

Within three years; contracts not in writing.

WEST VIRGINIA.—Within ten years; to recover real estate, contracts under seal, judgments, contracts in writing.

Within five years; contracts not in writing, except store accounts, where the action must be brought in three years.

WISCONSIN.—Within twenty years; judgments of courts of the State, contract under seal made in the State.

Within ten years; judgments of courts of another State, contracts under seal made in another State.

Within six years; all contracts not under seal.

WYOMING.—Within five years; contracts under seal contracts in writing.

Within four years; contracts not in writing.

CHAPTER V.

SALES OF PERSONAL PROPERTY.

Selling without Title—Essentials of a Sale—Seller's Lien —Sales on Credit—When Chattels are Worth $50— Delivery—Possession by the Seller—Fraud in the Sale— Stopping Goods in Transit—Sales of Stock—Sales on Installments—Auction Sales—Warranty—Must be Express—What is a Warranty—Expression of Opinion— Warranty May be Verbal—When Implied—Sales by Sample—Orders of Manufactured Articles—Remedy for Breach of Warranty—Article Cannot be Returned— Bill of Sale.

THE sale of a chattel is the exchange thereof for money. The exchange of one thing for another is not a sale. The smallness or inadequacy of the price compared with the real value of the thing sold is no excuse for the seller to refuse to deliver it.

Selling Without Title. The seller can give to the purchaser no better title than he has himself. If, therefore, the article sold really belonged to another, even though the seller believed himself the owner, the true owner can claim it and take it away from the purchaser without paying for it. A man is entitled to his own, wherever he finds it.

Essentials of a Sale. The agreement of the

parties, one to deliver the chattel, and the other to pay the price, is all that is necessary to pass the title of ownership. The buyer becomes owner even before he pays the money. If the chattel should be destroyed before it can reach the buyer, he must pay for it just the same.

The article sold need not be in the possession of the seller.

Seller's Lien. The seller has a lien on the article sold, while it remains in his possession, for the purchase money. He can refuse, notwithstanding that the title has passed, to give it over until the money is paid.

Sales on Credit. Where the sale is made on credit, the seller must deliver the article, and cannot demand the money until the credit expires.

If goods are sold at a certain price, to be delivered at a future day, and the market price should rise much higher, the goods must still be delivered at the contract price.

If the market price has declined, the buyer cannot for that reason refuse to pay the contract price.

When Chattels are Worth Over $50. When the article sold amounts in value to fifty dollars or more, the contract of sale to be binding on either party, must be in writing unless the goods are delivered or they are paid for either wholly or in part.

This writing need not be a bill of sale or a formal contract. Any letters or memorandums signed by the parties are sufficient.

This rule of law is very important to bear in mind, as without the written contract, the seller is at liberty to refuse to deliver, and the purchaser to receive or pay for the goods.

Delivery. The seller must deliver the chattels at the time and place agreed upon. He is liable for all damage occasioned by his delay. If no place is specified, he may deliver at the buyer's place of business.

Possession by the Seller. The fact that the seller retains possession after the sale gives him an apparent ownership and right to sell. Another purchaser, ignorant of the previous sale, would acquire a good title free from all claims of the first buyer. The latter would have a valid claim against the seller for his fraud, and could recover the money paid and damages.

Fraud in Sale. All contracts of sale where either party has been guilty of fraud may be rescinded or broken by the other party. Such fraud is instanced by a gross misrepresentation by the seller as to the quality of the goods sold, or by the buyer as to his financial soundness, etc.

Stopping Goods in Transit. Where the seller has shipped goods by water or by rail to the purchaser, and the purchaser becomes insolvent before the goods reach him, the seller on hearing of this, may order the carrier to stop the goods and not to deliver them.

Sales of Stock. Railroad and other stocks are

often sold by brokers for their principals, to be delivered at some future time, without the seller, at the time of the sale, owning a single share. This is a valid contract, and can be enforced by either party.

Sales on Installments. Many articles, such as furniture and sewing machines, are sold on installments. The article is delivered to the purchaser, on the condition that he is to pay the installments when they become due, that no title is to pass until all the installments are paid, and that if any one is not paid when it falls due, the seller may reclaim the article, and the installments paid are forfeited.

The seller is not legally entitled both to retake possession and also to forfeit the installments.

If the purchaser on the installment plan sells the article to another before all the money is fully paid, this buyer must either pay the amount remaining unpaid or give up the article. This is so, even if he paid the full price, in ignorance of the facts.

Auction Sales. Sales are often made by auction. The auctioneer is the agent of the seller, and binds him by any representations or warranties he may make at the time of the sale.

The highest bidder is entitled to the article as soon as the hammer falls. It is usually necessary for the purchaser to leave a deposit with the auctioneer.

The auctioneer cannot buy for himself. The seller can buy the article in for himself, but not if he has advertised or announced that the sale was to be "without reserve," or led the persons present to believe that there would be no "by-bidding."

A sale cannot be revoked after the hammer has fallen.

WARRANTY OF CHATTELS.

Must be Express. When personal property is sold, there is generally no warranty of quality by the seller implied, from the mere fact of the sale. The warranty must be in express words, and form a part of the contract of sale. Otherwise the goods may be absolutely worthless, and yet the buyer will have no remedy.

What is a Warranty? Any positive statements by the seller at the time of or before the sale constitutes a valid warranty, on which the buyer has the right to rely, and for which he may hold the seller responsible in damages if untrue.

These statements may be contained in printed circulars or advertisements.

The word "warrant" is not necessary.

Expression of Opinion. A mere expression of opinion by the seller as to the quality of an article, is not a warranty, unless it can be construed as a positive assertion. Buyers often imagine they are getting a warranty when they are not.

Warranty may be Verbal. While the warranty may be verbal, yet if the contract is in writing, the warranty must also be in writing.

When Warranty may be Implied. There are

some exceptions to the rule that the warranty must be express; they are where there is no opportunity for the buyer to inspect the goods. This variety of sales concerns goods at sea, to arrive or in transit.

Sales by Sample. There is an implied warranty that the bulk of the goods is equal to the sample shown.

Orders of Manufactured Articles. Where an article is ordered of a manufacturer for a special purpose, the manufacturer, when he furnishes the article, impliedly warrants that it is fit for that purpose.

Remedy for Breach of Warranty. On the breach of an implied warranty, the purchaser can return the defective article, and demand back his money.

Article Cannot be Returned. Where there is an express warranty, however, the article cannot be returned, but the purchaser may recover as damages the difference between the value of the article in its defective condition, and what it would have been worth if the warranty had been true, which is generally the price paid.

Bill of Sale. A bill of sale is a legal document in use in most of the States. It is useful where a number of articles are sold without being delivered, and it is also valuable as evidence of the sale.

FORM OF BILL OF SALE.

Know all men by these presents, That I, A. B., of ————, in the County of ————, and State of ————, party of the first part, in consideration of the sum of ———— dollars, to me paid by C. D., of ——————, party of the second part, the receipt whereof is hereby acknowledged, have bargained, sold, granted and conveyed, and by these presents do bargain, sell, grant and convey unto the said party of the second part, his executors, administrators and assigns, all the good and chattels, etc., (insert description and location of the mortgaged chattels).

To have and to hold the same unto the said party of the second part, his executors, administrators and assigns, forever. And I do for myself, my heirs, executors and administrators, covenant and agree, to and with said party of the second part, to warrant and defend the said described goods hereby sold, unto the said party of the second part, his executors, administrators and assigns, against all and every person and persons whatsoever.

In witness whereof, I have hereunto set my hand and seal, the —— day of ——— 18—.

Signed, sealed and delivered ⎞
    in the presence of   ⎠   (Signed) A. B.   (Seal.)
[Name of witness.]

CHAPTER VI.

PARTNERSHIP

Nature of—How Formed, Articles—Partners Bound by Articles—Duration—Articles not Binding on Others—Rights of Partners as to Each Other—Trustees for Each Other—No Right to Sue—Powers of Partners—To Buy and Sell—To Give Notes—Accomodation Paper—Papers Under Seal—Nominal and Silent Partners—New and Retiring Partners—Dissolution—Receiver Appointed When—Powers of Liquidating Partner—Notice of Dissolution—Executors, etc., of Deceased Partner—Rights of Creditors—Limited Partnership. FORMS: *Copartnership Articles—Notice of Dissolution—Certificate of Limited Partnership.*

A PARTNERSHIP is the association by two or more persons of their capital, labor or skill in a common enterprise for common profit. The partnership may exist for one transaction, or it may be continuing.

Nature of. There is a joint ownership of the firm property by all the partners, but joint ownership alone does not constitute a partnership. Merely sharing in the profits of the business does not make one a partner. Thus, a business manager, or confidential clerk, or other person who receives a percentage of the profits as part of his salary, or in addition to it, is not a partner, or liable to firm creditors as such.

The test of a partnership is a community of interest, an agreement to share both profits and losses, and a right to a voice in the direction of the affairs of the firm.

How Formed, Articles. A partnership may be formed by a verbal contract, but it is more usual and very expedient for the parties to draw up an agreement in writing, carefully defining the rights and duties of all the partners, the amount of capital contributed by each, the share of the profits which each shall be entitled to draw out, and the duration of the partnership. This instrument is known as the articles of partnership, and should be signed by all the members. A seal is not necessary but may be used.

Partners Bound by Articles. The partners executing the articles are bound by the terms and conditions therein stated. Although such articles are not absolutely essential to the partnership, yet having been executed, the instrument is the best evidence of the contract, and no partner can vary, contradict, or modify them by verbal evidence of a different understanding between the parties at the time the contract was made.

Duration. If no time for the duration of the partnership is mentioned in the articles, it may be dissolved at any time by any partner, and if not dissolved it continues indefinitely.   If the articles provide that the profits or the losses shall be divided "equally," they must be so divided, and not in proportion to the amount of capital each partner contributed to the firm.

Articles Not Binding on Others. Between the partners themselves the provisions of the articles are binding, and are the measure of the rights of each member of the firm. Thus the junior partner might be prohibited from making promissory notes in the firm name. But this is not binding upon third persons who have dealings with the firm, unless the articles are shown to them, or they are aware in some way of this restriction. They could hold the firm liable on such a note.

Rights of Partners as to Each Other. Each partner is expected to give a reasonable amount of his time and attention to the business of the firm. In case of his refusal or neglect to do so, the other partners may ask for a dissolution, and then re-organize without him. But if they go on with the business, and conduct and manage it themselves, without such formal dissolution, they cannot afterward claim, on an accounting, to deduct from his share of the capital and profits any commissions or extra compensation for any work they have done.

Trustees for Each Other. Partners are trustees for each other as among themselves, while they are agents of each other as to third persons. As trustees, therefore, everything they do must inure to the benefit of the firm. No partner can take advantage of his position as partner to obtain any private gain for himself.

If one partner, without the knowledge of the other partners, carries on another and separate business, in which he uses in any way the firm name or the firm credit, or his own credit as a member of the firm, the other partners have the right to claim a *pro rata* share of the profits of this other business.

No Right to Sue.   As a rule no partner can sue his copartner on any matter connected with the firm affairs, as long as the partnership continues.   He can, however, sue for any private or distinct debt.

Where there has been a balance struck, and an express promise by one partner to pay his copartner that balance, the latter can sue for it.   There are a few cases in which a partner has a right to arrest a copartner in a civil suit.

In cases where one partner is aggrieved by the conduct of the other partner, the only remedy is to apply to a court of equity for a dissolution of the partnership, and an accounting.

Powers of Partners.   Each partner is a general agent, with broad powers to act for and bind the firm.

To Buy and Sell.   He has the power to buy and sell goods, and to assign any or all of the property of the firm.

To Give Notes.   He can borrow money, and give the promissory notes of the firm as security for the loan.   He may compromise or release debts due the firm without the knowledge or consent of the other members.   He may pay any debts due from the firm in full, even if it takes all the assets of the partnership

The authority of a partner is confined to the general scope and custom of the business. While he may sign notes or checks and accept bills of exchange, this must be commercial paper in the ordinary course of the business of the firm. He cannot bind the firm by a note in favor of a private or individual creditor in payment of a private debt, without the consent of the other partners.

Accommodation Paper. Nor can one partner issue accommodation paper; that is, sign the note of another firm or individual, as surety or endorser, in the firm name, so as to bind the other partners without their knowledge and consent. In such a case, the partner signing would be personally liable, but not the firm.

Papers Under Seal. One partner cannot alone execute and bind the firm by any instrument under seal, except the release of a debt. All the partners must execute deeds and mortgages of the partnership property, powers of attorney, etc., in order to make them valid. One partner has no implied authority to submit a partnership matter to arbitration without his copartners' consent. One partner has no power to admit the service of legal papers, such as a summons or subpœna upon his copartner. Nor can he confess a judgment so as to bind the other partners.

In case the firm makes a general assignment of its property for the benefit of its creditors, all the partners must execute the deed of assignment. One partner alone has no power to make the assignment, unless expressly so directed by all the members of the firm.

Nominal and Silent Partners. A nominal partner is one who is so in name only, and has no interest in or control of the firm. Any person who allows his name to appear in the firm name, or represents himself as a member of the firm, when in reality he is not, is liable for the debts of the firm to persons who trust the firm on such representations.

A silent partner is just the reverse of a nominal partner, as he is a partner in fact, although his name does not appear. He is liable for the debts of the firm to the fullest extent when his connection is known.

A dormant partner is one who takes no part in controlling or directing the affairs of the firm.

New and Retiring Partners. A new partner on coming into the firm is only liable for the debts of the firm incurred subsequently to his becoming a member. He is not responsible for the debts of the old firm, unless he expressly assumes them.

A partner on retiring from a firm should give notice of that fact by publication in the newspapers. He should also mail a notice to all persons who are customers, or who have had dealings with the firm in the past. Otherwise they might continue business with the firm believing him to be a member still. If the firm fails, the retired partner is liable to all such persons who have claims against the firm and who have not received notice of his retirement.

Dissolution. When a partnership is formed for a definite period, it is dissolved by the expiration of that period.

The death or insanity of any partner operates as a dissolution.

The conviction of a partner on a criminal charge, and sentence to imprisonment for life dissolves the partnership.

If one partner becomes individually insolvent, and makes an individual assignment for the benefit of his private creditors, the partnership is thereby dissolved.

The partnership may also be dissolved at any time by mutual consent of all the members of the firm.

In case of misconduct of any member, the partnership is frequently dissolved by a court of equity.

Receiver Appointed, When. Whenever a partnership is dissolved by litigation, it is customary to appoint a receiver to take charge of the business, or to wind up the affairs of the firm. For these services he is entitled to commissions as compensation.

But, in most cases, where the relations of the several members are friendly, one or more or all of the partners are appointed to act for the others, and sign in liquidation.

Powers of Liquidating Partner. The liquidating partner does not have the powers of a partner in the former firm. All he has authority to do is to collect the debts due to the partnership and pay those owing by it.

He cannot issue notes in the name of the firm without the express consent of the other members.

For his services in settling the affairs of the firm, the liquidating partner cannot claim any extra compensation. The only way to secure any such compensation is to have an express agreement with the other partners.

Notice of Dissolution. Notice of the dissolution of the partnership, and the appointment of a receiver or a liquidating partner, should be given by publication in the newspapers, and by mailing such notice to other concerns having dealings with the dissolved firm. All debts must, after the receipt of this notice, be paid to the receiver or liquidating partner.

They must not be paid to the other partners, as they have no authority to receive such payment. The consequences of doing so is often to compel the debtor to pay the debt over again.

Executors, etc., of Deceased Partner. When there is a dissolution by the death of any partner, the representative of such partner, as his executor or administrator, has no right to any control of the affairs of the firm. All he is entitled to is the share due to that partner. If the executor, etc., be permitted by the surviving partners to meddle with the business, he becomes personally responsible for the debts of the firm.

Rights of Creditors. The partnership creditors are entitled to be paid their debts in full out of the assets or property of the partnership, before the individual creditors of any one partner can claim anything.

On the other hand the individual creditors of any partner may take his private property for the payment of their claims before the firm creditors have any rights to demand a share. The private property of each partner is responsible for the partnership debts, subject, however, to the rights of the private creditors.

If there is not enough private property to pay the individual creditors of any partner in full, and there is a balance due that partner from the firm, after the firm debts are paid, the individual creditors have a claim on that balance for the unpaid portion of their demands.

Real estate owned by a partnership is not subject to the dower of the widows of any of the members

Limited Partnership. A limited partnership is a partnership where the liability of some of the members for the debts of the firm is limited to the amount of capital they have put in.

In a general or ordinary partnership, all the members are liable for debts to the full extent of their private fortunes.

It is usually necessary in a limited partnership that at least one of the partners should be a general partner, and that the business should be carried on in his name. The other partners are called "special" partners. Their names do not appear in the firm name, but are usually printed in small letters in one corner of the sign, and letter-heads. They have no right to actively manage the affairs of the firm; if they do so, they are held as general partners.

A limited partnership is formed by filing certain certificates in the office of the Secretary of State and of the County Clerk. There must be advertisements of the partnership published in the newspapers for a certain time; and there are various other requirements which must be strictly complied with.

Such a partnership cannot be formed by the mere agreement of the parties.

FORM OF COPARTNERSHIP ARTICLES.

Articles of Agreement made the 1st day of May, one thousand eight hundred and eighty-one, *Between* A. B., of New York, and C. D. of the same place, witnesseth as follows: That the said parties to this agreement hereby agree to form with each other a partnership, under the firm name of B and D., for the purpose of engaging in and carrying on the business of [here state purposes of the partnership].

I. The partnership is to commence on the 1st day of June, 1881, and is to continue for the term of ten years.

II. The said A. B. agrees to furnish and provide the sum of $5,000 in cash.

III. The said C. D. agrees to furnish the stock of goods, machinery, fixtures, etc., now in the store of the said C. D., and also the lease of the said premises now occupied by him, which stock, machinery, lease, etc., shall be valued by the parties at the sum of $5,000.

IV. The capital stock so formed shall be used and employed in common between them for the carrying on of the said business, to their mutual benefit and advantage.

V. At all times during the continuance of their partnership, they and each of them, will give their entire time and attention, and to the utmost of their skill and power exert themselves for their joint interest, profit, benefit, and advantage.

VI. And the said parties shall and will at all times during the said partnership, bear, pay and discharge equally between them, all rents and other expenses that may be required for the support and management of the said business; and that all gains and profits of the said business shall be divided equally between them; and all losses incurred in or accruing to the said business in whatever way, or from whatever causes, shall be borne and paid by them equally.

VII. And it is agreed by and between the said parties, that there shall be kept at all times during the continuance of the said copartnership, perfect, just, and true books of account, wherein shall be entered all moneys by them or either of them received, paid, laid out and expended, in and about the said business, as also all goods, wares, commodities, and merchandize, by them or either of them bought or sold, by reason or on account of the said business, and all other matters and things whatsoever, to the said business and the management thereof in anywise belonging; which said book shall be used in common between the said copartners, so that either of them may have access thereto, without any hindrance of the other.

VIII. And also, the said copartners, once in each year, or oftener, if necessary, shall make, yield, and render, each to the other, a true, just, and perfect inventory and account of all profits or losses by each made or sustained, and the same account so made, shall and will clear, adjust, pay and deliver, each to the other, at the time, their just share of the profits, and pay and bear their just share of the expenses and losses so made as aforesaid.

IX. And the said parties hereby mutually covenant and agree, to and with each other, that during the continuance of the said copartnership, neither of them shall or will indorse any note, or otherwise become surety for any person or persons whomsoever, without the consent of the other of the said copartners. And at the end or other sooner dermination of their copartnership, the said copartners, each to the other, shall and will make a true, just and final account of all things relating to their said business, and in all things truly adjust the same; and all and every the stock and stocks, which shall be remaining, either in money, goods, wares, fixtures, debts or otherwise, shall be divided between them.

X. Each of the parties may draw out from the cash of the joint stock, the sum of one hundred dollars monthly, to his own use, the same to be charged in account, and neither of them shall take any further sum for his own separate use, without the consent of the other in writing; and any such further sum, taken with such consent, shall draw interest at the rate of six per cent. and shall be payable, together with the interest due, within ten days after notice in writing given by the other party.

In witness whereof, the parties hereto have hereunto set their hands and seals, the day and year first above written.

Sealed and delivered }
  in the presence of }   [Signatures] (Seal.)
  [Name of witness.]

FORM OF NOTICE OF DISSOLUTION OF PARTNERSHIP.

NEW YORK, May 1, 1885.

The copartnership heretofore existing under the firm name of Rutter & Brown is this day dissolved by mutual consent (or by limitation). Either party (or one exclusively) will sign in liquidation. GEORGE RUTTER,
JAMES BROWN.

FORM OF CERTIFICATE OF LIMITED PARTNERSHIP.

We, the undersigned, hereby certify that we do hereby commence a limited copartnership, as follows:

The firm name and style of said copartnership is John Parker & Co.

The general nature of the business to be transacted by the said copartnership is the buying and selling of grain and other produce on commission as brokers.

The names of the general and special partners composing the

said firm are as follows: John Parker, residing at No. 112 Smith Street, New York, and William Parker, residing at No. 112 Smith Street, New York, are the general partners of said firm, and George Williams, residing at No. 25 Bank Street, New York, is the special partner thereof.

The amount of capital which the said George Williams has contributed to the common stock of said copartnership is ten thousand dollars.

The period at which the aforesaid copartnership is to commence is the first day of January, 1885, and the period of the termination of said copartnership shall be the first day of January, 1888.

The principal office and place of business of said copartnership is to be in the City of New York.

Dated, New York, December 28th, 1884.

JOHN PARKER,
WILLIAM PARKER,
GEORGE WILLIAMS.

CHAPTER VII.

CORPORATIONS.

Kinds of Corporations—How Created—Powers of Corporations — Management — Stock—Franchise—Election of Officers—Control by State—Dissolution. FORMS: *Certificate of Incorporation—Power of Attorney to Transfer—Proxy to Vote—Certificate of Stock—Transfer of Stock.*

A CORPORATION is a body composed of individuals, so associated together as to form one person in the eyes of the law. It is an artificial, as distingushed from a natural, person.

A joint stock company is not a corporation, although it has many features in common. It is an association of individuals, but more in the nature of a partnership, and is not an artificial person. The members of such a company are liable as partners.

Kinds of Corporations. A sole corporation is one consisting of a single person.

A corporation aggregate is one consisting of more than one person.

Charitable or eleemosynary corporations are such as colleges or hospitals.

Public corporations are those organized for the

purpose of local government. A city, town, or county is a public corporation.

Private corporations include all corporations which are not public. The principal private corporations are railroad, telegraph, telephone, steamboat, and insurance companies, banks and manufacturing corporations

How Created. Corporations may be created by a charter granted by the Legislature. There are corporations in the United States acting under charters granted by the King of England before the Revolution.

In some States, certain classes of corporations may be organized under a general law. There are certain steps laid down, and by following these strictly, a specified number of persons may organize a corporation. Railroads and manufacturing companies are often formed in this way. It is generally necessary to file certain papers in the office of the Secretary of State and of the County Clerk, such as the certificate of incorporation, annual reports, etc. Corporations can now be formed in this way for almost any purpose.

Municipal or public corporations are always created by charter.

Powers of Corporations. A corporation has only the powers conferred upon it by its charter or the general law. Any act beyond its powers is void. Such an act is called "*ultra vires.*"

In New York every corporation as such, has power,

(1) to have succession by its corporate name for the period limited in its charter, and when no period is limited, perpetually; (2) to sue and be sued in a court of law; (3) to make and use a common seal, and to alter the same at pleasure; (4) to hold, purchase, and convey such real and personal estate, as the business of the corporation shall require, no' exceeding the amount limited in their charter; (5) to appoint such subordinate officers and agents as the corporation shall require, and to allow them a suitable compensation; (6) to make by-laws.

These are in addition to any special powers conferred on a particular corporation.

Management. Corporations act through agents, who are appointed or elected by the individuals composing the corporation. These agents, or officers, as they are called, are a president and a board of directors or trustees. The corporation is liable for the contracts and other acts of its officers, connected with the business. A majority of the directors control. It is necessary that the president should sign all contracts, deeds, mortgages, leases, and other instruments binding the corporation. Before he has authority to do this, he must obtain the consent of the directors by resolution and vote. The secretary often signs such instruments, as well as the president. The seal of the corporation should be affixed.

The officers can always be removed for cause. This is called amotion. A stockholder may often obtain an injunction to restrain the president or the directors from acting in a manner injurious to the corporation.

Stock. The stock is the capital of the corporation, and shares are the parts into which the stock is divided. A share is usually one hundred dollars in amount. Each share is evidenced by a certificate of stock. This is a paper certifying that A. B. owns one hundred dollars of stock

These shares may be transferred by one person to another by transferring the certificate. There is usually on the back of the certificate a blank form of power of attorney, authorizing a transfer. This may be filled up by the seller of the stock in favor of the buyer. The latter then obtains the title, and can compel the company to transfer the stock on the books. A stockholder has no right to vote or to receive dividends, unless his name appears on the books of the company as owner. Even such an owner cannot vote, if he has pledged or hypothecated his stock.

Preferred stock is stock on which dividends are declared in preference to ordinary stock.

Watered stock is a phrase applied to capital stock which has been increased in amount without warrant.

Franchise. A franchise is a right, generally exclusive in its nature, granted by the State to individuals or corporations. The franchise of a railroad company is the right to operate its road. The franchise has a value entirely distinct from the value of the plant or the ordinary property of the corporation. When a corporation sells its property, the buyer should expressly bargain for the franchise. Frequently a corporation is not allowed to sell its franchise, except by consent of the Legislature.

Liability of Stock-Holders.   The stock-holders of a corporation are usually not liable for the debts of the company beyond the amount of the stock held by them.   The holders of National Bank stocks, in case of the failure of the bank, are liable to double the amount of the face value of their stock; that is, each stockholder, in addition to the loss of his stock, may be assessed enough to pay all the debts of the bank, up to an amount equal to his stock.

There is no personal liability on the stockholders like that of partners, except that the stockholders may be sued personally for wages by the employes of the corporation.

Election of Officers.   The officers of a corporation are chosen by the stockholders by election.   Meetings are held for that purpose at certain times, designated by the by-laws.   Notice should be given by mail and by publication.   The holder of one share has one vote, and one stockholder has as many votes as he has shares.   The holder of a majority of the shares may elect all the officers.

If any stockholder is not present, he may give some member who is present a right to vote for him.   This is known as a proxy.   The right to vote by proxy must be conferred by the charter or the general law. It cannot be assumed.

Control by States.   The State which granted the

charter, or permitted the incorporation under a general law, has a certain right of control over a corporation. Through the Attorney-General, it can prevent it from exceeding its powers, or doing some unlawful act. It can even forfeit its charter for misconduct.

But the relation between the State and the corporation is that of a contract, and the State cannot pass any law which violates the obligation of a contract. With the internal management of the corporation, therefore, the State cannot interfere, nor can it change its charter or take away any of its rights.

Dissolution. A corporation may be dissolved by the expiration of the period limited in its charter, or by the consent of the members composing it, and the surrender of its charter.

It may also be dissolved by the decree of court. The action against a corporation to dissolve it is brought usually by the Attorney-General. The proceeding is called a "*quo warranto*." In New York and some other States, if a judgment is recovered against a corporation, and it is not paid, the judgment creditor can begin an action to dissolve the company.

It is usual on dissolution to appoint a receiver to wind up the affairs of the corporation.

FORM OF CERTIFICATE OF INCORPORATION OF A MAN-
UFACTURING CORPORATION.

(New York.)

STATE OF NEW YORK, ⎰
 COUNTY OF KINGS. ⎱ ss.

WE, the undersigned [names of incorporators], do by these

presents, pursuant to and in conformity with the act of the Legislature of the State of New York, passed on the seventeenth day of February, one thousand eight hundred and forty-eight, entitled, " An Act to authorize the formation of corporations for manufacturing, mining, mechanical or chemical purposes," and the several acts of the said Legislature amendatory thereof, associate ourselves together, and form a body politic and corporate, and do hereby certify:

1. That the corporate name of the said company is [name of company].

2. That the objects for which the said corporation is formed, are as follows:

[State them in general terms.]

3. That the capital stock of the said corporation shall be —————————— dollars, which shall be divided into ——— shares of one hundred dollars each.

4. That the said corporation shall commence on the ——— day of ———, in the year one thousand eight hundred and eighty ———, and shall continue in existence for the term of ——— years.

5. That the number of trustees of the said corporation shall be three, whose names are as follows, and who shall manage the concerns of the said corporation for one year:

[Names of trustees.]

6. That the names of the town and county in which the operations of said company are to be carried on are [name of town and county], and the principal place of business of the said corporation shall be in the town of ————————, in the County of Kings, and State of New York.

[Signatures.]

FORM OF POWER OF ATTORNEY TO TRANSFER.

(This may be indorsed on the certificate of stock, the blanks to be filled at pleasure.)

Know all men by these presents, that I, A. B., of —————————, do hereby constitute and appoint C. D., of ————————, my true and lawful attorney, for me, and in my name and behalf, to sell.

assign and transfer to ————, of ————, the whole, or any part of ——— shares of capital stock, standing-in my name, on the books of the ————— Company, and for that purpose to make and execute all necessary acts of assignment and transfer.

Witness my hand and seal, the —— day of ————, 18—.

Sealed and Delivered 〉
  in the presence of 〉 [Signature.] (Seal.)
[Witness.]

FORM OF PROXY TO VOTE.

Know all men by these presents, that I, A. B., of ——-———, do hereby appoint C. D., of ————, my attorney for me, and in my stead, to vote as my proxy, at any election of the directors (etc.) of the ————— Company, according to the number of votes I should be entitled to cast, if there personally present.

Witness my hand and seal, etc.

[As in last form.]

FORM OF CERTIFICATE OF STOCK.

The Eureka Manufacturing Company.

No. 931.   [Number of shares.]

This is to certify that A. B. is entitled to ————— shares of the capital stock of the ————— Company, of ————— dollars each, transferable only on the books of the said company, by the said A. B., or his attorney, upon the surrender of this certificate.

[Signature] President.   [Signature] Treasurer.

FORM OF TRANSFER OF STOCK.

Know all men by these presents, that I, A. B., of ————, for value received, have bargained, sold, assigned and transferred, and by these presents do bargain, sell, assign and transfer, unto C. D., of ——————, ————— shares of capital stock, standing in my name, on the books of the ————— Company; and I do hereby constitute and appoint the said C. D., my true and lawful attorney irrevocable, in my name or otherwise, but to his own use and benefit, and at his own costs and charges

to take all lawful ways and means for the recovery and enjoy
ment thereof.

    Witness my hand and seal; the ―― day of ――――, 18―.

      Sealed and delivered ⎱
        in the presence of ⎰   [Signature] (Seal.)
      [Witness.]

CHAPTER VIII.

AGENTS.

*General and Special Agents—Instructions—Brokers—
Commission Merchants—Advances—Lawyers—Fees—
Power of Attorney—Ratification—Liability of Agent to
Principal—Sub-Agents—Agents to Buy or Sell—Com-
pensation—Liability of Principal—Liability of Agents
to Third Persons—Dissolution of Agency—Form of
Power of Attorney.*

AN agent is one who acts for another, called the
principal. He differs from a servant or mere employe in that the latter does not represent his master or employer, and has no authority to bind him by
his contracts.

General and Special Agents. A special agent is
one who is authorized to do one particular thing, as
to sell a horse. He has no other implied powers and
cannot bind the principal, as by a warranty, when
such a power has not been given.

A general agent, however, is one who has a general
employment, or follows a line of business. His
powers are very broad, and the principal is responsible for all his acts done within the general scope of
the agency or business, whether the power was ex-

pressly given or not.   He has all the implied authority customary with the class of agents to which he
belongs.

Instructions. This authority may be limited by
the instructions of the principal, but private instructions to an agent, while they make him liable if he
violates them, do not affect third persons who deal
with him as such agent. Such persons have a right
to rely on the general authority of the agent, and
may hold the principal liable for the agent's acts and
contracts. If the instructions are shown to them,
however, the principal cannot be held on an unauthorized contract.

Examples of general agents are brokers, commission merchants, auctioneers, insurance and shipping
agents, business managers, etc.   Partners are general
agents of the firm.

Brokers. A broker is an agent employed to buy
or sell stock, grain, etc., for his principal.   He does
not have possession of the property as a rule.   He
must obey the direction of his principal as to selling
or buying, and if he does not, is liable for any loss.

Where stocks are bought "on a margin," as where
the principal furnishes ten per cent. of the amount,
and the broker the balance, and the market price
falls, the broker must give notice to the principal before he can sell to protect his advances.   If the principal does not furnish more "margin," the broker
may then sell with impunity.   In case he should sell
without notice, and the market price should rise, he

is liable to the principal for all the profits he might have made by holding the stock.

Commission Merchants. These agents have pos·session of the goods of their principals, with full power of sale, warranty, etc. They receive a commission for their services. Brokers act in the name of their principals, but commission merchants usually in their own name. They have power to mortgage or pledge the goods for their private debts, and the principals are bound. Wherever such an agent guarantees his principal a certain price for his goods, he receives a larger commission than usual. This is called a *del credere* commission.

Advances. In case of an advance made by the agent to the principal on the goods, the agent has a lien upon them for the amount, and can hold them till it is paid. Should the market price decline, he can sell, after giving notice to the principal, and waiting a reasonable time for him to make good the amount. This occurs in cases where the agent has been instructed not to sell below a certain price.

Lawyers. Attorneys-at-law have authority to bind their client in all matters pertaining to the suit in which they are retained or employed. They are bound to exercise proper skill and knowledge, and are liable for any damage occasioned by their negligence or ignorance.

Fees. Attorneys are entitled to reasonable fees, whether they succeed or not, and may sue their clients for them. If the amount has been fixed, beforehand they are entitled to that amount. If the client de-sires to change his lawyer, he must pay all the ex-penses and fees up to that time at least, and if the attorney has not been in fault, the fees to which he would have been entitled at the close of the case.

The parties cannot settle the case with each other out of court, without the consent of the attorney. If this is done, the attorneys may, in some States, go on with the case and enter up a judgment and collect it. They also have a lien on the papers for their services.

Power of Attorney. Wherever power is given to an agent to execute a deed or mortgage, or any paper requiring a seal, the authority to do this must also be under seal. This paper is called a power of at-torney, and the agent, an attorney in fact. Powers of attorney are frequently executed, even when not strictly necessary, in cases where authority of a general nature is conferred upon an agent. Persons dealing with such an attorney should examine the instrument to ascertain what his powers really are.

Authority may generally be given verbally or in writing.

Ratification. Wherever an agent has acted beyond his authority, the principal, even when not liable, may ratify the unauthorized act, and become responsible for it, as if he had authorized it. This is sometimes called " confirmation."

But the principal cannot ratify in part, and reject in part. He cannot accept the benefit and refuse the burden. He must ratify the act as a whole.

The principal, after once ratifying the act, cannot disavow it, if the ratification was made with full knowledge of the circumstances.

Liability of Agent to Principal. The agent is personally responsible, in damages, to his principal for any misconduct or negligence, resulting in loss.

He is bound to follow instructions. If he exceeds the authority given by them he is liable. If he has no instructions, he must follow custom and usage. But custom or usage will not justify an agent in disregarding instructions

Sub-Agents. As a rule an agent cannot delegate his authority to another. He may employ clerks and assistants but he becomes responsible for them. They are his agents, and not those of the principal.

Agent to Buy or Sell. An agent authorized to buy or sell cannot buy of or sell to himself without informing his principal. The opportunity for fraud would be too-great, and the fact that the agent charged himself a fair and reasonable price, makes no difference. The principal is not bound by such a sale and may disavow it.

Compensation. Agents are entitled to the compensation agreed upon, or if no specific amount was contracted for, to reasonable compensation. In many cases they have a lien upon goods of the principal in their possession for their services. They may also claim to be reimbursed for necessary expenses.

Liability of Principal. The principal is bound by, and is liable for, the acts of his agent, which he has given him the express or implied authority to do. He is responsible for the concealments and misrepresentations of his agent. Authority to sell in general terms does not imply authority to sell on credit, or to pledge or barter the goods; nor to warrant unless justified by custom. The principal is not bound in such cases.

Liability of Agent. The agent is liable to third persons where he has exceeded his authority, and the principal cannot be held. He is also liable where he makes the contract in his own name, and does not disclose who his principal is. He is of course liable when he is himself the principal, though he makes the contract as agent.

Dissolution of Agency. The authority of an agent is revocable by the principal at any time, except where the agent has some interest or ownership in the property intrusted to him, as in the case of a commission merchant who has made advances.

Wherever there is a power coupled with an interest, like a power of sale in a mortgage, the agency is not revocable, until the money is paid.

If the agent's authority is taken away without fault on his part, he may sue the principal for a balance of salary, commissions, or whatever damages he is entitled to.

The authority of an agent is always revoked by the death, insanity, or bankruptcy of the principal.

FORM OF POWER OF ATTORNEY.

Know all men by these presents, that I (or we) ———— (name of principal) ————— have made, constituted and appointed, and by these presents do make, constitute and appoint ————— (name of agent) ————— my true and lawful attorney for me and in my name, place and stead for the following purposes:

[Here define the powers delegated and the rights and authority conferred.]

giving and granting unto my said attorney full power and authority to do and perform all and every act and thing whatsoever requisite and necessary to be done in and about the premises, as fully to all intents and purposes, as I might or could do if personally present, with full power of substitution and revocation, hereby ratifying and confirming all that my said attorney or my substitute, shall lawfully do or cause to be done by virtue hereof.

In witness whereof, I have hereunto set my hand and seal the ———— day of —————, in the year one thousand eight hundred and —————.

Sealed and delivered }
  in the presence of }   Signed, [Name] (Seal.)
[Name of witness.]

STATE OF —————, }
COUNTY OF —————. } ss.

Be it known, that on the ———— day —————, in the year one thousand eight hundred and ———— before me ———— [a notary public, etc.,] personally came ————— to me known and known to me to be the person described in the above, and acknowledged the above letter of attorney to be his act and deed.

In testimony whereof, I have hereunto subscribed my name the day and year last above written.

[Signed] (Name of notary, etc.)

CHAPTER IX.

NEGOTIABLE PAPER.

NOTES: *Definition—Must be Payable to Order—Must be Payable in Money—Must not be on Condition—Essentials of a Note—Value Received—Interest—No Precise Form Necessary—Alteration—Forgery—Indorsement—Liability of Indorser—Indorsement in Full and in Blank—Without Recourse—Guaranteed Notes—Accommodation Paper—Days of Grace—Notes on Demand—Presentment for Payment—Protest—Notice to be Given—Defenses to Notes—Infancy—Usury—Alteration and Forgery—Want of Consideration—Fraud or Compulsion—Extending Time—Seal—Bills of Exchange—Definition—Negotiability—Foreign and Domestic—Sight Drafts, etc.—Acceptance—Acceptance supra Protest—Indorsement—Protest and Notice—Alteration, etc.* CHECKS: *No Days of Grace—Indorsement—Presentment for Payment—Certified Checks—Illegal Certification.*

NEGOTIABLE PAPER is a term applied to promissory notes, bills of exchange or drafts, and checks. By "negotiability" is meant that this kind of paper has most of the characteristics of money, so that it can be readily transferred from one person to another. A purchaser who buys a note or bill before maturity in good faith, and for a valuable consideration may often collect it of the maker, where the payee or other prior holders could not, as where the paper was without consideration.

PROMISSORY NOTES.

Definition. A promissory note is a written promise to pay another person or his order, either on demand or a certain number of days after date, a sum of money absolutely and without condition. The promisor is called the maker of the note; the person to whom the promise is made is the payee; and all subsequent holders of the note who write their names across the back in order to transfer it, are indorsers. The payee is the first indorser.

Must be Payable to Order. A note should be made payable to the *order* of the payee; otherwise it is not negotiable. A non-negotiable note, it is true, may be assigned like any other debt, but it has not then the characteristics of money. The purchaser takes it subject to all the defenses, such as fraud or want of consideration, which the maker could have made to the payment of the note, if it were still in the hands of the payee. It is not safe to take such notes.

A note payable to "bearer" is a good negotiable note, and requires no indorsement.

Must be Payable in Money. The note to be negotiable must also be payable in money. A note reading, "I promise to pay A. B. one thousand dollars' worth of lumber," is not negotiable.

Must not be on Condition. The promise to pay

must be absolute, and not depend on a contingency. If the note is to be paid on condition that the payee shall deliver certain goods or perform a certain act, the note is no more negotiable than any other ordinary contract. Still, such a note is assignable, if the purchaser is willing to take it.

Essentials of a Note. The essentials of a note therefore, are, first, the promise to pay; second, the payment to be in money; and, third, without any condition. The note should be dated, and signed at the end by the maker. If the maker signs as agent, he should write the name of his principal, as A. B. by C. D., agent. He should not sign C. D., agent. If he does, he will be personally liable.

Value Received. It is not necessary to use the words "for value received" in the note, but it is better to do so.

Interest. If the note is to carry interest, it must read so, as "with interest at —— per cent." If no interest is mentioned, none can be claimed by the holder. Should the note simply read, "with interest," without specifying the rate, interest will be computed at the legal rate. After maturity, all notes bear interest.

No Precise Form Necessary. It is not necessary to use any precise form in order for the paper to be a negotiable promissory note. Certificates of deposits issued by banks have all the essentials of a note. A paper reading, " Received of A. B. fifty dollars, to be returned on demand," is a good note. So is an " I. O. U."

Alteration. Any material alteration of a note, after delivery, by the payee or endorser makes it void. Anything written on the face of the note, as well as a change of what is already written, is an alteration. Changing the date or the place of payment, or the amount, or the name of the payee, are examples of alteration.

Forgery. In many cases alteration is also forgery. It is not necessary to constitute the crime of forgery that the maker's name should be forged.

An altered or forged note is void in the hands of everybody, even of a purchaser in good faith. A bank or individual who pays such a note loses the money. The maker is not liable.

Indorsement. Indorsement is effected by writing the name across the back of the note. A note payable to bearer need not be indorsed.

The payee of a note must indorse it in order to transfer it. If the note is again transfered, it need not be indorsed by the subsequent holders and sellers. Mere delivery passes the title. But it is usual and desirable for them to do so, and no one should take a note without securing the indorsement of the person selling it.

Liability of Indorser. If the maker does not pay the note at maturity, the indorser must. If there are several indorsers each is liable for the full amount.

An indorser who is compelled to pay can make ary

indorser prior to him re-imburse him for the amount so paid. The holder of a note, in case of non-payment, can sue one, any, or all of the indorsers.

Indorsement in Full and in Blank. An indorser may simply write his name across the back. He then indorses in blank. Or he may write, "Pay to A. B.," and then sign his name. A. B. will then be the only person to whom the note can be paid. It is no longer negotiable. This is called indorsement in full. If the indorsement in full reads, "Pay to the order of A. B.," the note will still remain negotiable and may be transferred any number of times, after A. B.'s indorsement.

Without Recourse. If an indorser writes the words, "Without recourse," after his name, he is relieved from any further liability. He cannot be compelled to pay, if the maker fails to do so. A note having such an indorsement is to be regarded with suspicion.

Guaranteed Notes. The payment of a note may be guaranteed by any third person by writing the following on the back of the note: "I hereby guarantee the payment (or collection) of the within note." The guaranty may be on a separate piece of paper.

Where the *payment* is guaranteed, the holder can compel payment by the guarantor immediately on the failure of the maker to do so.

Where only *collection* is guaranteed, the holder must first sue the maker and use all means of securing payment from him.

A note may also be guaranteed by the guarantor's writing his name below that of the maker and adding the word "surety."

Accommodation Paper. Any one who writes his name on the back of a note for the purpose of loaning his credit to assist the maker in negotiating the note, is an accommodation indorser. Although he receives no consideration for his indorsement, he is obliged to pay if the maker does not. Such paper, whether consisting of notes, bills of exchange or checks, is known as accommodation paper.

The fact that the holder knows that the indorsement was without consideration will not prevent his recovery, as it would in the case of ordinary business paper.

There are various other methods besides indorsement by which credit may be loaned. For instance, the accommodating party may make his own note payable to the order of the other party, or he may draw a draft in his favor, or he may accept the other's bill of exchange. All this is accommodation paper.

Days of Grace. All notes and bills have in addition to the time for which they are to run, three days of grace; that is, the maker has three days additional in which to pay the note or bill. If the last of the three days falls on Sunday, he must pay it on Saturday.

Notes on Demand. Notes on demand are due as soon as made. They have no days of grace.

Presentment for Payment. As soon as the note becomes due, it must be presented by the holder to the maker for payment. This demand should be made at the office or residence of the maker. If he is unable or refuses to pay, the note is said to be dishonored.

Protest. After dishonor the note should immediately be protested by some notary public. Sometimes a note contains the words, "No protest," "Protest waived," etc. It is not necessary to protest the note in these cases, though it is safe to do so.

Notice to be Given. A copy of the note, the certificate of protest, and a notice of non-payment should at once be mailed or sent to the maker and each of the indorsers. All this should be done within twenty-four hours. If any indorser does not receive these papers within a reasonable time, he is discharged from all liability. It is therefore very important that this should be promptly done. The notary usually sends the notices.

Defenses to Notes. When the maker or indorser of a note is sued, there are various defenses or excuses he may urge as reasons why he should not be compelled to pay it.

(1.) *Infancy.*—If the maker was under twenty-one years of age the note is void both as against him and against his father, unless given for necessaries.

(2.) *Usury.*—In States having a usury law, the note is absolutely void if given for a usurious consideration. No holder can enforce it, even though he was a purchaser in good faith, without knowledge of the usury, and had paid value for it.

(3.) *Alteration and Forgery.*—An altered or forged note is absolutely void, as before explained.

(4) *Want of Consideration.*—Where a note is given without consideration, it is only void as between the maker and the payee. A *bona fide* purchaser from the payee can collect it of the maker.

One who buys a note from the payee or any holder for less than the face value, can nevertheless recover the full amount from the maker.

(5.) *Fraud or Compulsion.*—A note obtained by fraud or threats cannot be enforced by the payee, but it is good in the hands of a purchaser before maturity.

Extending Time. Any agreement between the holder of a note and the maker to extend the time of payment after maturity, if the holder receives a sum of money for granting this extension, discharges all the indorsers from liability, and if the maker does not pay, the holder cannot sue the indorsers. This is therefore a dangerous practice.

Seal. A note with a seal is not negotiable. Such a note is good for the period of all sealed contracts.

BILLS OF EXCHANGE.

Definition. A bill of exchange is an order by one person on another, who has funds of the first on deposit, to pay to some third person, or order, a certain sum of money. The person making the order is called the drawer of the bill; the person on whom the order is made is the drawee; and the person to whom the money is ordered to be paid is the payee. Sometimes the drawer and payee are the same person.

Bills of exchange are also known as drafts.

Negotiability. The rules stated in regard to the negotiability of promissory notes also apply to bills of exchange. They must be payable to the order of the payee or to bearer; they must be payable in money and not on condition.

Foreign and Domestic. When the drawer lives in one country or State, the bill is a foreign bill of exchange; when they both live in the same State, it is a domestic bill.

Foreign bills are usually made out in sets of three referred to as first of exchange, second of exchange, and third of exchange, all of the same tenor and date, one of which being accomplished or paid, the others are void.

Sight Drafts, etc. Bills of exchange may be drawn, payable at sight, a certain number of days after sight, or after date.

Acceptance. When a bill of exchange is presented to the drawee, the latter, if he concludes to honor it, writes the word "accepted," and the date, and signs his name in red ink across the face of the bill.

A draft so many days after sight, must be presented twice, first for acceptance, and afterward for payment.

It is usual for the holders of bills of exchange to

present them to the drawee for acceptance as soon as possible, no matter when they are payable.

A bill of exchange, even though drawn a number of days after date, becomes due at once, if it is not accepted. The holder can immediately demand payment of the drawer.

The drawee of a bill is not liable until he has accepted it, even though he has funds of the drawer in his possession. The holder cannot sue him for refusal to accept. The drawer, however, can sue for the injury done to him.

Acceptance Supra Protest. If the drawee resuses to accept a bill when presented, any friend of the drawer can accept for his honor in order to prevent the bill from becoming due at once. He would then be an accommodation acceptor, and if obliged to pay the bill, would have a claim against the drawer for repayment.

Indorsement. Bills of exchange are transferred in the same way as notes, by indorsement. The bill may be indorsed in full, in blank, or without recourse. It is absolutely necessary that the payee should indorse the bill, and it can then be transferred from one person to another without further indorsement, though it is customary and desirable to obtain the indorsement of every holder.

Protest and Notice. The rules in regard to protest and timely notice of non-payment or non-acceptance are the same as in the case of promissory notes.

Alteration. etc. What has been said in regard

to the alteration and forgery of notes is also true of bills.

A check is an order on a bank to pay another person, or order a sum of money. In form and effect it is a bill of exchange.

No Days of Grace. A check is due on demand and has no days of grace. If dishonored, no protest for non-payment is necessary.

Indorsement. If a check is payable to the order of some person named, the latter must indorse it. A check payable to "bearer" or "cash," needs no indorsement. The bank is justified in paying such a check to any holder who presents it. If the holder was a thief or a finder, it is the loss of the true owner.

Banks will not pay the checks unless they can identify the holder or know the signature of the payee to be genuine. If the payee's name be forged or the amount of the check raised, and the bank pays it, it is the loss of the bank

Presentment for Payment. A check should be presented for payment at the bank as soon as possible after its receipt, usually within twenty-four hours. It is very unsafe to delay, as in case the bank should fail, the holder of the check would have no right to demand payment of the maker.

Certified Checks. Where a bank has funds on hand to meet the check, and the holder does not desire immediate payment, the bank will certify the check. This is equivalent to the acceptance of a bill of exchange, and gives the holder of the check a claim against the bank. By certification the bank assumes the debt and promises to pay it.

The president and cashier have authority to certify checks. Assistant cashiers, tellers and clerks usually have no such power, unless it is an established usage for them to do so.

Illegal Certification. By the laws of the United States, National Banks have no right to certify checks, unless the drawer of the check has sufficient money deposited in the bank to meet it. There is a heavy penalty for the violation of this provision.

State banks and private bankers are not within this prohibition.

FORM OF A NEGOTIABLE PROMISSORY NOTE.

ST. LOUIS, June 1, 1885.

Thirty days after date (or on demand) I promise to pay to John Doe or order (or bearer) one thousand dollars (with interest). Value received.

$1,000. RICHARD ROE.

FORM OF A BILL OF EXCHANGE.

(Sight Draft.)

BOSTON, April 1, 1883.

At sight, pay to the order of William Morris, five hundred dollars, and charge the same to account of

$500. SMITH & JONES.

To Messrs. Brown & Brother, New York.

NON-NEGOTIABLE NOTE.

St. Louis, June 1, 1885.

Thirty days after date, I promise to pay to John Doe one thousand dollars (with interest) for value received.

$1,000.   Richard Roe.

ANOTHER FORM.

Chicago, August 10, 1885.

Ten days after sight (or ten days after date) pay to the order of Cardwell & Company three hundred dollars, and charge the same to my account.

$300.   John N. Smith.

To Williamson & Son, Cleveland.

FORM OF CHECK.

Albany, May 8, 1885.

Pay to Henry Brown or order one hundred and fifty dollars.

$150.   Charles R. Thorne.

To National Bank of Adams.

New York, July 1, 1884.

Bank of America.

Pay to bearer (or cash) fifty dollars.

$50.   Williams & Co.

INDORSEMENT IN FULL.

Pay to Williams & Randolph.

H. K. Kennedy.

Or

Pay to the order of Willliams & Randolph.

H. K. Kennedy.

FORM OF NOTARY PUBLIC'S CERTIFICATE OF PROTEST.

United States of America,)
   State of ———,   } ss.
   County of ———.   )

On the —— day of ——, 18—, at the request of [name of holder of note or bill], I, John Doe, a Notary Public of the State of

New York, duly commissioned and sworn, did present the original promissory note (or bill of exchange), hereunto annexed, to ———, the maker [or the drawee or the acceptor] at his office, No. 20 Wall Street, in the City of New York, and demanded payment [or acceptance], who refused to pay (or accept) the same. Thereupon I, the said Notary, at the request aforesaid, did protest, and by these presents do publicly and solemnly protest, as well against the maker and indorsers of the said note (or the drawers and indorsers of the said bill) as against all others whom it may concern, for exchange, re-exchange, and all costs, damages and interest already incurred, and to be hereafter incurred for want of payment (or acceptance) of the same.

This done and protested in the City of New York aforesaid, in the presence of ——— and ———, witnesses.

In testimonium veritatis.

[Seal of Notary.]   (Signature.)

                                              Notary Public.

FORM OF NOTICE OF PROTEST OF NOTE.

To Messrs. A. & B.:

Please take notice that a promissory note made by John Jones, for one hundred dollars, dated June 1st, 1885, payable three months from date, in favor of yourselves, and indorsed by you, has been presented by me at the office of the said John Jones, at Meridan, and payment being duly demanded, and refused, whereupon, by direction of the holder, the same has been protested, and payment thereof is requested of you.

                              (Signature.)

                              Notary Public

FORM OF NOTICE OF PROTEST OF BILL.

To John Jones, Esq.:

Please take notice that your bill for two hundred dollars, at ten days from sight, dated May 15th, 1884, drawn on Richard Roe, has this day been protested for non-acceptance.

                              (Signature.)

                              Notary Public.

CHAPTER X.

COMMON CARRIERS.

Rights and Duties—Lien of Carrier—Regulations—Liabilities—Goods in Transit—Bills of Lading—Carrier of Passengers—Baggage—The Check System—Unchecked Baggage—Injuries from Negligence—Liable to Travelers—When Person is Killed—Contributory Negligence—Stoppage in Transitu—Carrier must Obey—When Bill of Lading is Transferred—Consignment to Agent. TELEGRAPHS: *Duty to Send—Partiality—Secrecy—Delivery—Liability for Negligence—Conditions in Blanks—Insuring Accuracy—Receiver of a Telegram.*

A COMMON carrier is one who undertakes, for hire, to transport the goods or the persons of those who choose to employ him, from place to place. In former times the phrase "common carrier" was used principally of stage-coaches, but now it applies also to railroads, steamships, steamboats, express companies, tow-boats, cabs, ferries, etc.

Rights and Duties. Common carriers differ from private carriers in this respect, that they are obliged to take the goods of anyone who may offer them on his paying the price. If they refuse they are liable for all the damage as by delay. Carriers are, of course, entitled to a reasonable compensation, but

their rates must be uniform. They cannot discrimi-
nate. Sometimes railroads endeavor to evade this, by
taking full rates from those they desire to favor and
then refunding a part by way of "rebate." This is
unlawful.

Carriers of persons are not allowed to refuse passage to persons on account of their color. Heavy
damages can be recovered against them in such cases,
beyond the mere pecuniary loss.

Railroads, steamboats, etc., are bound to provide
proper vehicles and accommodations for their passengers. When trains or boats are advertised to start at
a particular time, the company must see that this is
done. If there is a time-table, they must run in accordance with it, and the company cannot inconvenience the passenger by deviating from it arbitrarily
without notice.

Lien of Carrier. Common carriers have a lien on
the goods of shippers for the freight, and on the baggage of passengers for the fare. They may hold them
until the charges are paid, and if no one claims them,
after waiting for a reasonable time, usually a year,
they can advertise and sell the articles at auction. All
large railroads have such sales every year.

Regulations. Carriers have the right to make
reasonable regulations, such as that a passenger must
buy a ticket before entering the train or else pay a
larger sum. The passenger is bound to obey this and
all other rules of the company so long as they are

reasonable. He need not, however, obey an unreasonable rule.

Liabilities. In regard to the goods intrusted to his care, the carrier is an insurer, that is, if the goods are lost, stolen, burned, or injured in any way, he is responsible for them, whether the loss was due to his carelessness or not. He insures against everything except what is called "the act of God or the public enemy." By this expression is meant everything caused by purely natural agencies, such as a flood, or a storm of wind or rain, lightning, freezing, or capture by an enemy in time of war. For losses by these means he is not liable, but he is for all others.

Goods in Transit. This liability, however, is only cast upon the carrier while the goods are *en route*, not while they are stored in the depot or freight-house. Thus, if the goods were to burn while on their passage, the carrier is always liable, and cannot plead that it was not his fault. But if the goods had arrived at their destination, and were stored in the depot until the consignee saw fit to come and take them away, and the depot burned, the carrier would not be responsible for the goods unless the fire could be proved to have been caused by the negligence of himself or his servants. By usage, however, he remains liable as a common carrier for twenty-four hours after the goods arrive.

Bills of Lading. It is customary for common carriers, through their freight agents, to issue bills of lading to the shipper or forwarder. This paper contains a receipt for the goods, and states the conditions on which the carrier sends them. The latter usually stipulates that he will not be responsible for delay or for any loss by fire, or for transportation on connecting lines, or for negligence of employes; in fact, he excuses himself from very nearly all his rightful responsibilities. If the forwarder accepts this bill of lading, he impliedly agrees to its conditions. He may, however, refuse to accept the paper, and yet insist upon and compel the carrier to take the goods. He has, at least, the legal right to do this, although practically it may put him to much inconvenience, and he may find it to his interest to submit.

Carrier of Passengers. Common carriers of persons are responsible for the baggage of passengers when the latter give it into their possession. The usual method is to have it " checked." The company is then liable in the same way as it is for merchandise or goods carried on a freight train.

Baggage. Baggage consists of trunks, valises or parcels of any description, containing the articles which a traveler might naturally be expected to take with him. He would not be expected to carry valuable diamonds in large quantities, and the company would not be liable for the loss unless the passenger had informed the agent as to the contents. But it is liable for all ordinary articles.

The Check System. The brass check which the passenger receives for his baggage often has a notice stamped upon it to the effect that the company's liability for the trunk, or valise, etc., is limited to $100. The carrier seeks to give the check the same effect as a bill of lading. But the mere acceptance of the check is not an acceptance of the condition as it is in a bill of lading, unless the passenger has his attention called to it and agrees to abide by it. The company may, therefore, be liable to a much larger amount.

Any one who presents the check at the place to which the baggage was checked has an apparent right to it, and the company is justified in delivering it to him. If the baggage agents have reason to believe that the holder is not the true owner, they may refuse, but they do so at their peril. If they do deliver it in good faith, and the real owner subsequently appears, the company is not responsible. It is the owner's fault that he lost his check.

Unchecked Baggage. A passenger who does not check his baggage, but takes it into the car with him, does so at his own risk. The carrier is under no obligation to look after it, or any liability to pay for it in case it is stolen or lost.

In case of the loss of checked baggage where the carrier is liable, the owner may show and prove what the contents and their value were by his own evidence alone.

Injuries from Negligence. Carriers of passengers are liable to the latter for personal injuries occasioned by the negligence of their employes. They are not, however, liable even in such a case to a gratuitous passenger or one traveling upon a pass. Neither are they liable to their employes who may be injured, such as engineers or brakemen. These are not passengers, and a master is not liable for injuries to a servant due to the fault of a fellow servant. The conductor of a train has the right to eject a passenger for the non-payment of fare, but he cannot do it while the train is in motion. The company would be liable in damages for the injury thus occasioned.

Liable to Travelers. The carrier, as a railroad company, for instance, is also under a duty to be careful as to those who are not passengers; that is, to those traveling on the high-roads where they cross the track. It should have signs erected at these crossings, and should take other precautions, such as blowing the whistle, ringing the bell, or in case the railroad runs through a thickly populated region, or a city, by stationing flagmen to give warning, fencing the tracks in, or hanging sliding gates which may be lowered when a train passes.

The degree of care to be exercised is much greater in a city, and the trains should run at a less rate of speed than in the country. Horse railroads are also bound to take great care not to injure other vehicles, or pedestrians, and the cars must not be driven at an excessive speed. If the company omit to take these ordinary and reasonable precautions, and any-one is injured, it is liable to him for the damage caused both to his person and his property. If the damage was occasioned by the negligence of the carrier's employes, the company is responsible also for that.

When Person is Killed. If a person is killed, his administrator may sue the company and recover damages for the benefit of the widow and children. The limit of the company's liability in such a case is usually $5,000. But if a person be merely injured there is no limit to what he may recover. The amount lies in the discretion of the jury.

Contributory Negligence. If the passenger or other person injured is guilty of negligence which contributes to produce the injury, he cannot recover damages of the carrier, even if the latter was also negligent. The carrier or his employes may be grossly careless, and the passenger only slightly so, yet if the injury would not have occurred without this slight negligence on his part, he has no redress. He may, for instance, stand on the platform of a train in motion. This is not excessively careless, yet if he should be thrown off and injured it is his own fault. Or a person might step on the track thoughtlessly, although aware that a train was nearly due at that point, and if the engineer should heedlessly run him down without trying to reverse the engine and stop the train, the company is not liable. Railroad companies are seldom, if ever, liable for injuries to persons who walk on or along the track, unless the latter are traveling on a high-road, where they have a right to be at a point where it crosses the track.

Stoppage in Transitu. The seller or consignor of goods has the right at any time to order the carrier to stop the goods in transit and not to deliver them to the consignee or buyer in case of the latter's insolvency. This is called the right of stoppage in transitu. The value of this right is that the consignor can regain possession of the property and save himself from loss by reason of the buyer's failure.

If the goods should be delivered to the consignee the seller could then only come in with the other creditors for a *pro rata* share of the debtor's assets, the goods being reckoned as part of those assets

Carrier Must Obey. The carrier on receiving this notice either by letter, telegram, or any other way, is bound to obey it, and if he afterward gives the goods to the consignee, he must make up the difference between the *pro rata* dividend of the assets and the price of the goods to the consignor.

The phrase "transit" refers not merely to the time the goods are on the passage, but also after they have arrived at their destination, while they are in the freight depot or warehouse of the common carrier. They may be stopped at any time before they are actually delivered to the consignee.

When Bill of Lading Has Been Transferred. There is one exception to the consignor's right of stoppage in transitu. This is where the bill of lading is sent to the buyer as consignee, and he transfers it by indorsement to one who buys in good faith and for a valuable consideration. The title to the goods is at once vested in the assignee of the bill of lading In this one respect a bill of lading is, like a bill of exchange, negotiable.   The holder has a better right to demand and receive the goods than his own assignor—the insolvent consignee.   Notwithstanding the insolvency the consignor cannot now stop the goods, and must take his chances of recovering his debt from the consignee alone.

Consignment to Agent.   The way for the consignor to avoid this possible loss is to consign the goods to his own agent and send the bill of lading to him at the place of destination of the goods.   This agent may then hold the goods until the buyer pays for them or he may make some other arrangement within his authority. This method is much more prudent and safe wherever it is practicable, than to consign directly to the buyer.

TELEGRAPHS.

Telegraph companies are regarded as practically common carriers.

Duty to Send.   A telegraph company is bound to receive and transmit any message delivered to its operators.   If it refuses, or receives the message and willfully or carelessly neglects to send, it is liable for all the damage occasioned thereby.   It is not compelled, however, to send an immoral or indecent message, or one so long as to interfere with the ordinary business of the company.

Partiality.   Messages must be sent in the order

in which they are received. Any partiality to one person which causes injury to another, as by delay, makes the company liable.

Secrecy. Another duty of a telegraph company is secrecy. It is bound not to disclose, nor allow its employes to disclose, the contents of any telegram. But the officers or operators of the company may be subpœnaed to produce any particular telegram in court at a trial, or to testify as to its contents, and they are then protected from liability.

Delivery. It is the duty of the company to deliver the message to the right person after it has been transmitted. The delivery must be prompt. But in case the telegram has not been paid for, it can refuse to deliver it until the charges are paid. An extra charge may sometimes be demanded for delivery when made outside the " free delivery limits " of the terminal office. These limits may be prescribed by the company. If the person cannot be found, the company should give speedy notice of the fact to the sender of the message.

Liability for Negligence. The message must be sent accurately, just as it is written, and the company is responsible for the mistakes of its operators. Thus a change of the word " sacks " of salt into " casks," where the word was plainly written, causing the consignment of a much larger quantity of salt than was intended, made the company liable for the loss.

Conditions in Blanks. All telegraph companies now have blank forms, at the top of which are printed

certain conditions or terms to which the sender impliedly agrees by writing his message below. These
may vary the ordinary liabilities of the company.
The principal condition is to the effect that the company will not be liable for mistakes, delays, non-
delivery, whether caused by negligence or not, unless
the sender orders it *repeated*, that is, telegraphed back
for comparison. For this the company demands half
rates additional. Unless the sender does this, he
cannot recover of the company in case of loss. Even
if repeated, it is usually stipulated that he only re-
covers fifty times the cost of the telegram.

Insuring Accuracy. In addition to this precaution, correctness may be insured to any amount by
stating the amount of risk, and paying one per cent.
on that amount for distances under 1,000 miles, and
two per cent. for greater distances.

There is also a provision that the claim must be
presented in writing sixty days after sending the
message.

Receiver of a Telegram. The receiver of a telegram cannot recover from the company for any loss to
him caused by negligence or delay, as he has no contract with the company, and it is under no legal obligations to him of any nature.

CHAPTER XI.

MASTER AND SERVANT.

*Duties of Employer—Liability of Employer—Contractors
—Wages—Wrongful Discharge—Must Seek Other
Employment—Services of Minor Child—Loss of Services
—Apprentices.*

A SERVANT is one who renders personal services to
another, generally for compensation. The word applies not only to servants in the household, but to
clerks, laborers, and all other employes.

If the term of service be for less than one year, the
contract may be merely verbal; if it is to last for a
longer time, it must be in writing in order to be binding on either party.

Duties of Employer. It is the duty of the master
or employer to furnish his employe with proper tools
and machinery. If he exposes the employe to dangerous machinery, without informing him of the
danger, the employer is liable in damages for any injury which may occur from that cause. If the employe was aware of the danger, the master is not
liable.

The employer must also employ suitable and competent fellow-workmen. If he has a workman whom

he knows to be negligent, he must either discharge him or inform the other workmen; otherwise, he is liable for the consequences of such workman's negligence where the co-servants are injured.

Liability of Employer. The employer is liable for the wrongful acts of his employe producing injury to others, if those acts are done in the course of the ordinary employment. Thus a railroad company is liable to passengers and travelers on its highway for the negligence of its conductors or engineers, while running trains on the road. The employer is not liable for the acts of his employes disconnected with the employment.

Co-servant. It is a familiar rule of law that the master is not responsible to his servant for the acts of a fellow-servant, in the same cases where he would be liable to other persons. If a servant is injured through the carelessness of another servant, he may sue the latter for damages, but not the master. Superintendents, managers, overseers, etc., are not regarded as co-servants of inferior employes, although they are employed by the same master. Employers are, therefore, liable to their employes for the negligence of such persons.

Contractors. A contractor is not an employe in the legal sense. He alone is responsible for his own acts and acts of his workmen. In case the other party exercises control, however, he, as well as the contractor, will be liable. In order to distinguish between a contractor and a servant in any case where there is doubt, the tests are, whether the person follows an independent employment or trade, whether he has the direction and control of the work, whether he selects the workmen and pays them their wages. Such a person is a contractor, and not a servant.

Wages. It is the duty of the servant or employe to faithfully and fully perform the services for the entire term or period of service. If he does not do this he cannot recover his wages or any part of them. If the contract of the servant is to work for a certain time, as six months, and he leaves willfully and without cause before the six months have expired, he is entitled to nothing from the master. If he is rightfully dismissed by the master before that time, as for dishonesty, incapacity, or misconduct, the master is under no obligation to pay him anything.

If the contract is by the month and the wages are payable monthly, in cases where the servant leaves or is discharged, he is entitled to all the wages due for for the months completed. For the part of the month he has just served, however, he cannot claim proportionate wages, but loses them entirely. If the contract were for the year, he might serve eleven months and yet have no right to claim compensation for the services actually rendered. He must perform the entire contract. A contract for the year, with the wages payable monthly, is not a monthly hiring.

If the servant is prevented from serving by sickness or other valid cause, he does not lose his wages for that reason. He may still claim them of the employer. If he dies, his representatives may recover the reasonable value of the services already rendered.

The death of either party dissolves the contract. Should the master die his representatives are not bound to continue the employment of the servant for the remainder of the term. They may discharge him at once on paying him the wages due up to the time of the master's death.

Wrongful Discharge. If the servant be discharged by the master without good cause during the continuance of the term of the contract, he can sue the master for damages. If he is unable after such a dismissal to obtain employment elsewhere, the amount of damages would be the amount of the wages or salary for the remainder of the term of service.

Must Seek Other Employment. It is the duty of the servant to reduce the damages by accepting any similar employment, if he can obtain it. If the salary or wages of his new position or employment are greater than his former position, he can only recover nominal damages. If they are less, he can recover the difference between them. If the servant should refuse to search for, or accept, a new position, he cannot recover of his former master. But he is not obliged to accept a position of another, especially an inferior, grade.

It is advisable for a servant so discharged, whether he finds new employment or not, to wait until the contract period is up before suing for damages.

Services of Minor Child. The parent is entitled to the services of his minor child. If the child serves in the household, the parent is entitled to its services gratuitously; this is true even if the child is an adult, unless there is an express promise to pay for such services.

If a minor child is in the employment of some other person, the parent is entitled to its earnings, and may demand them of the employer. The employer cannot refuse to pay his wages to the parent, If he continues to pay them to the child, the parent may recover them from the employer. The parent. however, may " emancipate " his child, and give him the right to receive and retain his earnings.

Loss of Services. The employer has the right to the services of his employe for the period of the contract. If anyone wrongfully deprives him of those services, as by enticing the employe away, he may sue such person for damages. It is on the ground of loss of services that a father can sue the seducer of his daughter.

Apprentices. An apprentice is one who is bound by indenture to some person to learn a trade. A person of full age may bind himself as an apprentice. An infant may be so bound, with his own consent, by his parent or guardian, until he is twenty-one, or for a shorter period.

Orphan asylums, overseers of the poor, and other officials frequently have power to bind poor children as apprentices, even against their own consent.

The apprenticeship may be effected by indenture, or by any instrument, in writing. No particular form is essential. The child must sign the instrument and also the master. The consent of the parent or guardian should be indorsed upon it.

The master has the general rights of a parent. He may punish the apprentice for misconduct, and compel him to work. He is also entitled to his earnings and services without compensation. In return he is obliged to teach him his trade.

The system of apprenticeship is falling into disuse.

CHAPTER XII.

MARRIAGE AND DIVORCE.

Contracts to Marry in the Future—Breach of Promise—What Proof Necessary—Promise Inferred—Time—Excuses for Refusal—Infant's Promise not Binding—Seduction—Essentials of Marriage—No Ceremony Necessary—Who Can Perform Ceremony—Marriage Settlements—Must be in Writing—Divorce, Absolute and Limited—Alimony—Right to Dower—Custody of Children—Right to Re-Marry—Place of Marriage—Grounds of Divorce—Recrimination—Forgiveness—Collusion—Neglect to Prosecute—Separation by Consent—Obligation to Support—Residence—Courtesy—Dower—Property Rights of Married Women.

Contracts to Marry in the Future. Mutual promises by a man and a woman to marry at some future day constitute a valid contract.

Breach of Promise. If either party refuse to carry out the contract, he or she is guilty of breach of promise, and may recover damages of the other party. It is not very often, however, that the man sues the woman, though he has the right.

What Proof Necessary. In case of a lawsuit for breach of promise of marriage, where the party sued—the defendant—denies the promise, it is next to impossible to prove it by direct evidence, as there is one oath against another, and witnesses are not usually present at the time such promises are made.

Promise May be Inferred. The promise is, therefore, nearly always inferred from circumstances, such as constant visits, presents, declarations of the parties, the reception of the man by the woman's parents or friends as her betrothed without any objection from him, etc.

Time. When a person promises to marry another without specifying any time, he will be guilty of breach of promise, unless he stands ready to fulfill his engagement within a reasonable time. Five years, unless the parties are very young, would be unreasonable.

Excuses for Refusal to Keep the Promise. A refusal may be justified on the ground of the bad character or conduct of the other party; poor health of either party is sometimes a good excuse, but not generally. If the woman were a widow, or divorced, and concealed this fact from the man, this justifies a refusal to marry on his part.

Infant's Promise Not Binding. If either party is an infant, that is, under twenty-one years of age, he or she is not bound by the promise to marry, and cannot be sued for breach of promise. The infant may break the contract at any time it pleases with legal impunity.

Seduction. Seduction of a woman under a promise of marriage, and subsequent refusal to marry on his part, is a crime, and is punished by severe penalties, as by imprisonment and fine. A marriage of the parties after the trial is commenced, and before the verdict is given, will save the accused from conviction.

MARRIAGE.

Essentials of the Marriage Contract. Marriage is a civil contract, and is entered into by the mere consent of the parties. If the man says " I marry you," and the the woman says " I marry you," this is a valid marriage in most of the States. A marriage will often be inferred from circumstances, such as co-habitation, and the introduction of the woman by the man as his wife.

No Ceremony. No ceremony is necessary or any priest, minister, or magistrate. In this case, how-ever, it is advisable to have witnesses. Marriage is not a religious contract in the United States.

Who Can Perform Ceremony. Clergymen of all denominations, judges, mayors. aldermen, justices of the peace, and magistrates generally, may perform the ceremony if there is one.

Licenses are required in a few States.

Marriage Settlements. These are common in England, but rare in this country. They are settle-ments on or gifts of property to the wife, either by the husband or his father or her father, in considera-tion of the marriage.

Must Be In Writing. Any promise by any per-son to make some settlement of this kind, must be in writing, in order to be enforceable after marriage.

Divorce, Absolute and Limited. Divorce is a dissolution of the marriage by law.

It may be absolute, in which case the bonds of matrimony are entirely sundered and the parties are free to marry again; or limited, in which case the parties are merely separated.

Alimony. Where there is a divorce for the husband's fault, he is obliged to still furnish money for the support of his wife, or former wife, in proportion to his means. This is called alimony.

Right to Dower. If the divorce is granted for the woman's fault, she is not entitled to dower; but if for the husband's fault, she can still claim it.

Custody of the Children. The innocent party is generally entitled to the custody of the children, unless they are very young, when the mother may be awarded possession.

Right to Re-Marry. After an absolute divorce the innocent party always has the right to marry some other person.

In a few States, including New York, the party in fault cannot marry during the lifetime of the other, and may be punished for doing so. In most States both parties may marry again.

The Place of Marriage and Divorce. If the marriage is valid in the place where it was made, it is valid everywhere, even though it would not have been valid if it had been celebrated in the latter place. So with divorce This affords a method of evading the strict laws of one State, as the guilty party may remove into another State, having a laxer law, and after obtaining the divorce, may marry again.

Grounds for Divorce. These differ very much in the different States, as will be seen by the "Summary" at the end of the chapter. In New York absolute divorce is only granted for one cause—adultery. In other States, valid causes are adultery, force, fraud, duress, insanity, or impotence at the time of the marriage, consanguinity, desertion or abandonment, cruelty, neglect to support or provide, bigamy, incompatibility of temper, habitual intemperance, such conduct as renders it unsafe or improper for the parties to live together.

Recrimination. Where either husband or wife applies for a divorce on any ground, particularly adultery, it will not be granted if the applying party has been guilty of the same fault. This countercharge on the part of the defendant is called recrimition.

Condonation or Forgiveness. If the innocent party has forgiven the guilty party after the commission of the offense, with full knowledge of the fact, and has voluntarily cohabited with the other, the divorce will not be granted. A subsequent offense, however, will revive the right to the divorce.

Collusion. The decree of divorce will not be made where there is any evidence which tends to show that the parties have conspired to obtain the divorce.

Neglect to Prosecute. The neglect for a long time to bring an action for divorce will be regarded as tantamount to forgiveness, and a divorce will be refused.

Separation by Act of the Parties. Husband and wife cannot divorce themselves, but they can agree to separate. It is well in such a case to draw up articles of separation, and have them executed by both parties. There is usually a provision that the husband shall regularly provide a certain amount for the wife's support. This is an amicable arrangement, and cannot be made without the consent of both parties.

Obligation to Support. In case of marriage the husband is obliged to support his wife, to furnish necessaries, such as food, clothing, etc. She can bind her husband by contracts with tradesmen.

There is no such obligation after divorce, except for the alimony decreed by the court.

Residence to Get a Divorce. In order to be entitled to apply for and obtain a divorce, is is necessary for the person so applying to have resided in the State a certain time, usually at least one year. The period varies in the different States, as will be seen by the summary.

Curtesy. By the common law a husband of a woman who dies leaving real estate is entitled to the use for life of such real estate, provided there was a child born during the continuance of the marriage.

This is still the law in most of the States. In New

York the wife can deprive her husband of curtesy by conveying the land by deed, or disposing of it by will. The husband has no interest whatever in the land of his deceased wife, unless there has been a child of the marriage. It is not necessary that the child should be still alive.

Dower. Dower is the right of a widow to a life-interest in one-third of her deceased husband's land. Dower does not refer to personal property. There is no way in which a husband can deprive his wife of her right to dower. If he sells or mortgages the land, the grantee or mortgagee takes the deed or mortgage subject to the right of dower. She may release her dower by joining with her husband in signing the instrument, or by executing a deed of release.

Some States have abolished dower. These are California, Colorado, Kansas, Louisiana, Minnesota, Texas, Arizona, Dakota, Idaho and Utah. There is usually some provision made for the widow in place of dower in these States.

Property Rights of Married Women. All the property, real and personal, owned by a woman at the time of her marriage, and all the property acquired by her after that time by gift, purchase or will, belongs to her alone. It is her "sole and separate estate." Her husband has no rights over it. It is not liable for his debts.

She has a right to sell, mortgage, and make contracts concerning this separate property, in most

States, without her husband's consent. In some States he must join with her in signing deeds, mortgages, etc. She can keep a bank account and give checks upon the deposits. She can generally sue and be sued alone on matters connected with her property. In most States, she is permitted to carry on business in her own name. She alone is then liable for her debts. Her husband is only liable for debts which are contracted by her for "necessaries," food, clothing, shelter, etc.

A husband is never bound by his wife's contracts for articles which are not necessary.

DIVORCE LAWS.

The following is a summary of the divorce laws of the various States:

ALABAMA.—Either absolute or partial, for these causes: (1) Impotency; (2) adultery; (3) voluntary abandonment for two years; (4) for imprisonment in the penitentiary for two years, the sentence being for seven years or longer; (5) commission of the crime against Nature before or after marriage; (6) habitual drunkenness of the husband, if not existing to the knowledge of the wife at the time of the marriage; (7) pregnancy of the wife at the time of the marriage if without his knowledge or agency; (8) actual violence to the wife, committed by the husband and attended with danger to life and health; (9) reasonable apprehension of such violence.

ARIZONA.—A person applying for a divorce must have been a resident of the Territory six months. Divorce absolute and from bed and board for these causes: (1) Impotency at the time of the marriage; (2) when the female was under fourteen and the marriage was without consent of parents; (3) adultery; (4) extreme cruelty; (5) where consent was obtained by force or fraud; (6) the conviction of either party of a felony after marriage; (7 when the judge decrees the case to be within the reason of the law; (8) habitual intemperance; (9) willful desertion for one year.

ARKANSAS.—Causes: (1) Impotency; (2) willful desertion for one year without cause; (3) where either party had a husband or wife living at the time of the marriage; (4) where either is convicted of felony; (5) habitual drunkenness for one year; (6) intolerable cruelty; (7) adultery.

The party applying must have resided one year in the State.

CALIFORNIA.—Causes: (1) Adultery; (2) extreme cruelty; (3) willful desertion for one year; (4) willful neglect for one year; (5) habitual intemperance for one year; (6) conviction of felony.

The plaintiff must have been a resident of the State six months.

COLORADO.—Causes: (1) Natural impotency at time of marriage; (2) husband or wife living at time of marriage; (3) adultery; (4) willful desertion and absence for one year; (5) willful desertion and absence from the State without intention of returning; (6) failure of husband to support for one year; (7) habitual drunkenness for one year; (8) extreme cruelty; (9) conviction of felony.

Plaintiff must have resided one year in the State.

CONNECTICUT.—Causes: (1) Adultery; (2) fraudulent contract; (3) willful desertion for three years with total neglect of duty; (4) seven years' absence; (5) habitual intemperance; (6) intolerable cruelty; (7) sentence to imprisonment for life; (8) any crime involving a violation of conjugal duty and punishable by imprisonment in State's prison.

The plaintiff must have resided three years within the State.

DAKOTA.—Causes: (1) Adultery; (2) extreme cruelty; (3) willful desertion; (4) willful neglect; (5) habitual intemperance; (6) conviction for felony.

Willful desertion or neglect, or intemperance, must have been for one year.

The plaintiff must have resided ninety days in the Territory.

DELAWARE.—Causes: (1) Adultery; (2) desertion for three years; (3) habitual drunkenness; (4) impotency at time of marriage; (5) extreme cruelty; (6) conviction for felony. Either absolute or

from bed and board, at discretion of court, for (1) fraud in con
tracting the marriage, or (2) willful neglect to provide.

Divorces of residents of the State obtained in other States, for
causes not permitted in Delaware, will be of no force in Delaware.

DISTRICT OF COLUMBIA.—Causes: (1) Adultery; (2) cruel treatment; (3) willful desertion and abandonment for three years.   Divorce may be either partial or absolute.

Plaintiff must have resided two years in the district.

FLORIDA.—Causes: (1) Where either party party had a husband
or wife living at time of marriage; (2) within the degeees of relationship forbidden; (3) impotency; (4) adultery; (5) extreme
cruelty; (6) habitual indulgence in violent and ungovernable
temper; (7) habitual intemperance; (8) willful, obstinate, and continued desertion for one year.

Plaintiff must have resided in State two years.

No partial divorce granted.

GEORGIA.—Causes: (1) Intermarriage within prohibited degrees
of affinity; (2) mental incapacity at time of marriage; (3) impotency at time of marriage; (4) force, fraud, or menace, in obtaining the marriage; (5) pregnancy of wife at time of marriage unknown to husband; (6) adultery; (7) willful and continued
desertion for three years; (8) conviction for crime and sentence to
penitentiary for two years or longer; (9) cruel treatment; (10)
habitual intoxication.

Divorce may be either absolute or partial.

IDAHO.—Causes: (1) Impotency at time of marriage; (2) where
the female was under fourteen and married without the consent
of her parents; (3) adultery; (4) extreme cruelty; (5) habitual
intemperance for two years; (6) willful desertion for one year;
(7) willful neglect to provide; (8) fraud or force in obtaining the
marriage; (9) conviction for felony and sentence for two years or
longer

The plaintiff must have resided six months in the Territory.

ILLINOIS—Causes: (1) Impotence; (2) bigamy, (3) adultery; (4)
desertion or drunkenness for two years; (5) attempt on the life of

the other; (6) extreme and repeated cruelty; (7) conviction of felony.

The plaintiff must have been a resident of the State one year.

INDIANA.—Causes: (1) Adultery; (2) impotency; (3) abandonment for two years; (4) cruel and inhuman treatment; (5) habitual drunkenness; (6) failure to provide for two years; (7) conviction of an infamous crime.

The plaintiff must have resided two years in the State.

IOWA.—Causes: (1) Adultery; (2) willful desertion for two years; (3) conviction for felony; (4) habitual drunkenness; (5) inhuman treatment; (6) pregnancy of the wife at time of marriage, unless known to the husband.

Marriages may be *annulled* for (1) marriage within prohibited degrees; (2) impotency at time of marriage; (3) where either party had a husband or wife at time of marriage.

Plaintiff must have been a resident for one year.

KANSAS.—Causes: (1) Former marriage; (2) abandonment for one year; (3) adultery; (4) impotency; (5) pregnancy of wife by other than her husband; (6) extreme cruelty; (7) fraud in contracting the marriage; (8) habitual drunkenness; (9) gross neglect of duty; (10) conviction of felony.

The plaintiff must have resided in the State one year.

KENTUCKY.—Causes: (1) Impotency; (2) living separate for five years; (3) abandonment for one year; (4) adultery; (5) conviction for felony; (6) concealment of loathsome disease existing at time of marriage; (5) force, fraud, or duress in obtaining the marriage; (6) habitual drunkenness for one year; (7) cruelty and inhuman treatment of wife by her husband for six months; (8) outrageous and ungovernable temper of husband; (9) pregnancy of wife by another man, without husband's knowledge, at time of marriage.

The plaintiff must have resided in the State one year. No divorce granted for acts done outside the State unless they were causes where done.

LOUISIANA.—Causes: (1) Habitual intemperance; (2) excess; (3) cruelty; (4) adultery; (5) conviction of crime; (6) abandonment

(7) public defamation; (8) attempt on the life of the other; (9) where either party has fled from justice.

MAINE.—Causes: (1) Adultery; (2) impotency; (3) extreme cruelty; (4) desertion for three years; (5) habitual drunkenness; (6) cruel or abusive treatment; (7) willful neglect to provide.

The plaintiff must have resided in the State one year.

MARYLAND.—Causes: (1) Adultery; (2) abandonment for three years; (3) fornication by wife before marriage.

These are the causes for absolute divorce, yet the court may decree that the guilty party shall not marry during the lifetime of the other.

Partial divorces are granted for: (1) Vicious conduct; (2) cruelty; (3) abandonment; (4) desertion.

MASSACHUSETTS.—Causes: (1) Adultery; (2) impotence; (3) extreme cruelty; (4) desertion for three years; (5) habitual intoxication; (6) cruelty; (7) neglect to provide proper support; (8) sentence to imprisonment for five years.

The plaintiff must have resided five years in the State, unless both parties were residents of the State at the time of the marriage. If the cause occurred out of the State, the parties must have prior thereto lived together in the State, or one of them must have lived here when the cause occurred

MICHIGAN.—Causes: (1) Adultery; (2) physical incompetence at the time of the marriage; (3) sentence of imprisonment for three years or more; (4) desertion for two years; (5) habitual drunkenness.

Any resident of the State whose husband or wife has obtained a divorce in another State may apply for a divorce, which will be granted in the discretion of the circuit court.

Imprisonment for life dissolves the marriage without any need for a divorce.

Partial divorce is granted either forever or for a limited time for (1) extreme cruelty and desertion and (2) for neglect to provide proper support.

MINNESOTA.—Causes for absolute divorce: (1) Adultery; (2) impotency; (3) cruel and inhuman treatment; (4) sentence of imprisonment in State's prison; (5) willful desertion for three years; (6) habitual drunkenness for one year.

Causes for limited divorce: (1) Cruel and inhuman treatment; (2) such conduct of the husband as may render it unsafe or improper for the wife to cohabit with him; (3) abandonment of the wife by the husband.

The plaintiff must have resided in the State one year.

MISSISSIPPI.—Causes: (1) Within prohibited degrees of affinity; (2) impotency; (3) adultery; (4) sentence to the penitentiary; (5) willful and continued desertion for two years; (6) habitual drunkenness; (7) insanity or idiocy at time of marriage; (8) habitua cruel and inhuman treatment marked by personal violence; (9) bigamy.

The plaintiff must have resided in the State one year.

MISSOURI.—Causes: (1) Impotency at time of marriage and still continuing; (2) wife or husband by former marriage still living; (3) adultery; (4) willful absence for one year; (5) conviction of a felony; (6) habitual drunkenness for one year; (7) cruel and barbarous treatment that endangers the life of the other; (8) such indignities as to render the condition of the other intolerable; (9) because husband is a vagrant; (10) conviction of husband previous to marriage for felony or infamous crime; (11) pregnancy of wife by another man at the time of the marriage.

NEBRASKA.—Causes: (1) Adultery; (2) abandonment for two years; (3) habitual drunkenness; (4) physical incompetence at time of marriage; (5) sentence of imprisonment for three years or longer; (6) extreme cruelty; (7) neglect to provide.

The plaintiff must have resided in the State six months.

NEVADA.—Causes: (1) Impotency at the time of marriage and continuing to the time of divorce; (2) adultry; (3) willful desertion for one year; (4) conviction of felony or infamous crime; (5) habitual gross drunkenness contracted since the marriage; (6) extreme cruelty; (7) willful neglect of the husband to provide proper support for one year.

The plaintiff must have resided in the county of the State where the action is brought six months.

NEW HAMPSHIRE.—Causes: (1) Impotency; (2) adultery; (3) extreme cruelty; (4) conviction of crime punishable by imprisonment for more than one year, and actual imprisonment on such conviction; (5) treatment seriously injuring health; (6) treatment endangering reason; (7) absence for three years without being heard of; (8) habitual drunkness for three years together; (9) refusal to cohabit for six months together; (10) when wife has resided out of the State separate from her husband ten years without his consent.

The defendant must be served *personally* with the papers if the parties are residents of another State. If only one party, as the plaintiff, resides in the State, he must actually reside there one year.

NEW JERSEY.—Causes: (1) Adultery; (2) bigamy; (3) willful and continued desertion for three years; (4) within prohibited degrees.

Partial divorce is granted for extreme cruelty.

Plaintiff must reside in the State three years.

NEW MEXICO.—Causes: (1) Abandonment; (2) cruel and inhuman treatment; (3) adultery.

Strict proof is required in all cases.

NEW YORK.—Causes for annulling marriage: (1) Where female was under fourteen and married without the consent of parents; (2) former husband or wife living; (3) idiocy or insanity; (4) force, fraud or duress in obtaining marriage; (5) physical incapacity.

Cause for absolute divorce: Adultery only. The plaintiff may re-marry but not the defendant.

Causes for limited divorce or separation: (1) Cruel and inhuman treatment; (2) abandonment; (3) neglect to support; (4) conduct rendering it unsafe and improper for defendant to cohabit with plaintiff.

NORTH CAROLINA.—Causes: (1) Adultery; (2) impotency; (3) pregnancy of wife at time of marriage without husband's agency or knowledge.

Limited divorce for: (1) Abandonment; (2) cruelty; (3) such indignities to the person of the other as to render his or her condition intolerable and life burdensome; (4) habitual drunkenness.

OHIO.—Causes: (1) Former husband or wife living; (2) willful absence for three years; (3) adultery; (4) impotence; (5) extreme cruelty; (6) fraud in obtaining the marriage; (7) any gross neglect of duty; (8) habitual drunkenness for three years; (9) imprisonment in the penitentiary under sentence; (10) the procurement of a divorce without the State by the other party.

OREGON.—Causes: (1) Impotency; (2) adultery; (3) conviction of felony; (4) habitual gross drunkenness of two years; (5) willful desertion for three years; (6) cruel and inhuman treatment; (7) personal indignities rendering life burdensome.

The plaintiff must have been a resident of the State for one year.

PENNSYLVANIA.—Causes: (1) Incapacity of procreation; (2) former marriage with husband or wife still alive; (3) adultery; (4) willful desertion for two years; (5) cruel treatment of wife by husband, or such personal indignities as to render her condition intolerable, and which have forced her to withdraw from his house; (6) incestuous marriage is void; (7) fraud, force and coercion in contracting the marriage; (8) conviction for felony and sentence for two years; (9) cruel treatment of husband by wife, such as to render his condition intolerable.

The plaintiff must have resided in the State one year.

RHODE ISLAND.—Causes: (1) Conviction of murder or arson; (2) absence for many years without knowledge; (3) impotency; (4) adultery; (5) extreme cruelty; willful desertion for five years; (6) continued drunkenness; (7) neglect of husband to provide necessaries; (8) other gross misbehavior, and wickedness repugnant to and in violation of the marriage covenant.

SOUTH CAROLINA.—No divorce for any cause permitted.

TENNESSEE.—Causes: (1) Impotency; (2) bigamy; (3) adultery; (4) willful desertion or absence for two years; (5) conviction of crime and sentence; (6) attempt by one party to take the life of the other; (7) refusal of wife to remove with her husband to this State, and willfully absenting herself from him two years; (8)

pregnancy of the wife at the time of marriage by another person without husband's knowledge; (9) habitual drunkenness.

Limited divorce or absolute for (1) cruel and inhuman treatment by husband; (2) indignities to her person; (3) abandonment; (4) refusal to provide for her.

The applicant for divorce must have resided within the State two years.

TEXAS.—Causes: (1) Impotency; (2) adultery; (3) abandonment for three years; (4) excess, cruel treatment or outrage, if such ill-treatment is of such a nature as to render their living together insupportable; (5) conviction for felony.

The applicant must be an actual inhabitant of the State and a resident of the county six months.

UTAH.—Causes: (1) Impotence; (2) adultery; (3) willful desertion for more than a year; (4) willful neglect to provide necessaries; (5) habitual drunkenness; (6) conviction for felony; (7) extreme cruelty.

VERMONT.—Causes: (1) Adultery; (2) sentence to imprisonment for three years or more; (3) intolerable severity; (4) absence of seven years and not heard of during that time; (5) willful desertion for three years; (6) willful neglect to provide necessaries.

The parties must have lived together as husband and wife within the State, and the applicant must have resided in the State one year next preceding the application.

The defendant, in case a divorce is granted, cannot marry again within three years; is liable to imprisonment for between one and five years.

VIRGINIA.—Causes: (1) Adultery; (2) impotency; (3) consanguinity; sentence to confinement in penitentiary; either party a fugitive from justice two years; (4) willful desertion and abandonment for five years; (5) pregnancy of wife at time of marriage by another man without knowledge of husband; (6) where the woman had before marriage been notoriously loose

Limited divorce decreed for (1) cruelty; (2) reasonable apprehension of bodily harm; (3) abandonment or desertion.

The plaintiff must be a resident of the State.

WEST VIRGINIA.—Causes: (1) Adultery; (2) impotency; (3) willful abandonment for three years; (4) sentence to penitentiary; (5) pregnancy of wife at time of marriage by another person without husband's knowledge; (6) where wife had unknown to husband been notoriously a prostitute before marriage; (7) where the husband had been notoriously immoral.

Marriages may be annulled for these causes, *i. e.*, (1) where a white person and a negro are married; (2) former husband or wife living; (3) consanguinity; (4) insanity; (5) where the male is under fourteen or the female under twelve years of age.

Limited divorce for (1) cruel and inhuman treatment; (2) reasonable apprehension of bodily hurt; (3) abandonment; (4) habitual drunkenness.

The plaintiff or one of the parties must have resided in the State one year.

WISCONSIN.—Causes: (1) Adultery; (2) impotency; (3) sentence of three years or more; (4) cruel and inhuman treatment; (5) willful desertion for one year; (6) habitual drunkenness for one year; (7) entire and voluntary separation for five years.

Plaintiff must have resided in the State one year.

PROVINCE OF ONTARIO, CANADA.—There is no divorce court. A special act of Parliament must be passed. Adultery is the only ground.

FORM OF ARTICLES OF SEPARATION BETWEEN HUSBAND AND WIFE.

This Indenture, made the ——— day of ———, one thousand eight hundred and ———, between A. B. of the first part, and his wife of the second part, and [name of trustee], as trustee of the said [name of the wife], of the third part;

Whereas, divers disputes and unhappy differences have arisen between the party of the first part and his wife, for which reason they have consented and agreed to live separate and apart from each other during their natural life.

Now, therefore, this Indenture witnesseth, that the said party of the first part in consideration of the premises, does hereby cov-

enant, promise and agree, to and with the said trustee, and to and
with his said wife, that it shall and may be lawful for her, his said
wife, at all times hereafter, to live separate and apart from him,
and that he shall and will allow and permit her to reside and be in
such and such place or places, and in such family or families, and with
such relations, friends and other persons, and to follow and carry
on such trade or business as she may from time to time choose or
think fit; and that he shall not, nor will at any time, sue, or suffer
her to be sued, for living separate and apart from him, or compel
her to live with him; nor sue, molest, disturb or trouble any other
person whomsoever, for receiving, entertaining or harboring her;
and that he will not, without her consent, visit her, or knowingly
enter any house or place where she shall dwell, reside or be, or
send, or cause to be sent, any letter or message to her; nor shall
or will, at any time hereafter, claim or demand any of her money,
jewels, plate, clothing, household goods, furniture or stock-in-
trade, which she now has in her power, custody or possession, or
which she shall or may, at any time hereafter, have, buy or procure, or which shall be devised or given to her, or that she may
otherwise acquire, and that she shall and may enjoy and absolutely dispose of the same as if she were a *femme sole* and unmarried;
and further, that the said party of the first part shall and will well
and truly pay, or cause to be paid, for and toward the better
support and maintenance of his said wife the sum of ————
dollars, to be paid to her said trustee monthly, for her benefit and
use. And the said trustee, in consideration of the sum of one
dollar to him duly paid, does covenant and agree, to and with the
said party of the first part, to indemnify and bear him harmless of
and from all debts of his said wife, contracted, or that may hereafter be contracted by her, or on her account; and if the said party
of the first part shall be compelled to pay any such debt or debts,
the said trustee hereby agrees to repay the same on demand, to
the said party of the first part, with all damage and loss he may
sustain thereby.

In witness whereof, the said parties have hereunto affixed their
hands and seals, this ———— day of ———— 18—.

[Signatures.]   [Seal.]

CHAPTER XIII.

PARENT AND CHILD.

Rights of the Parent—Custody—Adoption—Method of Adoption—Right to Punish—To Educate—Right to Earnings—Emancipation—No Right to Child's Property—Right to Services—Liabilities of the Parent—To Support the Child—Even Illegitimate Child—Children Must Support Parent Sometimes—Where a Child has Property of its Own—Liable for Necessaries—What are Necessaries—Not Liable for Non-necessaries—Nor for Willful Acts—Nor Crimes—Illegitimate Children—Subsequent Marriage makes Legitimate—Effect of Illegitimacy—May Inherit from Mother—Guardians.

In very ancient times the parent of a child, particularly the father, was regarded as possessing almost absolute rights. With the progress of modern ideas of the family, these rights have become very much limited, and the relations of parent and child carefully defined.

Rights of the Parent—Custody. The parent is entitled to the custody of his minor child as against all the world. No one has the right to take the child and retain him against the wishes of the parent; nor has the child himself any right to leave his parent and live away from home. He can be compelled to return. If a relative or other person keeps him and refuses to give him up, the parent may obtain a writ of " habeas corpus," directing such person to produce the child in court; and the rights of the parties are then decided by the judge, who must order the child to be given up to the parent, unless there be some strong reason, such as cruelty or drunkenness on the part of the parent, which would make it improper to do so.

Adoption. Any child, whether its parents are living or not, may be adopted. In that case the parent is no longer entitled to the custody, but the adopting person is. The child cannot be adopted without the consent of its parents, if they are living, but the consent, having once been given, cannot be revoked. If the child is over fourteen years of age, it must also consent to the adoption. Under any circumstances the court has the right to refuse to permit the adoption if it considers that the person petitioning is not a proper person to have the custody.

Method of Adoption. The usual method of adopting a child is to draw up a written petition addressed to a court, reciting the facts which make the adoption necessary or desirable. This must generally be sworn to. Then the parties come before the court, and if the judge is convinced from the testimony that there is no valid objection, he will order that the child be adopted. The adopting person is then entitled to all the rights of a natural parent, and the child owes him the same duties as it would to its father or mother, had it not been adopted.

To Punish. The parent has the right to punish his child, as by administering corporal punishment, provided he does not carry it so far as to be guilty of cruelty. Brutality, even of a parent, will be punished by the law.

To Educate. It is the parent's right and his duty to educate his child. In some States there are laws making it obligatory upon the parent to send his child to some public or private school a certain number of weeks in the year (in New York fourteen weeks, eight of which must be consecutive).

Right to Earnings. The parent is entitled to all the earnings of his minor child. If the child refuses to hand them over to his parent, the latter may notify the child's employer to pay the wages of the child to *him*. If the employer, notwithstanding, continues to pay them to the child, the parent may sue and recover them of the employer.

"Emancipation." The parent, however, may "emancipate" his child; that is, he may give him the right to receive his own earnings, and he cannot then demand them of the employer. This "emancipation" may either be express or it may be implied from the silent acquiescence of the parent.

No Right to Property of the Child. Although a parent may claim the earnings of his child on the ground that he is obliged to support it, he has no right to the property of the child acquired by gift, or by a legacy in a will, or in any other way.

If a parent should appropriate any of his child's property, he would be just as guilty of theft as any-one else who might take it wrongfully, and he could not excuse himself on the ground that it was only a fair compensation for the support he had given the child. The latter could sue his parent for the value of the property appropriated, and have him arrested for the crime as well.

Right to Services. The parent has a right to the services of his child, about the household for instance, and the child has no claim for compensation; not even if it is an adult. It is on this ground that a father or mother is allowed to sue for the loss of the child's services where the latter is enticed away from home. In case a daughter residing at home and ren-dering services, no matter how slight, is seduced, the parent may sue the seducer for damages on the ground of the loss of his daughter's services. The daughter herself cannot sue because of her consent. *" Volenti non fit injuria."*

The amount of damages recoverable by the parent is not the mere value of the daughter's services. The injury to the honor and reputation of the family is taken into consideration, and very heavy damages— thousands of dollars—sometimes are given.

Liabilities of the Parent to Support. The prin-cipal duty of a parent is to support his child, certain-ly during its minority. It is provided in England by statute that one who marries a widow with children by a former husband is obliged to support them until they are sixteen years of age. But this is not generally the law in the United States.

Even Illegitimate Children. It is a parent's duty to support even an illegitimate child. Such a child has legally no father, but his putative father, as he is called, may be compelled by the Overseers of the Poor to furnish the child with reasonable support, so that it shall not become a "burden on the parish."

Children Must Support Parent. On this same ground an adult child must support an indigent parent who is incapable of taking care of himself.

When Child has Property of its Own. If the child has means of its own, such as a legacy left to it by a will, the father must still support the child from his own means, and cannot make any demand against the child's property. In case, however, the parent is poor or has other children who have claims upon him, he may apply to a court of equity for permission to use some of the child's property for its support and education. The court may then order the guardian of the child's property, who may be the father himself or some other person, to use a certain amount for those purposes.

Liable for Necessaries. The parent is liable to tradesmen and others who furnish "necessaries" to his child; this is true, even though he has given notice that he will not pay the debts of his children, or be bound by their contracts. He is under an obligation to support his child, and he cannot get rid of it in any way.

What are Necessaries? By "necessaries" are meant generally all those things that are necessary to life, such as food, clothing and shelter, and even some things not absolutely necessary, but which are proper and suitable for a child occupying the social position to which his parent's means entitle him. The same things which might be regarded as necessaries for the son of a wealthy man would not be necessaries for the son of a man without wealth.

Not Liable for Non-Necessaries. But in no case is a parent liable for unnecessary articles, like costly jewelry, purchased by his child

Nor For Willful Acts. Nor is the parent responsible to others for damage occasioned by the willful or wrongful acts of his child. The child alone is responsible for such acts

Nor Crimes. The parent of course cannot be held for a crime committed by his child, but the latter, if it has arrived at the age of discretion, usually seven years, is just as liable to be punished as any older person.

Illegitimate Children. All children born in wedlock are legitimate, unless it is proved that the husband could not possibly be the father. The adultery of the wife cannot affect the legitimacy of the child. He is conclusively presumed to be the child of the husband.

It makes no difference how soon after the marriage the child is born. A child born the same day as the marriage, if subsequent to the ceremony, is legitimate, provided there is good reason for believing that the husband is the father. This is the law in New York.

Subsequent Marriage Makes Legitimate. In many of the States of the Union a subsequent marriage of the father and mother, no matter how long after the birth of the child, makes it legitimate. These States are Maine, Vermont, Massachusetts, Connecticut, Maryland, Virginia, Ohio, Indiana, Illinois, Missouri, Georgia, Alabama, Mississippi, Louisiana and Kentucky.

Effect of Illegitimacy. The only legal effect of illegitimacy of any consequence is that the child cannot inherit property from his father; nor from his mother, if she have any legitimate children. He may, of course, take a legacy given to him by his putative father's will, but if there is no will he cannot inherit.

May Inherit from Mother. If his mother leaves no legitimate children, he may inherit her property, and if he dies before his mother, without children of his own, his mother is entitled to his property. With the exception of this disability, an illegitimate child has every natural and civil right.

Guardians. A guardian is one who has control of the person or the property of an infant, or both. He may be appointed by a direction of the parent in his will, in which case he is called a testamentary guardian.

Sometimes a guardian is appointed by a court of equity, or a surrogate.

If he has possession of his ward's property, he is required to give bonds. If a child is over fourteen he may petition for the removal of his guardian and have another appointed.

The rights and duties of guardians are similar to those of parents.

They cannot sell or dispose of the child's land without obtaining an order of court.

At the termination of the guardianship they must account, and they are personally liable for any misuse of their ward's money or for letting it lie idle.

They are entitled to certain commissions as compensation for their services.

When an infant sues or is sued, it is necessary to have a special guardian appointed for the purpose of protecting his interests in the suit. This guardian is generally a lawyer and is called a guardian *ad litem*.

CHAPTER XIV.

PATENTS, COPYRIGHTS AND TRADE-MARKS.

PATENTS: *New and Useful Invention—Subject of a Patent—Who May Obtain a Patent—Duration of a Patent—The Application—The Petition—The Specification—Contents Of—The Claim—Disclaimer—The Oath—The Drawings—Model and Specimens—Amendments—Drawings for Designs—Re-issue—Appeals—Caveat—Assignment--Licenses—Rights of a Purchaser—Infringement—Fees.* COPYRIGHT: *Nature Of—Who Can Apply—Duration Of—How Acquired—Notice—Infringement—Assignment.* TRADE-MARKS: *Nature Of—Who Has the Right to Use—Registration—What is a Good Trade-mark—Words of Quality and Description—Fraud—Sale—Infringements.* FORMS: *Petition—For Re-issue—Oath — Specification — Disclaimer — Assignment.*

A PATENT is a grant by the United States of an exclusive right to manufacture and sell an invented article for a limited period.

Invention Must be New and Useful. In order to entitle an inventor to a patent, his invention must be new and useful. If it is merely an application of an old invention, the patent will not be granted. It must not have been known or used in this country by others.

If patented or described in any printed publication in this or any foreign country before his invention or discovery thereof, and if in public use or on sale for more than two years prior to his application, the applicant cannot obtain a patent.

Subject of a Patent. A patent may be obtained for the invention or discovery of any new and useful art, machine, manufacture, or composition of matter, or process, or any new and useful improvement thereof.

New and original designs for a manufacture, bust, statue, or for the printing of fabrics may be patented.

Who May Obtain a Patent. The patent is generally issued to the original inventor himself. If he dies, his executor or administrator may make the application, and take out the patent in his own name. It may also in case of assignment before the issue of the patent be issued directly to the assignee.

Aliens, that is, citizens of another county, may have their inventions patented in the United States.

Duration of Patent. A patent, when granted, is good for seventeen years. After that time, the invention is free and open to the public

No patent granted after March 2, 1861, can be extended except by act of Congress.

A foreign inventor, who has patented his invention in his own or any other country, can obtain a patent here only for the unexpired period which his foreign patent has to run.

The duration of a design patent may be for the term of three and a half, seven, or fourteen years.

The Application. Applications for a patent must be made to the Commissioner of Patents. A complete application comprises the petition, specification, oath, and drawings, and the model or specimen when required, and the first fee of $15. The petition, specification and oath must be written in the **English** language.

It is desirable that all these papers, etc., should be deposited in the office at the same time. The application will not be placed upon the files for examination until all the parts, except the model or specimen, are received. A delay of two years after filing the petition in completing the application acts as an abandonment.

The Petition. The petition is a communication duly signed by the applicant and addressed to the Commissioner of Patents, stating the name and residence of the petitioner, and requesting the grant of a patent for the invention, therein designated by name, with a reference to the specification for a full disclosure thereof.

The Specification. The specification is a written description of the invention or discovery, and of the manner and process of making and using the same. It is required to be in such full, clear, concise, and exact terms as to enable any person skilled in the art or science to which it appertains to make and use it.

Contents of. The specification should contain the following: 1st. Preamble, giving the name and residence of the applicant, and the title of the invention; and if the invention has been patented in any country, a statement of the country or countries in which it has been so patented, giving the date and number of each patent. If the patent has no number it will be so stated under oath. 2d. General statement of the object and nature of the invention. 3d. Brief description of the drawings, showing what each view represents. 4th. Detailed description explaining fully the alleged invention, and the manner of constructing, practicing, operating, and using it. 5th. Claim or claims. 6th. Signature of inventor. 7th. Signatures of two witnesses.

The Claim. The claim is part of the specification, and requires great knowledge, care, and skill to draw it properly. It is a clear and accurate statement of what is original in the invention, and must not include too much or too little. A mere principle or law of Nature cannot be claimed, but a process or machine involving such a principle may be.

Disclaimer. Whenever through inadvertence, accident, or mistake, and without any fraudulent intention, the claim embraces more than the inventor was the original discoverer of, the patent remains good for what is original, provided the inventor files in the Patent Office a " disclaimer " of what he was not entitled to claim, without unreasonable delay. The disclaimer must be in writing attested by witnesses.

The Oath. The applicant for a patent must make oath or affirmation, that he does verily believe himself to be the original and first discoverer of the art, machine, manufacture, composition, or improvement for which he solicits a patent, and that he does not know, and does not believe that the same was ever before known or used. He must state of what country he is a citizen, and where he resides. The form of the oath is slightly changed when the application is made by an executor or administrator.

The Drawings. The applicant for a patent is required by law to furnish a drawing of his invention, where the nature or the case admits of it. The drawing must be signed by the inventor, or his attorney in fact, and attested by two witnesses. It should show every feature of the invention covered by the claims.

Models and Specimens. If the examiner finds a model necessary or useful, he must file a written certificate to that effect, and the applicant must furnish one. The model should be neatly made of durable material, metal being preferable. It must exhibit every feature of the machine which forms the subject of claim. A working model is often desirable.

When the invention or discovery is a composition of matter, the applicant, if required by the Commissioner, must furnish specimens of the composition. Where the article is not perishable, a specimen of the composition claimed, put up in proper form to be preserved, must be furnished.

Amendments. Amendments may be made by the

applicant before or after the first rejection. They may be made as often as there are any reasons offered for the rejection of the application. The amendments are written on separate pieces of paper.

Drawings, etc., for Designs. When a design can be sufficiently represented by a drawing or photographs, a model will not be required. Wherever a photograph or an engraving is employed to illustrate the design, it must be mounted upon Bristol board, 10x15 inches in size, and properly signed and witnessed. The applicant will be required to furnish ten extra copies of such photograph or engraving (not mounted) of a size not exceeding seven and a half inches by eleven.

Re-issue. A re-issue is granted when the original patent is invalid or void by reason of a defective or insufficient specification, or from excessive claim, provided the error arose from inadvertence, accident or mistake, and without fraudulent intention.

There must be filed with the petition for a re-issue, a statement setting forth the defects of the specification, and an oath that the errors arose without any fraudulent or deceptive intention.

Appeals. Appeals may be taken by applicants from the decision of the examiners to the examiners-in-chief, then to the Commissioner, and then to the Supreme Court of the District of Columbia, and the Supreme Court of the United States.

Caveat. A caveat is a notice given to the Patent Office by an inventor of his claim to an invention he has not matured or finished, in order to prevent the grant of a patent to another for the same or a similar invention without notice.

Any citizen of the United States, or an alien who has been a resident for one year, may file a caveat. The caveat should set forth the object and distinguishing characteristics of the invention, and pray protection of the caveator's right, until he has matured his invention. The paper is filed in the confidential archives, and preserved in secrecy. The caveat must comprise a specification, an oath, and a drawing, if possible.

The caveat continues in force only for one year, and may be renewed by payment of a second fee of ten dollars.

If, within the year, any application is filed interfering with such caveat, notice is given to the caveator to file a complete application within three months.

Assignment. Every patent or any interest therein is assignable by an instrument in writing.

The assignment may be of the inventor's entire interest, or of the right to manufacture and sell the article, or to use the process, within a certain territory.

It must be recorded in the Patent Office within three months from its date, or it will be void as against a subsequent purchaser or mortgagee for value without notice.

Licenses. A license to manufacture or use the patented article indefinitely, or for a limited time may be given. The license may be oral or written.

Rights of a Purchaser. The purchaser of a patented article or machine is entitled to use it, and may repair it from time to time, But he cannot make or construct another like it. He is at liberty to sell it to anyone he pleases, even in a territory for which another person has taken an assignment of the patent, or of an exclusive right to sell.

Infringement. During the period for which the patent is granted, no one but the inventor and his assigns have a right to manufacture and sell the patented article.

If any other person does so, he is guilty of infringement.

The only method of relief against an infringer is an action in the United States Circuit Courts, which have jurisdiction of patent cases. The patentee can obtain an injunction compelling the infringer to stop such manufacture and sale, and to account for the profits already made. A temporary injunction is frequently obtained at the beginning of the case, before it has been decided on the merits.

Fees. Nearly all the fees payable to the Patent Office are positively required by law to be paid in advance—that is, upon making application for any action by the office for which a fee is payable. For the sake of uniformity and convenience, the remaining fees will be required to be paid in the same manner:

The following is the schedule of fees and prices of publications, etc., of the Patent Office:

On filing each original application for a design patent for
    three years and six months $10 00

On filing each original application for a design patent for
    seven years 15 00

On filing each original application for a design patent for
    ourteen years 30 00

On allowance of an application for a design patent, no
    further charge.

On filing each caveat 10 00

On filing each original application for a patent   .   .   15 00

On allowance of an original application for a patent,
    except in design cases 20 00

On filing each disclaimer 10 00

On filing every application for the re-issue of a patent   .   30 00

On filing each application for a division of a re-issue   .   30 00

On allowance of an application for the re-issue of a patent,
    no further charge.

On filing every application for an extension of a patent   .   50 00

On the granting of every extension of a patent   .   .   50 00

On filing an appeal from a primary examiner to the
    examiners-in-chief 10 00

On filing an appeal from the examiners-in-chief to the
    Commissioner 20 00

For manuscript copies of records in the English language,
    for every one hundred words or fraction thereof   .   10

If certified, for the certificate additional   .   .   .   25

For copies of drawings not in print, the reasonable cost
    of making them.

For uncertified copies of the specifications and accompany-
    ing drawings of all patents which are in print:

Single copies   25

Twenty copies or more, whether of one or several patents,
    per copy   10

For twenty coupon orders, each coupon good until used
    for one copy of a printed specification and drawing   2 00

For certified copies of patents, whether in manuscript or in print:

For the specification, for every one hundred words or fraction thereof	10
For the drawings, if in print	25
For the drawings, if not in print, the reasonable cost of making them, as above.	
For the certificate	25
For the grant	50
For certifying to a duplicate of a model	50

For abstracts of title to patents or inventions:

For the certificate of search	1 00
For each brief from the digests of assignments . .	20
For copies of matter in any foreign language, for every one hundred words or fraction thereof , ' .	20
For translation, for every one hundred words or fraction thereof	50
For recording every assignment, agreement, power of attorney, or other paper, of three hundred words or under	1 00
For recording every assignment, agreement, power of attorney, or other paper of over three hundred words and under one thousand words	2 00
For recording every assignment, agreement, power of attorney, or other paper of over one thousand words	3 00

COPYRIGHT.

Copyright is the exclusive right which may be obtained by an author or publisher to print and sell copies of his work for a limited period.

Subject of Copyright. A copyright may be obtained for any book, map, or chart, dramatic or musical composition, engraving, cut, print, photograph, or negative thereof or of a painting, drawing, chromo, statue, statuary and of models and designs intended to be perfected as works of the fine arts.

The name of a newspaper cannot be copyrighted, but it may be registered and protected as a trade-mark.

Who Can Apply. The author, inventor, designer, or proprietor of anything subject to copyright, or the executors, administrators, or assigns of such persons may apply for a copyright.

No one who is not a citizen of the United States, or resident therein, can obtain a copyright. Foreign authors are denied the privilege.

The right conferred is the sole liberty of printing, reprinting, publishing, completing, copying, executing, furnishing and vending the book, map, etc., and in case of a dramatic composition, of publicly performing or representing it, or causing it to be performed or represented by others.

Authors may reserve the right to dramatize or translate their own works. This has no force beyond the United States.

Duration Of. Copyrights are granted for the term of twenty-eight years. At the expiration of this period, the author, inventor or designer, if still living, or his widow or children, if he is dead, may have the copyright extended for the further term of fourteen years.

The application for this renewal must be made within six months after the original copyright expires. The steps to be taken are the same as in the case of the original copyright, except that within two months after the renewal a copy of the record must be printed in one or more newspapers published in the United States. If this is not done, other persons cannot be sued for infringement.

How Acquired. The necessary steps in obtaining a copyright are as follows: The applicant must, before publication, deliver at the office of the Librarian of Congress, or deposit in the mail addressed to the Librarian of Congress, at Washington, D. C., a printed copy of the title of the book or other article or a description of the painting, drawing, chromo, statue, statuary, etc., for which he desires a copyright.

Within ten days after publication he must deliver or send by mail two copies of such copyright book, or other article, or in case of a painting, drawing, statue, statuary, etc., a photograph of the same.

The Librarian then records the name of the copyrighted book, or other article, in a book kept for that purpose, for which he is entitled to a fee of fifty cents. The copyright is then complete.

The failure on the part of the proprietor of any copyright to deliver or deposit in the mail, either of the published copies, or description, or photograph makes him liable to a penalty of twenty-five dollars, to be recovered of him by an action in any district court of the United States. Such an omission does not make the copyright void.

Notice. The proprietor of a copyright must give

notice thereof by inserting in each of the copies of every edition published, on the title page, or the page immediately following, if it be a book, or if a map, chart, musical composition, etc., by inscribing upon some visible portion thereof the words, "Entered according to act of Congress, in the year 18—, by A. B. in the office of the Librarian of Congress, at Washington;" or these words at his option: "Coyprighted, 18—, by A. B."

Every person who inserts such a notice, or one of similar purport, in or on any book, etc., for which he has not obtained a copyright, is liable to a penalty of $100, one-half for the person who may sue for such penalty, and one-half to the use of the United States.

Infringement. Any person who prints, publishes, or imports, or sells, or exposes to sale a copy of any copyrighted book forfeits every copy thereof to the proprietor of the copyright, and is liable to pay him whatever damages may be recovered in a civil action.

In the case of maps, musical compositions, engravings, etc., the infringer forfeits to the proprietor all the plates, and every sheet either copied or printed. Besides this he also forfeits one dollar for every sheet found in his possession; and in case of a painting, statue, or statuary, ten dollars for every copy so found.

The consent of the proprietor of the copyright may be obtained by an instrument in writing, signed by him in the presence of two or more witnesses.

Any person publicly performing or representing

any dramatic composition for which a copyright has been obtained, without the consent of the proprietor thereof, or his heirs or assigns, is liable for damages therefor, not less than $100 for the first, or $50 for any subsequent performance. Dramatic compositions are also protected independent of copyright.

Assignment. A copyright may be assigned by any instrument in writing. The assignment must be recorded in the office of the Librarian of Congress within sixty days after its execution. Otherwise it is void as against any subsequent purchaser or mortgagee for a valuable consideration without notice.

TRADE-MARKS.

A trade-mark is a name or device used by the manufacturer, proprietor, or seller of goods in connection with goods sold by him, to indicate that they are made by him, or that he has the exclusive right to sell them. Trade-marks frequently have great value, and secure to the owner the profits arising from the sale of the goods bearing the mark.

Who Has the Right? The person who has chosen a trade-mark has the exclusive right to use it. A foreigner can claim protection for his trade-mark in the United States as well as a citizen. It is not necessary to take any special steps to secure a trade-mark, as in the case of a patent or a copyright.

Registration. But it is desirable to have the trade-mark registered in the patent office at Washington. This is done as follows:

1. By causing to be recorded in the patent office the names of the parties and their residences and places of business, who desire the protection of the trade-mark.

2. The class of merchandise and the particular description of goods comprised in such class, by which the trade-mark has been or is intended to be appropriated.

3. A description of the trade-mark itself, with fac-similes thereof and the mode in which it has been, or is intended to be, applied and used.

4. The length of time, if any, during which the trade-mark has been used.

5. The payment of a fee of twenty-five dollars, in the same manner, and for the same purpose as the fee required for patents.

6. The compliance with such regulations as may be prescribed by the Commissioner of Patents.

7. The filing of a declaration under the oath of the person, or of some member of the firm, or officer of the corporation, to the effect that the party claiming protection for the trade-mark has a right to the use of the same, and that no other person, firm or corporation has the right to such use, either in the identical form, or having such near resemblance thereto as might be calculated to deceive, and that the description and fac-similes presented for record are true copies of the trade-mark sought to be protected.

Trade-marks remain in force thirty years. The

forms of application will be furnished by tne Patent Office when requested.

Prints and labels may also be registered on payment of a fee of six dollars. The registration continues in force twenty-eight years.

What is a Good Trade-Mark? A valid trademark may consist of the name of the manufacturer, but he cannot prevent another person of the same name from using it on goods of his own.

The trade-mark may be any device, emblem or symbol not already in use, which may be selected.

The name of the place where the goods are manufactured is a good trade-mark.

The best and safest kind of a trade-mark is some unusual word in combination with an unusual device. An ordinary device like a star or a cross cannot be claimed as a trade-mark to the exclusion of its use by others.

Words of Quality. Words which denote the quality, nature, kind, description, ingredients, composition, etc., of an article, do not constitute a good or valid trade-mark, because language cannot be appropriated by one individual in this way.

Such words as "superior," "superfine," etc., cannot be protected. Every one has the right to use them.

Fraud or Dishonesty. Any fraud or dishonesty on the part of the owner of a trade-mark, such as an attempt to mislead the public as to the quality or maker of the goods, or any misrepresentations in the label, have the effect of making void a trade-mark in other respects good. The courts will refuse to protect such a trade-mark, or to enjoin other persons from its use.

Sale. A trade-mark is a property-right and may be the subject of sale. There must be no circumstances, however, which would lead the public to believe that the original owner was still the manufacturer or seller of the goods. The sale of a business usually carries with it the exclusive right to use the trade-mark, even if no express contract is made.

Infringement. Any person who uses or employs on his own goods the trade-mark of another, for the purpose of taking advantage of the other's reputation, or for any other reason, may be compelled to stop such use and sale of the goods so marked, and to account to the owner of the trade-mark for the profits made.

It is not necessary to constitute infringement that the same identical mark be used. There may be considerable difference. A merely colorable imitation, or a resemblance so close as to deceive or to cause a superficial observer to take one for the other, is an infringement.

FORM OF PETITION.

To the Commissioner of Patents:

Your petitioner, A. B., a citizen of the United States, residing at Poughkeepsie, in the County of Dutchess, and State of New York, prays that letters patent be granted to him for the improvement in [subject of invention], set forth in the annexed specifications. A. B.

PETITION FOR RE-ISSUE.

To the Commissioner of Patents:

Your petitioner, A.B., a citizen of the United States, residing at G., in the County of M., and State of N., prays that he may be allowed to surrender the letters patent for an improvement in force-pumps, granted to him May 10, 1885, whereof he is now sole owner, and that letters patent may be re-issued to him, for the same invention upon the annexed amended specification. With this petition is filed an abstract of title duly certified, as required in such cases.   A. B.

CAVEAT.

The petition of A. B., a citizen of the United States, residing at L., in the County of M., and State of N., represents:

That he has made certain improvements in cotton-gins, and that he is now engaged in making experiments for the purpose of perfecting the same, preparatory to applying for letters patent therefor. He therefore prays that the subjoined description of his invention may be filed as a caveat in the confidential archives of the Patent Office.

OATH.

[To follow specification.]

STATE OF ——————, }
COUNTY OF ——————. } ss.

A. B., the above named petitioner, citizen of ——————, and resident of ——————, in the County of ——————, and State of ——————, being duly sworn, deposes and says that he verily believes himself to be the original and first inventor of the improvement in the force-pumps, described and claimed in the foregoing specification; that the same has not been patented to himself, or to others, with his knowledge or consent; that the same has not to his knowledge been in public use or on sale in the United States for more than two years prior to this application, and does not know and does not believe that the same was ever known or used prior to his invention thereof.

[Inventor's full name.]

Sworn to and subscribed before me this 10th day of June, 1884.
[Signature of notary.]   (Seal.)

SPECIFICATION.

To all whom it may concern:

Be it known that I, A. B., of ————, in the county of ————, in the State of ————, have invented a new and improved mode of preventing steam boilers from bursting; and I do hereby declare that the following is a full and exact description thereof, reference being had to the accompanying drawings and to the letters of reference marked thereon.

The nature of my invention consists in providing the upper part of a steam boiler with an aperture in addition to that for the safety-valve, which aperture is to be closed by a plug or disk of alloy which will fuse at any given degree of heat, and permit the steam to escape should the safety-valve fail to perform its functions.

To enable others skilled in the art to make and use my invention, I will proceed to describe its construction and operation. I construct my steam boiler in any of the known forms, and apply thereto gauge-cocks, a safety-valve and the other appendages of such boilers; but, in order to obviate the danger arising from the adhesion of the safety-valve, and from other causes, I make a second opening in the top of the boiler, similar to that made for the safety-valve, as shown at A, in the accompanying drawing, and in this opening I insert a plug or disk of fusible alloy, securing it in its place by a metal ring and screws, or otherwise. In general, I compose this fusible metal of a mixture of lead, tin and bismuth, in such proportions as will insure its melting at a given temperature, which must be that to which it is intended to limit the steam; it will, of course, vary with the pressure the boiler is intended to sustain.

I surround the opening containing the fusible alloy by a tube B, intended to conduct off any steam which may be discharged therefrom.

When the temperature of the steam in such a boiler rises to its assigned limit, the fusible alloy will melt and allow the steam to escape freely, thereby securing it from all danger of explosion.

What I claim as my invention, and desire to secure by letters patent, is the application to steam boilers of a fusible alloy which will melt at a given temperature and allow the steam to escape, as herein described, using for the purpose the aforesaid metallic compound, or any other substantially the same, and which will produce the intended effect. A. B.

Witness.

DISCLAIMER.

To the Commissioner of Patents:

Your petioner, A. B., a citizen of the United States, residing at L., in the County of M., and State of N., represents that in the matter of a certain improvement in printing presses, for which letters patent of the United States, No. 75,000, were granted to C. D., on the 12th day of June, 1879, he is [here state interest of disclaimant]; and that he has reason to believe that, through inadvertence, the specification and claim of said letters patent are too broad, including that of which said patentee was not the first inventor. Your petitioner, therefore, hereby enters his disclaimer to that part of the claim in said specification which is in the following words, to-wit:

"I also claim the sleeves, A B, having each a friction-cam, C, and conncted respectively by means of chains or cords, K L and M N, with an oscillatory lever to operate substantially as herein shown and described."

Witness, A. B.

C. D.

ASSIGNMENT OF ENTIRE INTEREST IN PATENT.

Whereas, I, A. B., of L., County of M., State of N., did obtain letters patent of the United States for an improvement in car-wheels, which letters patent are numbered 95,000, and bear date the 5th day of June, in the year 1869, and whereas, I am now the sole owner of said patent and of all rights under the same, and whereas, E. F., of R., County of S., State of N., is desirous of acquiring the entire interest in the same.

Now, therefore, to all whom it may concern, be it known that for and in consideration of the sum of five thousand dollars to me in hand paid, the receipt whereof is hereby acknowledged, I, the said C. D., have sold, assigned, and transferred, and by these presents do sell, assign and transfer unto the said E. F. the whole right, title, and interest in and to the said improvement in car-wheels, and in and to the letters patent therefor aforesaid; the same to be held and enjoyed by the said E. F. for his own use and behoof, and for the use and behoof of his legal representatives, to the full end of the term for which said letters patent are or may be granted, as fully and entirely as the same would have been held and enjoyed by me had this assignment and sale not been made.

In testimony whereof I have hereunto set my hand and affixed my seal at L., in the County of M., and State of N., this 25th day of July, 1878.

In presence of,   A. B.   [Seal.]
    W. X.,
    Y. Z.

CHAPTER XV.

INSURANCE.

Kinds of—Insurance Companies—Re-insurance—Double Insurance—The Policy—Valued and Open Policies—Insurable Interest—Mortgagee May Insure—Creditor's May—Insurance Agents—No Authority to Waive Proofs of Loss — Warranties — Representations — Hazardous Trades—Occupancy—Care — Negligence—Alterations—Alienation—May Lease or Mortgage—Representations in Life Insurance—The Premium—Assignment—Policies Payable to Wife—Proof of Loss—Mutual Companies—Form of Proof of Loss.

INSURANCE is an indemnity for loss, either of property or life. The loss incurred on buildings or goods usually is that arising from fire, and the policies are called fire policies, even though other perils are enumerated, such as damage from water. Marine insurance applies to vessels and their cargoes, and is very different from ordinary fire insurance. It is treated of in the chapter on Shipping.

Insurance Companies. Any person may be an insurer, but usually such business is carried on by insurance companies—corporations with large capitals. Still, a contract by one man to pay another a sum of money, in case of the loss of or injury to the latter's property, is a good and valid contract, even if it is oral and never committed to writing.

Re-insurance. Insurers may, after they have insured another, re-insure their own risk. Insurance companies often re-insure in another company at a smaller premium for their own protection.

But the first insured who holds the policy of the first company has no claim against the second company—the re-insurer—even if the first company is insolvent, and cannot pay the loss

Double Insurance. By double insurance is meant the case where property is insured in more than one company. It is generally necessary to get the consent of the first company before the insured can take out a second policy elsewhere. Otherwise the first policy will be void.

The insured is entitled in any event to recover as insurance only the amount of his loss and not the face of the policy. If, therefore, he is insured in several companies for more than his loss, or if the loss is total, for more than the value of the premises, each company is only liable proportionately to the amount of risk each carried.

The holder of the policy, however, is entitled to demand full payment from each company until his loss is satisfied, and then the companies so paying will have a claim on the other companies which have not paid their share for that share.

The Policy. The contract of insurance with its various conditions is embodied in the " policy," which

differs, of course, with different companies. No
peculiar form is necessary. The usual questions are
asked of the applicant, and together with the written
answers are filed in the office of the company, which
then issues the policy. Some companies issue an
informal variety of policy known as "accident tickets," usually for short periods, as a voyage or journey; for example, the following: "This Company
will pay the holder of this ticket —— dollars a week
in case of injury from accidents; or, in case of death,
—— dollars to his legal representatives." This,
though very short, is nevertheless a perfectly valid
policy.

Valued and Open Policies. Policies may either
be *valued*, that is, they may state the amount of risk
taken, or *open*, in which case the amount of loss
proved is the amount the company is obliged to pay.
Time policies state the period for which they are to
run. Life insurance policies are, of course, always
valued policies.

Insurable Interest. Any person may insure his
own life or property in favor of anyone he mentions.
But no one else can effect such insurance unless he
has an insurable interest in the other person. Anyone who might possibly be dependent upon another
for support has such an interest as to entitle him
to insure the other's life for his own benefit; that
is, to take out a policy payable to himself. A child
has this interest in the life of his father or mother,
even though not actually dependent upon them for

support; also a father in the life of his son, or a sister in the life of her brother, or a brother in the life of his brother.

If a child is supported by anyone not a relative such child would have an insurable interest.

A creditor also may insure his debtor's life up to the amount of the debt, which is, of course, the extent of his interest. He can effect such insurance and make it payable to himself, or any person he names, without giving the debtor thus insured any right or control over the policy. An employe even can insure his employer's life for his wages.

Any interest in property gives a person possessing such interest the right to insure it, whether he is the true owner or not.

Mortgagee may Insure, Thus one holding a mortgage can insure the premises as well as the owner. The owner may also insure up to the full value of the property, so that two persons may hold policies on the same premises at the same time. It is usually the duty, however, of the owner to insure.

Creditors, etc. Persons who hold personal property as collateral security, or by way of pledge, as a pawnbroker, for instance, have the right to insure. Creditors, those holding property under a lease, or having a mechanic's lien, may also take out policies to protect themselves. Executors and administrators are usually under a duty to insure the property of the estate.

Insurance Agents. Insurance is effected almost

always by agents of the company, and, on the ordinary principles of agency, the company is bound by the acts and representations of their agents. The insured has the right to hold the company responsible for very nearly everything the agent says or does, whether the company has given him the authority or not.

Thus there is a list of questions always put to the applicant in regard to his health or the condition of his property, etc. The agent might consent to waive some of these questions, or to issue the policy in cases where all the answers were not satisfactory. The company cannot afterward refuse to pay the loss on the ground that it had given the agent no right to do these things.

No Authority to Waive Proofs of Loss. There are some things, however, that the agent cannot do. If the policy itself, which is delivered to the insured, contains certain provisions or directions, as that, for instance, the insured is to file "proofs of loss" in the office of the company, the agent cannot dispense with this necessity. And in general both parties, the company and the insured, must abide by the language and terms of the policy, as a formal written document is of much higher importance than the mere verbal declarations of an agent. As a matter of caution, everyone should read his policy very carefully before completing the contract.

Sometimes there is a provision in the policy that the insurance agent shall be considered entirely as the agent of the insured. This would take away the liability of the company for the acts of such an agent.

Warranties. A warranty is a statement of fact made by the insured and contained in the policy itself, and forming a part of it. If it is incorrect or untrue in the slightest particular, whether material or immaterial, the policy is void, and the insured cannot recover his loss, though he has paid his premiums.

For instance, in a life policy the statement of the applicant's age is a warranty, and if in reality he were older or younger, in which latter case the premiums might have been smaller and the statement might therefore seem to be immaterial; the policy, nevertheless, is absolutely void.

Representations. The answers to most of the questions usually put to the applicant are not included in the policy itself, but are written on a separate paper and filed by the company. These answers are known as "representations," and if any of them are false, the policy is not thereby rendered void, unless the statement was material and important; so material, perhaps, that the company was deceived, and such that if it had known the truth it would not have issued the policy.

Hazardous Trades. A frequent warranty in fire insurance policies is that the building shall not be used for hazardous or extra-hazardous trades or manufactures, such as the making of gunpowder or chemicals. If the owner allows the building to be used in that way, either at the time of insuring or subsequently, he forfeits the insurance.

Occupancy. Another important warranty is in regard to occupancy; it is agreed that if the building ceases to be occupied, the policy is to be considered as suspended. It is, therefore, dangerous to leave an insured building vacant. A mere temporary absence or vacancy for a day or so, however, would not usually affect the policy.

Care. It is generally necessary for the insured to take great care in connection with the heating and lighting arrangements. He must place zinc mats under the stoves, and see that the pipes and flues are in good safe condition. Otherwise he cannot recover of the company in case of fire.

Negligence. It is a peculiar rule about insurance, however, that although the owner or his servants, or employes, were negligent, and this negligence lead indirectly to the fire, the company cannot refuse on this ground to pay the insurance money, provided the conditions of the policy had not been violated.

Alterations. It is not safe for the owner of a building, after taking out a policy, to make any extensive or serious alterations, without obtaining the written consent of the company. Such alterations may often increase the risk and danger of fire.

Alienation. In fire policies there is almost always a provision that if the insured *aliens*, that is, sells the premises, the policy becomes void. The owner by selling loses his insurable interest. He would not lose anything, even if the property should be destroyed, and there is no reason why the insurance money should be paid to him.

If the purchaser of the property desires to continue the policy, the proper thing to do is for the seller—the holder of the policy—to obtain the permission of the company and assign the policy to the purchaser. It is not always necessary to obtain permission to assign, but it is safer to do so.

May Lease or Mortgage. Leasing the premises to a tenant or mortgaging them is not an "alienation," which makes the policy void under this clause. If the mortgage is foreclosed and the property sold, however, the insurance is at an end. Mortgaged personal property—chattels—may be insured and the insurance is good so long as the owner retains possession, but not after foreclosure and sale.

Representations in Life Insurance. When one applies for an insurance on his life, he is asked certain questions in regard to his general health and his habits. These questions should be answered fully, fairly and honestly, as they are very material. Any willfully untruthful statement vitiates the policy. At the same time a person may often be mistaken in regard to himself, and consider himself a healthy man, when he really is not. It is hardly possible that all the answers should be strictly true, and so, if some of them are slightly incorrect, the policy is not void.

An honest belief in the truth of his answer is all that is required of the applicant.

There are certain conditions in life policies, just as in fire policies, which, if they happen, make the policy void. For instance, the company is not liable in case the person insured commits suicide—" dies by his own hand "—or dies at the hand of justice for crime, or of *delirium tremens*, or from the effect of intemperance in any form.

If the person whose life is insured should kill himself while insane, this would not render the policy void, unless there is a special clause to that effect.

The Premium. The premium is the commission paid to the company in consideration of the insurance. It varies very much with the value of the property, its locality, its liability to be destroyed. In cities, for instance, the rates are higher in the dry-goods districts, than in the residential districts.

Life insurance rates also vary with the age and health of the individual. There is a difference between the rates of the different companies, some seeking to attract the public by lower premiums. As a rule the best and safest companies are those which charge the highest premiums.

The first premium is usually paid when the policy is issued, and if it is not, the policy as a rule does not take effect until it is paid. Any failure to pay subsequent premiums when they come due, either forfeits the policy, together with the previous premiums, or suspends it as long as they remain unpaid. In case the provision in the policy is that the policy shall be forfeited, a subsequent acceptance of the premium by the company would be a waiver of the condition as to forfeiture and the policy would come into force again. The company is not obliged, however, to accept it.

Assignment. There is usually a provision both in life insurance and fire insurance policies that any assignment of the policy, without application to the company and their written consent, avoids it. Subject to this provision, the holder of a policy may assign it at his pleasure. Either a fire or life policy may be assigned to a creditor as collateral security for a debt. The balance of the insurance money in such a case would go to the legal representatives of the insured after the creditor had satisfied his debt.

Policies Payable to Wife Cannot be Assigned. A policy taken out by a man and made payable to his wife or his children cannot in many States be assigned by him even with the consent of the company or under any circumstances whatever. It is for the benefit of a wife, and she is regarded as possessing a peculiar interest in the policy.

In many States, her consent and signature to the assignment would not deprive her of her right to demand the insurance money. An assignment may be made by an indorsement on the policy as " Pay to ——— ———." Sometimes the company on the surrender of the old policy will insure a new policy payable to the assignee.

Proof of Loss. After the loss of the property by fire, the insured should immediately prepare, "the proofs of loss." These are usually in the form of an affidavit, stating the facts and the amount of loss, and must be signed and sworn to by the insured.

There is generally a provision in fire policies that unless these proofs of loss are filed in the office of the company within sixty days after the fire the company will not be liable. This is, therefore, a matter of great importance.

Mutual Companies. Within a few years, a large number of life insurance companies have been organized on the mutual system. They start with small capitals or none at all. There are certain fees due from each member who is insured, the amount of the fees varying with the amount of the insurance. In case of death every member is liable to an assessment which varies in amount in the same way. If the assessments are not paid the policy is forfeited. These companies do not offer the safest kind of insurance, for, as the death-assessments become more frequent, many members drop out, making the assessments still larger on those that remain, until the company becomes insolvent.

PRELIMINARY PROOFS OF LOSS.

STATE OF ———, ⎱ ss.
COUNTY OF ———. ⎰

To the Mutual Insurance Company:

Be it known, that on this day of ———, 18—, before me [name of notary public or magistrate] duly commissioned and sworn, and residing in the town of ————, in the County and State aforesaid, personally appeared [name of the insured], who, being duly sworn, deposes and says that the following statement contains a particular, just and true account of his loss in the words and figures following, that is to say:

I. That on the — day of ———, 18—, the Mutual Insurance Company, by their policy of insurance, numbered ———, issued by them, did insure the party herein and therein named against loss or damage by fire, to the amount of ———, for the term of one year from the — day ———, 18—, to the — day of ———, 18—, at noon.

II. That in addition to the amount covered by said policy of said company, there was no other insurance thereon. [Or if any, state what.]

III. That the actual cash value of the property so insured amounted to the sum of ——— dollars, at the time immediately preceding the fire, as will appear by the annexed schedule, showing a full and accurate description of each kind of property, and the value of the same, with the damage or loss on each stated separately.

IV. That the property insured belonged to [name of insured].

V. That the building insured, or containing the property destroyed or damaged, was occupied in its several parts by the parties hereinafter named [and for the following purposes] to wit: [Here state who they were.]

VI. That on the—day of ———, 18—, a fire occurred by which the property insured was injured or destroyed to the amount of ——— dollars, as set forth in the statement and the several schedules and papers hereunto annexed, which the deponent declares to be a just, true and faithful account of his loss, so far as he has been able to ascertain the same.

And the insured claim of the Mutual Insurance Company the sum of $———.

VII. That the fire originated [here state circumstances]. And the said deponent further declares that the said fire did not

originate by any act, design or procurement on his part or in con-
seqence of any fraud or evil practice done or suffered by him, and
that nothing has been done by or with his privity or consent to
violate the conditions of insurance, or render void the policy
aforesaid.

Sworn to before me }
this — day of ——, 18—. }   (Signature of insured.)

[Signature of notary public.]

CHAPTER XVI.

INSOLVENT AND GENERAL ASSIGNMENTS.

Insolvent Assignments—Voluntary—Involuntary—Discharge from Debts—General Assignments—When Assignment is Void—Preferences—Partnership Assignments—Power to Sell—Other Powers of Assignee—Acceptance of Assignee—Assignee's Bond—Assignee may Resign—Revocation of Assignment—Assignee's Commissions—Acknowledgment—Filing and Recording—Inventory and Schedules—Where Filed—Notice to Present Claims—Proof of Claim—Assignee's Report. COMPOSITIONS: *Verbal Arrangement not Binding—In Writing under Seal—Who must Sign—Fraud by Debtor—Partner's Authority—Performance by Debtor—Summary of Law of Different States.* FORMS: *General Assignment—Clause Giving a Preference—Another Form—Assignee's Bond—Composition Deed.*

WHEN a debtor finds himself unable to pay his debts in full there are generally two courses of action open to him. He may either go into bankruptcy under the insolvent law, or he may make a general assignment for the benefit of his creditors.

These insolvent and general assignments are governed by the statutes of each State, as the Bankruptcy Law of the United States has been repealed.

Insolvent Assignments. Under insolvent laws,

the debtor can go into bankruptcy voluntarily, or he
he can be forced into it by his creditors.

Voluntary. In voluntary bankruptcy, it is the
usual method for the debtor to present a petition to
some court, usually the County Court, stating the fact
that he is insolvent, and that he is willing to surrender all his property for equal distribution among
his creditors.

In some States it is necessary to obtain the consent
of a certain amount of the creditors in number or
value or both. In New York two-thirds of all the
creditors must consent.

With this petition must be presented an inventory
of all the debtor's assets, and a schedule or list of his
creditors and the amount of the debts due to them.
All these papers must be under oath.

An assignee is named either by the debtor or the
creditors, and sometimes by the judge. The assignee
takes possession of the property, sells it, and dis-
tributes the proceeds among the creditors under the
discretion and order of the court.

Involuntary. In involutary bankruptcy the creditors petition that the debtor be declared a bankrupt
and an assignee appointed. This petition can be
made whenever debts have been due and unpaid for
a considerable time, and when there is evidence that
the debtor is in reality insolvent, and cannot meet his
obligations. In some States it is necessary for a
majority, or a greater or less number of creditors, to
sign the petition.

Discharge from Debts. The great advantage of an insolvent assignment is that the debtor obtains an absolute discharge from his debts, whether the creditors consent to it or not. No matter what the percentage or *pro rata* share of each creditor is, the whole debt is wiped out, and the debtor can engage in business again without any old debts hanging over him. This is not true of a general assignment.

General Assignments. A general assignment is a deed or conveyance by the debtor of all his property, except that exempt from execution, to any person selected by him, in trust for the benefit of creditors. This person is the assignee, and the creditors have no voice in his appointment. The creditors, moreover, cannot interfere or prevent such assignment, and their consent is not necessary. Some States do not permit such assignments to be made, as will be seen by the Summary.

When Assignment Void. The assignment must be for the benefit of *all* the creditors, and not a part or class of them; otherwise it is void.

There also must be nothing which tends to hinder, delay, or defraud creditors.

A power granted to the assignee to sell on credit makes the assignment void.

Any reservation of an interest to the debtor, by which he is to receive any of the property before all the debts are paid in full, is fraud ; although the debtor may retain property exempt by law from the payment of debts.

A provision in the assignment requiring a creditor to give a release of the whole debt on receiving his share of the assets, makes the assignment void.

Also, a provision allowing the debtor to continue the business.

Also, a power to the assignee to lease or mortgage.

Also, a provision for the payment of debts which are in reality fictitious.

Preferences. The debtor may, in many of the States, provide that one debt or several debts shall be paid in full, before any others are paid at all. If the assets are only sufficient to pay these preferred debts, the other creditors will receive nothing. But in a majority of States preferences are forbidden, and all the creditors share equally. A provision for a preference in such States sometimes make the assignment void as a whole; sometimes only the provision is void, and the rest of the assignment is valid.

A limited partnership or a corporation cannot give a preference even in those States where preferences are allowed.

Wages of employes are preferred in all the States.

Partnership Assignments. When a copartnership makes an assignment, all the partners must sign. Such an assignment may be of the partnership property only, or it may include the individual property of each member of the firm. But the private property must be used to pay the private debts of such member in full, before it can be applied to the firm debts.

Firm property cannot be assigned to pay individual

debts of any member, except subject to firm debts. But one member may make an individual assignment to pay his private debts, and include therein his interest in the partnership property. His share of the partnership debts must be paid in full out of his share of the partnership property, before it can be used to pay his private creditors.

A partnership assignment cannot be made to a member of the firm.

Power to Sell. An assignment should always contain a clause granting a power of attorney to the assignee to sell the property, either at public or private sale.

It is very dangerous, however, for the assignee to sell at a private sale. The sale should be as public as possible, at auction, and notice should be given beforehand.

The assignee would have the right under this clause to execute deeds and bills of sale.

The assignee, being a trustee, cannot purchase the property for himself, nor can he employ an agent to bid it in. Such a sale can be set aside by the debtor or the creditors.

Other Powers of Assignee. The assignee has power, and it is his duty to collect all debts. He can sue or bring actions in the courts for that purpose.

He may redeem mortgages and give satisfaction pieces.

He has the power to pay taxes, insurance and rent.

He also has power to employ agents to act for him

But it is neither desirable or safe for him to employ the debtor as such agent.

He has a right to assets of the debtor situated in another country or State, and may sue for them in that State.

Acceptance of Assignee. A clause is sometimes put into the assignment, by which the assignee accepts the trust. In this case the assignee should sign and execute the assignment as well as the assignor. This is not absolutely essential but very advisable.

Assignee's Bond. Before the assignee can take possession of the property, or do any act in relation to it, he must give a bond, generally to the people of the State, conditioned that he will perform his duties and execute his trust fairly and honestly.

The bond must be for a sum of money double in amount the value of the assigned property. Two bondsmen or sureties must also qualify on the bond for a like sum.

This bond is filed in court with the other papers.

Assignee may Resign. If there are more than one assignee, they must act jointly. Any assignee may resign at any time on showing good cause. The court will then appoint a " receiver," whose duties are the same as those of the assignee. If an assignee is guilty of misconduct, he will be removed.

Revocation of Assignment. After the acceptance of the assignment by the assignee, it cannot be revoked by the assignor or debtor. Nor can it be altered in any manner by the assignee.

Assignee's Commissions. The assignee is entitled to certain compensation for his services. This compensation is known as commissions.

Sometimes they are fixed by the assignor, but they must be reasonable.

Usually the law fixes the amount of commissions. In some States, including New York, they are at the rate of five per cent. on all money received and paid out.

Acknowledgment of Assignment. The debtor or assignor must acknowledge the assignment before a notary public or other proper officer in the same manner as a deed to be recorded. If the assignee signs the instrument, he must also acknowledge it.

Filing or Recording. Within a certain number of days after the date of the assignment, usually twenty, it must be filed in some public office. In New York and many other States the proper place is the office of the County Clerk of the county where the debtor resides.

If the assignment embraces real estate, a copy should also be filed in the office of the Register or Recorder of Deeds.

If there is property of the debtor in other counties, copies should also be filed in the County Clerk's office of those counties.

In some States it is the duty of the debtor or assignor to attend to the filing. In others it is delivered to the assignee, who must see that it is filed within the proper time.

Neglect to file within the time prescribed, in many of the States, makes the assignment void.

Inventory and Schedules. It is necessary for the debtor to file with the assignment, or within a certain number of days after, a true and complete inventory of his property or assets. This must be sworn to. If the inventory is false, the debtor can be punished for perjury.

There must also be a schedule under oath, containing a list of the creditors and their residences, and the amount and character of the debts due to them. This schedule is often included in the inventory.

Where Filed. The inventory and schedules are in some States filed in the same office as the assignment. In most of the States, however, they are filed in the office of the Clerk of the Court, usually the County Court having jurisdiction.

Notice to Present Claims. It is one of the first duties of the assignee to give notice to the creditors to present their claims to him in writing under oath within a certain time.

This is done by publication of such a notice in newspapers designated by the court, and mailing a copy of the notice to each creditor. In New York the notice must be published once a week for six weeks, and the claims must be presented within thirty days after the last publication.

Proof of Claim or Debt. The creditor on receiving the notice should at once send to the assignee a copy of the bill, with an affidavit that it a just and true debt.

The result of failure on the part of the creditor to do this within the time specified is to deprive him of any right to share in the assets in the hands of the assignee.

Even if the creditor receives no actual notice his claim is barred, as the publication is constructive notice, and he is bound by it.

Assignee's Report. The assignee has a certain time within which to sell the property and convert it into money, and to collect the debts and claims due to the assignor. He must then render a report to the court, which will order him to distribute the assets among the creditors.

In all cases the assignee acts under the direction of the court. If he is in doubt, he may apply for information. Sometimes he will be given authority to compromise and release debts due to the debtor's assigned estate.

COMPOSITIONS.

A composition is an arrangement by a debtor with his creditors by which the latter receive a certain portion or percentage of their debts in full satisfaction. The debtor is absolutely discharged from further liability for the balance, without either making an assignment, or going into bankruptcy, or even suspending business in any way.

Verbal Arrangement not Binding. A mere verbal promise by the creditor or creditors to accept the sum offered, does not constitute a composition. The creditors are not bound by their oral promise, since it is without consideration, and they can sue the debtor for the balance of the debt at any time.

In Writing Under Seal.   The contract, to be valid and binding, must be in writing, under seal.   It is called a composition-deed.   The creditors must agree to release the debtor on receipt of the amount at which the debt is compromised.

Who Must Sign.   The debtor should sign the composition.   It is not necessary that all the creditors should be parties, although it is very desirable.   A composition between a debtor and any portion of his creditors is binding.   In States where preferences are not allowed there should be no provision in the composition whereby those creditors who sign are to receive more than the other creditors who do not.

Fraud by Debtor.   Any misrepresentation by the debtor as to his assets, with intent to defraud his creditors, makes the composition void.

A secret promise to give one creditor an undue advantage, as by giving him further securities, by way of inducement for him to sign the composition, is a fraud upon the other creditors and makes it void.

Partner's Authority.   Any one member of a firm has the implied authority to bind the firm by the composition of any debt or debts

Performance by Debtor.   The debtor must fulfill the conditions and terms of the composition to the letter. He must pay the dividends on the precise day named, and keep any other promise strictly. If he fail in this, the creditors can repudiate the composition, and claim the whole amount of the debt.

SUMMARY OF THE LAW OF ASSIGNMENTS IN THE VARIOUS STATES.

ALABAMA.—Preferences are not allowed. If the assignment directs a preference this does not make the assignment itself void, but all the assets are distributed equally.

ARKANSAS.—Before the assignee can take possession, sell, or in any way control the assigned property, he must file in the office of the Clerk of the Probate Court a complete inventory and description of the property. He must also execute a bond to the State of Arkansas, in double the value of the property, with sureties, conditioned that the assignee shall execute the trust, and pay the proceeds of the sale of the property to the creditors mentioned in the assignment.

The assignee must file his accounts every year in the same office. Within one hundred and twenty days after the execution of the bond, the assignee must sell the assigned property at public auction, on thirty days notice.

CALIFORNIA.—Assignments are void if preference is given to one class of debts over another; or if they tend to coerce any creditor into releasing or compromising his claim; or provide for the payment of false or fraudulent claims; or give the assigning debtor any right or interest in the property before all debts are paid; or tend to delay creditors in obtaining their money; or exempt the assignee from liability for misconduct.

The assignment must be acknowledged and certified in the same way as a deed; otherwise it is void.

A verified inventory of all creditors, their residences, the debts owing to them, and of the property assigned, must be filed by the debtor within twenty days after making the assignment. The assignment must be recorded within twenty days in the Recorder's office, where the debtor resides. The assignee must give his bond in a sum to be fixed by the County Judge within thirty days after the date of the assignment.

There is also an insolvency law, under which the debtor can petition for a discharge from his debts, provided they are over three hundred dollars in amount ; and the creditors, or any five of them, can compel an involuntary bankruptcy.

COLORADO.—The ordinary rules of the common law are in force. There are no statutes on the subject of assignments or insolvency.

CONNECTICUT.—Preferences are not allowed. The wages of mechanics and laborers for work done within three months are preferred over all other debts, to the amount of one hundred dollars in each case.

Any creditor with a claim of at least one hundred dollars, which he cannot collect after suit and execution, can apply to a Court of Probate for the appointment of a trustee in insolvency of the debtor's property. If this application is granted, the trustee takes possession. An allowance is made to the debtor for the support of his family. If he pays seventy per cent. of all debts, he receives a full discharge.

DAKOTA.—Preferences are not allowed. The assignment is void if it prefers creditors; if it tends to coerce any creditor into releasing or compromising his claim, or if it provides for the payment of any false or fraudulent claim. The assignment does not discharge the debtor without the consent of all the creditors.

The assignment must be acknowledged and certified in the same manner as a deed of real estate. The debtor must make a full and true inventory, which he must swear to. The assignment and inventory must be filed with the Register of Deeds of the county where the debtor resides, within twenty days after the date of the assignment.

The assignee's bond must be given to the Territory, and in double the value of the assigned property. It must be filed within thirty days in the same office as the inventory.

DELAWARE.—Preferences are not allowed. Assignments should be acknowledged before a Notary Public, and filed in the office of the Register of the Court of Chancery. Within thirty days after the date of the assignment, the assignee must file a sworn schedule of the assigned property. The Chancellor appoints two appraisers, who file an inventory and appraisement. The assignee must give a bond to the State of Delaware, with sureties, in double the value of the property as appraised. The assignee must render his account one year from the date of the bond.

DISTRICT OF COLUMBIA.—Preferences allowed. The common law prevails. No statutes on insolvency.

FLORIDA.—Preferences allowed. No insolvent laws.

GEORGIA.—Preferences allowed, except that limited partnerships cannot make preferential assignments. Any reservation in the assignment of a benefit to the debtor, or to any person for him, makes it void.

IDAHO.—Preferences are not allowed. The assignment is not valid unless it is of all the debtor's property, and for the benefit of all his creditors. The acceptance of a dividend by a creditor operates as a full discharge of the debtor.

There is an insolvency law, which provides that the debtor may draw up a petition to the District Court. A schedule of his property and debts should be annexed. If the petition is allowed, an assignee is appointed by the creditors. The assignee must give the usual bond. The assignment should be filed with the Clerk of the Court.

ILLINOIS.—Preferences are not allowed. If a preference is given in the assignment, it does not make it absolutely void, but the assets are distributed proportionately.

The assignment must be acknowledged and recorded in the county where the debtor resides.

An inventory of the creditors, the debts owing to them, and the property assigned, must be annexed to the assignment by the debtor. The assignee must file his sworn inventory in the County Court, and give bonds in double the value of the property. He then gives notice, by publication for six weeks, for creditors to present their claims in writing under oath.

These claims should be presented within three months. The assignee's commissions are left to the discretion of the court.

INDIANA.—The assignment must be acknowledged and recorded within ten days in the office of the Recorder of the county where the debtor resides. A schedule of all the property assigned should be annexed to the assignment, with an affidavit that nothing has been withheld or transferred, and no judgment has been confessed to defraud or delay creditors. The assignee must give a bond in double the value of the property. He must file a complete inventory within thirty days. Within twenty days after filing the inventory he must file an appraisement made by two householders. The assignee should sell the property as soon as possible, giving thirty days notice. His report should be made within six months. If there are no contested claims, the money is paid to the clerk for *pro rata* distribution.

IOWA.—Preferences not allowed. The assignment must be for the benefit of all the creditors. The debtor should annex to the assignment a sworn inventory of all his property, and a list of his creditors, and the debts owing to them.

The assignment must be acknowledged and recorded in the county where the debtor resides. The assignee should file a full inventory and valuation of the property with the Clerk of the District or Circuit Court. He must give a bond in double the value of the property with one or more sureties. Notice to the creditors to present their claims should be published for six weeks, and a copy should be mailed to each creditor. The claims should be sent to the assignee within three months.

KANSAS.—Preferences are not allowed. The assignment must be acknowledged and certified, and recorded in the office of the Register of Deeds of the county where the debtor resides. A sworn inventory of the property must be filed within thirty days after the date of the assignment, in the office of the Clerk of the District Court. A sworn schedule of the debts, the names of the creditors and their residences must be filed on the day of executing the assignment in the same office. If this is not done, the assignment is void. The creditors are notified, within two days after the schedule is filed, of the fact of the assignment, and they have the right to convene at the Clerk's office and choose an as· signee. The assignee appointed by the debtor only has the custody of the property until the election or appointment of another by the creditors or the judge. The assignee must give a bond in double the value of the property. He has six months in which to adjust and allow claims presented, and one month afterward, he may pay them *pro rata.*

The assignment does not operate as a discharge of the debtor, and he is still liable for the unpaid balance of all debts.

KENTUCKY.—Preferences are not allowed. The assignment must be acknowledged, filed and recorded, like a deed, in the office of the County Clerk of the county where the debtor resides. The assignee must execute a sufficient bond with surety approved by the County Court, and take an oath to faithfully perform his duties. The inventory of the assignee must be filed in the County Court within sixty days, and he must render a report of sales within two years from the time of qualification. The notice to present claims must be published in a newspaper for a period fixed by the court. Claims may be proved at any time before the assets are distributed.

LOUISIANA.—A debtor cannot assign his property to his creditors and obtain a discharge from his debts, without their unanimous consent.

By the Insolvent Law, a debtor may surrender his property and obtain a full discharge, provided a majority of his creditors in number and amount agree thereto.

MAINE.—No preferences allowed. The assignment must be acknowledged. The assignee must give a bond within ten days to the Judge of the Court of Probate of the county where the debtor resides. Within twenty days he must file an attested copy of the assignment and an inventory of all the property in his possession. The assignee must also give notice of his appointment by publication, to be continued for three weeks, within fourteen days after the date of the assignment. Creditors may prove their claims in the usual way.

The assignment may contain a release providing for the discharge of the debtor from his debts.

There is also an Insolvent Law by which a debtor owing $300 may obtain a discharge from his debts on application to the Probate Judge by petition, stating his inability to pay his debts and his willingness to assign his property for the benefit of his creditors. The judge issues a warrant, and the sheriff takes possession of the property.

Involuntary proceedings to compel the debtor to assign may be commenced by two or more creditors owning one-fourth of the claims against him. Other creditors are notified, a meeting is held, and the creditors elect an assignee. This assignee must give a bond.

An allowance may be made to the debtor for support out of the estate pending proceedings.

MARYLAND.—Under the Insolvent Law a debtor may apply to the Circuit Court of the county where he resides, stating that he is insolvent, and offering to give up all his property for the benefit of his creditors. Accompanying the petition there should be a schedule of the property and a list of the creditors and the debts owing to them. All these papers must be verified by affidavit.

Any debtor who departs from the State with intent to defraud creditors, or conveys any property in contemplation of insolvency with the intention of giving a preference, or delaying or defrauding his creditors, or confesses a judgment, or fraudulently stops payment of his negotiable paper and fails to pay it for twenty days, may be declared an insolvent on the petition of one or more creditors whose claims aggregate $250.

A preliminary trustee is appointed. Notice is then given by mail and publication to the creditors to elect a permanent trustee.

Assignments giving preferences are not allowed, except that wages and salaries to clerks, servants and employes, for the three months preceding the assignment, may be preferred.

The debtor is absolutely discharged from his debts by insolvent proceedings commenced either by himself or his creditors.

MASSACHUSETTS.—General assignments are not allowed.

Under the Insolvent Law the debtor may petition the Judge of Insolvency of the county where he resides.

A creditor having a claim of one hundred dollars or more may also petition that the debtor be adjudged insolvent where the debtor has removed himself or any of his property from the State with intent to defraud creditors, or concealed himself to avoid arrest or attachment, or made any fraudulent payment or conveyance, or where his negotiable paper is fourteen days overdue, or he is insane or insolvent.

Schedules of his debts and assets, under oath, must be filed by the debtor. The creditors elect the assignee.

Wages due operatives, servants, and employes, to an amount in each case of one hundred dollars, for labor performed within one year prior to the insolvency are paid first; also physicians' fees amounting to fifty dollars within six months.

The debtor is discharged from his debts, but in order to obtain the discharge in cases where the estate does not pay fifty per cent. the debtor must file the assent in writing of a majority of his creditors in number and amount within six months after the date of the assignment.

MICHIGAN.—Preferences are not allowed. A provision for a preference makes the assignment void.

The assignment must be acknowledged, and the original, or a copy, with a schedule of the property assigned and a list of the creditors, and the assignee's bond must be filed in the office of the Circuit Court Clerk within ten days after making the assignment. The assignee's inventory must be sworn to. The bond runs to the assignor and the creditors, and must be in double the amount of the assigned property, with sureties.

Claims of creditors must be proved within ninety days by an affidavit to be filed in the Circuit Clerk's office. The assignee must give notice by mail to each creditor within ten days. He must have the property appraised by two persons as soon as possible after the assignment. The assignee's report must be filed in three months.

Under the Insolvent Law the debtor must present a petition

signed by himself and two-thirds of his creditors, accompanied by a true account of all his creditors, debts, and an inventory of his property. The debtor may be discharged, and the assignment and discharge must be filed in the Register's office.

MINNESOTA.—The assignment must be acknowledged and filed in the office of the Clerk of the District Court for the county where the debtor resides. Within ten days after making the assignment, the debtor must file a sworn inventory containing a list of the creditors, the debts due to them, and also a complete inventory of his property. The assignee must give a bond to the State of Minnesota, with two sureties, in double the value of the assigned property. This bond must be filed within five days after the inventory, or the assignment is void. Notice must be published and sent by mail to each creditor. Claims of creditors must be sworn to.

The wages of servants, laborers, mechanics, and clerks for services performed within three months prior to the date of the assignment, are entitled to be paid in full before other debts.

It is a question whether preferences are legal.

MISSISSIPPI.—No statutes on assignments. The common law prevails. Preferences are allowable.

MISSOURI.—Preferences are not allowed. The assignment must be acknowledged and recorded with the Recorder of Deeds of the county where the debtor resides. With the assignment must be filed an affidavit of the debtor, setting forth 'the nature and value of his property. Within three days the assignee must give a bond with two sureties in double the value of the assigned property. Within fifteen days he must file an inventory of the property in the clerk's office of the Circuit Court of the county where the debtor resides. The judge appoints two persons to appraise the estate. Within three months after the date of the assignment the assignee must appoint some time and place where he will hear and allow demands, and four weeks' notice of this must be sent to the creditors. The failure of a notified creditor to present his demand will preclude him from obtaining a share of the property.

Dividends must be declared one month after the allowance of demands.

MONTANA.—There has been no legislation on this subject, and the rules of the common law prevail. Preferences are, therefore, allowable.

NEBRASKA.—No preferences are allowed in the assignment, except for the wages of laborers to the amount of one hundred dollars. The assignment must be recorded in the office of the Recorder of Deeds within thirty days.

Within thirty days after the execution of the assignment, the assignee must file in the office of the Clerk of the District Court of the county, an inventory of the assigned property, with an affidavit that it is a full and complete inventory of all the property that has come to the knowledge of the assignee. The District Courts appoint three appraisers and the assignee is obliged to file a bond in double the appraised value of the property. The assignee must at once publish a notice of his appointment, and the creditors have six months in which to present their claims.

Assignees must file statements with the Clerk of the District Court every six months.

The assignment does not discharge the debtor.

NEVADA.—General assignments not in use. Under the Insolvent Law, the debtor may file a petition with the Judge of the District Court, with a schedule containing the names of creditors, the debts due to them, and a complete inventory of the debtor's property. There is then a meeting of the creditors appointed by the judge, to show cause why the debtor should not be discharged. The creditors select the assignees. On demand of any two creditors, the assignees must report. Concealment of property or books, or alterations of books, with intent to defraud creditors is fraudulent, and will prevent the debtor from obtaining a discharge.

NEW HAMPSHIRE.—Preferences are not allowed.

The assignment must be under seal and must be sworn to and acknowledged. Within ten days after the date of the assignment the assignee must file in the office of the register of probate a copy of the assignment with a schedule of the property, and a list of creditors, and the debts owing to them.   Both debtor and assignee must swear to this schedule.   The assignee must give a bond to the Judge of Probate with sureties, within five days after filing the schedule.   The assignee must give notice of the assignment by publication.   The creditors have six months to file their claims under oath in the Probate Office.   One year from the time of appointment the assignee is required to settle his account in the Court of Probate, and a *pro rata* distribution of the assets is ordered.

NEW JERSEY.—Preferences are not allowed.

The assignment must be acknowledged.   The debtor must annex to the assignment an inventory under oath of his property, and a list of creditors and the debts owing to each.   The inventory and list of creditors must be proved before the Surrogate and recorded in his office.

The assignee must give three weeks' notice by publication in two papers for creditors to present their claims.   He must present an inventory, under oath, of the property to the Surrogate, and give bonds in double the amount of the valuation to the Ordinary of the State.

After all this is done, the assignment may be recorded in the office of the County Clerk or Register.

The creditors have three months to present their claims; if they do not present them they are not entitled to share in the assets after that time.   The assignee must render his final account within one year.   Wages of clerks, minors, mechanics, and laborers are preferred debts to an amount not exceeding $300 to one person. The landlord's claim for rent for one year is also preferred.   If the debtor have a family, goods to the amount of $200 are reserved to him.

There are also Insolvent Laws.

NEW YORK.—Preferences are allowed.

The assignment must be acknowledged, and recorded in the office of the Clerk of the County where the debtor resides.   If real estate is conveyed in the City of New York it must also be filed in the Register's office.

The assignee must file a written assent to take the trust, duly acknowledged. A sworn inventory, containing the name of the debtor, the names and residences of the assignee and creditors, the nature and amount of the debts owing to them, and of the property assigned, must be filed by the debtor in the County Court, (or, in New York City, the Court of Common Pleas) within twenty days from the date of the assignment. If the debtor fails to do this, the assignee has ten days further in which to file an inventory.

Within thirty days after the filing of the assignment, the assignee must publish a notice in the newspapers, once a week for six weeks, for creditors to present their claims within thirty days of the last publication; a copy must be mailed to each creditor. If any creditor does not present his claim, duly sworn to, within that time, he loses his right to a share in the assets.

The assignee must file his bond in an amount designated by the judge, within thirty days after the filing of the assignment and in the office of the County Clerk. The assignee has no power to sell before giving this bond, but he may take possession. He has one year in which to account. The judge may allow the assignee to compromise claims. The assignee is entitled to five per cent. on the sum which has come into his hands, as commissions.

Limited partnerships are not allowed to give preferences in case of assignment, nor moneyed corporations.

There is also an Insolvent Law by which debtors can be discharged on obtaining the consent of two-thirds of his creditors in amount in value. They must sign the petition.

NORTH CAROLINA.—Preferences are allowed. Under the Insolvent Laws a debtor may present a petition to the Superior Court, stating the usual facts. The petition should be accompanied by a schedule of the creditors and the debts, and a sworn inventory of the property. The creditors have thirty days to object. If no one makes the objection, the debtor is discharged and a trustee is appointed.

The debts of the debtor are not discharged by these proceedings or by an assignment, and his after-acquired property is liable for the balance of any debts still unpaid in full.

OHIO.—Preferences are not allowed.

The assignee must, within ten days after the delivery of the assignment to him, appear before the Probate Judge of the county where the debtor resides, and file the assignment, or a copy, in the Probate Court. He must execute a bond to the State of Ohio. Fifty per cent. of the creditors in value may elect a trustee in place of the assignee. Within thirty days after giving the bond the assignee must publish a notice of his appointment in a newspaper, and must file an inventory of the property, which must be sworn to, and an appraisement made by three appraisers appointed by the court, also under oath. There must also be filed a schedule of all the debts of the debtor and a list of the creditors.

Claims of creditors must be presented within six months after the publication of the notice. Wages up to $100 in amount in each case due and earned within six months prior to the assignment are preferred to all other debts. Dividends are payable eight months after the appointment of the assignee. Notice of payment is given by publication. The assignment and acceptance of dividends by creditors does not discharge the debtor from liability for the balance of the debt remaining unpaid.

OREGON.—The assignment is void unless made for the benefit of all the creditors and in proportion to their several claims It must be acknowledged and recorded in the county where the debtor lives. An inventory, under oath, of his property, his creditors, and the debts owing to them must be annexed to the assignment by the debtor. The assignee must also file an inventory, under oath, of all the property which has come into his possession, and its value. Notice must be given to the creditors. Claims must be presented by the creditors within three months after the notice, or they lose their right to share in the assets. The debtor is not discharged from liability for the payment of the balance of the debts remaining unpaid.

PENNSYLVANIA.—Preferences are not allowed. Stipulations for

a release in the assignment are void. The assignment must be acknowledged, and recorded in the office of the Recorder of Deeds in the county where the debtor resides, within thirty days after its execution. The assignee has thirty days in which to file an inventory in the Court of Common Pleas, with an affidavit that it is full and complete. He must give a bond with two sureties in double the appraised value of the property. His account must be filed within one year. The wages of minors, mechanics and laborers, up to $200 in each case, are paid in full before other debts. Fraudulent assignments are punished by fine and imprisonment.

RHODE ISLAND.—Preferences are not allowed, except for the wages of labor performed within six months, and not exceeding one hundred dollars to any one person.

If a debtor makes an assignment giving other preferences, three or more creditors, holding at least one-third in value of the debts, may petition the Supreme Court, stating the facts. The court will appoint a receiver, and direct an equal distribution among all the creditors who come in and prove their claims.

The debtor is not discharged unless the creditors voluntarily agree to it.

SOUTH CAROLINA.—If a debtor assign all his property and reserves nothing for himself, he can prefer such creditors as he pleases. The assignees must call the creditors together within ten days after the assignment, and they may then name an agent or agents, equal in number to the assignees, to act with them.

If no agent is appointed the assignee or assignees can act alone. He or they must report to the creditors every three months. The assignee's commissions are five per cent. for receiving and two and one-half per cent. for paying out money.

Under the Insolvent Law a debtor may obtain a discharge from his debts by petitioning the Court of Common Pleas. There must be a sworn schedule accompanying the petition. The creditors have thirty days in which to object to the discharge. If they accept the dividends the debtor is discharged from the entire debt.

TENNESSEE.—Preferences are allowed. The assignment must

be acknowledged and registered. It must contain a schedule of the debts and assets. The assignee must give a bond in the value of the property, if the value exceeds $500.

The assignee must make a perfect schedule of the assets assigned. His commissions cannot exceed five per cent.

TEXAS.—Preferences are not allowed. The property is distributed among the creditors in proportion to their claims, even if there is a direction for a preference. The assignment must be acknowledged and recorded. An inventory of the creditors and the debts owing to them, and of the debtor's property, sworn to, should be annexed to the assignment. Within thirty days from the date of the assignment, the assignee must give public notice of the assignment by publication and by mail. Creditors have six months to present their claims. It is the duty of the assignee to put the assignment on record, and give a bond with sureties. Whenever the assignee has enough property on hand to pay a dividend of ten per cent. he must do so. The assignee is entitled to reasonable compensation, to be fixed by the Judge of the County or District Court.

UTAH.—Preferences are allowed. No statutes. The common law prevails.

VERMONT.—Assignments must be for the benefit of all the creditors in proportion to their several claims. They must be acknowledged and a copy filed in the County Clerk's Office. The assignment must be accompanied by an inventory of the property and a list of the creditors and the debts due to them. The assignee cannot be a creditor. He must execute a bond to the Probate Court of the county.

Under the Insolvent Law, the debtor, or any creditor, may petition the Probate Court. A full discharge is not granted unless the assets amount to thirty per cent. of the debts, or a majority of the creditors assent.

The wages of employes, clerks and house-servants, to the amount of fifty dollars, for work done within six months, are preferred to all other debts.

VIRGINIA.—Preferences are allowed. The property is assigned

to a trustee. The debtor will not be discharged unless his creditors assent. There are no Insolvent Laws.

WASHINGTON TERRITORY.—The debtor may petition the District Court. There must be annexed to the petition a sworn
schedule of the creditors and the debts owing to them; also an inventory of the property. The creditors elect the assignee, who
gives a bond. The debtor is discharged, unless he has been guilty
of fraud.

WEST VIRGINIA.—Preferences are allowed. The assignment
must be acknowledged, and filed in the Office of the Clerk of the
County Court of the county where the property assigned is
situated. No inventory is required to be filed, except, on the sale of
property, an inventory of the property sold. The assignee is not
required to give a bond, nor any notice for creditors to present
claims. The assignee has a reasonable time in which to declare
dividends. He is entitled to five per cent. commissions. The
debtor is not discharged.

WISCONSIN.—Preferences are allowed. The assignee must
deliver to the County Judge a bond executed to the Clerk of the
Circuit Court in the value of the property. The bond and a copy
of the assignment must be filed with the Circuit Clerk; and within
ten days after such filing the assignee must also file an inventory
of the assets, a list of the creditors and the debts due to them.
Failure to file makes the assignment void. The assignee must
give notice by publication and by mail for the creditors to present
their claims within twelve days after the date of the assignment.
The creditors then have three months in which to send in their
sworn claims. If they fail to do this, they forfeit the dividend.
Within six months the assignee must report. A power to sell on
credit in the assignment makes it void.

There is an Insolvent Law, under which the debtor may present
a petition to the Circuit Court, stating the usual facts with schedule
and inventory. The debtor may be discharged unless creditors
dissent, and the assignment is recorded in the office of the Register
of Deeds.

WYOMING.—Under the Assignment Law, creditors who accept

the dividend must release the debtor from further liability.   The assignee must give a bond in an amount fixed by the Probate Judge.

FORM OF A GENERAL ASSIGNMENT FOR THE BENEFIT OF CREDITORS.

Know all men by these presents, That I [or we],—(name of party assigning),—party of the first part, for value received, have sold, and by these presents do grant, assign, and convey unto (name of assignee), party of the second part,

[Here insert a description, in general terms, of the property assigned, as "all the property, credits, claims, demands, due and owing or to become due, fixtures, furniture, stock in trade of every kind and description, whatsoever belonging to me and now in my store at," etc.]

To have and to hold the same unto the said (name of assignee), his executors, administrators and assigns forever, to and for the use of (all my creditors) hereby constituting and appointing (name or assignee) my true and lawful attorney irrevocable in my name, place and stead, for the purposes aforesaid, to ask, demand, sue for, attach, levy, recover and receive all such sum and sums of money which now are, or may hereafter become due, owing and payable for or on account of all or any of the accounts, dues, debts, and demands above assigned, giving and granting unto the said attorney, full power and authority to do and perform all and every act and thing whatsoever requisite and necessary, as fully, to all intents and purposes, as I might or could do, if personally present, with full power of substitution and revocation, hereby ratifying and confirming all that the said attorney or his substitute, shall lawfully do, or cause to be done by virtue hereof.

In witness whereof, I have hereunto set my hand and seal the —— day of ———, one thousand eight hundred and eighty ——.

Sealed and delivered)
   in presence of   }   (Signed)   (Name of party.)   [Seal.]

[Name of witnesses.]

FORM OF CLAUSE IN ASSIGNMENT GIVING A PREFERENCE TO SOME CREDITORS.

To pay all and singular the debts set forth and enumerated in a schedule hereunto annexed, marked " Schedule A," in full. After payment in full of all the debts designated in ' Schedule A," as above directed, the said party of the second part shall, out of the residue, pay all and singular all the other debts and liabilities of the party of the first part in full. If the residue be not sufficient to pay and discharge all such debts and liabilities in full then the said party of the second part shall distribute the said residue among the remaining creditors ratably and in proportion.

[Insert this in preceding form.]

ANOTHER FORM OF GENERAL ASSIGNMENT FOR THE BENEFIT OF CREDITORS.

This Indenture, made this —— day of ———, in the year one thousand eight hundred and ———, between (name of debtor), of ———, party of the first part, and ———, of ———, party of the second part, *Witnesseth,* that, whereas the party of the first part is indebted to divers persons in sundry sums of money which he is unable to pay in full, and is desirous of providing for the payment of the same, so far as in his power, by an assignment of all his property for that purpose. *Now,* therefore, the said party of the first part, in consideration of the premises, and of the sum of one dollar to him paid by the party of the second part, upon the ensealing and delivery of these presents, the receipt whereof is hereby acknowledged, has granted, bargained, sold, assigned, transferred, set over, and by these presents does grant, bargain, sell, assign, transfer and set over unto the said party of the second part, his heirs, executors, administrators, and assigns, all and singular, the lands, tenements, hereditaments, appurtenances, goods, chattels, stock, promissory notes, debts, claims, demands, property and effects of every description belonging to the party of the first part, wherever the same may be, except such property as is exempt by law from levy and sale under execution, to have and to hold the same and every part thereof unto the said party of the second part, his heirs, executors, administrators and assigns.

In trust, nevertheless, to take possession of the same, and to sell the same with all reasonable dispatch, and to convert the same into money, and also to collect all such debts and demands hereby assigned as may be collectible, and with and out of the proceeds of such sales and collections:

1. To pay and discharge all the just and reasonable expenses, costs and charges of executing this assignment, and of carrying into effect the trust hereby created, together with a lawful commission to the party of the second part for his services in executing said trust.

2. To pay and discharge in full, if the residue of said proceeds are sufficient for that purpose, all the debts and liabilities now due or to grow due from the said party of the first part, and if the residue of said proceeds shall not be sufficient to pay the said debts and liabilities and interest moneys in full, then to apply the said residue of said proceeds to the payment of said debts and liabilties ratably and in proportion.

3. And if after the payment of all the said debts and liabilities in full, there shall be any remainder or residue of said property or proceeds, to repay and return the same to the said party of the first part, his executors, administrators and assigns.   And in furtherance of of the promises, the said party of the first part does hereby make, constitute and appoint the said party of the second part, his true and lawful attorney, irrevocable, with full power and authority to do all acts and things which may be necessary in the premises to the full execution of the trust hereby created, and to ask, demand, recover and receive of and from all and every person or persons all property, debts, demands, due, owing and belonging to the said party of the second part, and to give acquittances and discharges for the same, to sue, prosecute, defend and implead for the same, and to execute, acknowledge and deliver all necessary deeds, instruments and conveyances.

And the party of the first part does hereby authorize the said party of the second part to sign the name of the said party of the first part to any check, draft, promissory note or other instrument in writing which is payable to the order of the said party of the first part, or to sign the name of the party of the first part to any instrument in writing, whenever it shall be necessary so to do to carry into effect the object, design and purpose of this trust.

The said party of the second part does hereby accept the trust created and reposed in him by this instrument, and covenants and agrees to and with the said party of the first part, that he will faithfully and without delay execute the created trust according to the best of his skill, knowledge and ability.

In witness whereof, the parties to these presents have hereunto set their hands and seals, the day and year first above written.

Sealed and delivered ⎱ (Signed) (Name of debtor.) [Seal.]
in the presence of ⎰ (Signed) (Name of assignee.) [Seal.]

If acknowledgment be necessary it may be made in this form:

State of ——,   ⎱ ss.
County of ——.   ⎰

On this —— day of ——, in the year one thousand eight hundred and ——, before me personally came (names), to me known and known to me to be the individuals described in and who executed the above instrument, and each for himself acknowledged that he executed the same.

(Name of Notary Public.)

FORM OF ASSIGNEE'S BOND.

Know all Men by these Presents, that we (name of asignee) and (name of surety) and (name of surety), of the City of ——, are held and firmly bound unto the people of the State of ——, in the sum of —— dollars, lawful money of the United States of America, to be paid to the said people; for which payment, well and truly to be made, we bind ourselves, our heirs, executors and administrators, jointly and severally, firmly by these presents. Sealed with our seals.

Dated the —— day of ——, one thousand eight hundred and ——.

Whereas (name of debtor), has made an assignment of his property in trust to the above bounden (name of assignee), for the benefit of his creditors, dated the ——— day of ———, one thousand eight hundred and ———.

Now, therefore, the condition of this obligation is such, that if the above bounden (name of assignee), shall faithfully execute and discharge the duties of such assignee, then this obligation to be void, else to remain in full force and virtue.

Sealed and delivered }	(Signed) (Name of assignee.) [Seal.]
in the presence of }	(Signed) (Name of surety.) [Seal.]
(Name of witness.)	(Name of surety.) [Seal.]

COUNTY OF ———, SS.

(Name of surety), one of the sureties to the foregoing bond, being duly sworn, says, that he is a resident and freeholder within this State, and that he is worth the sum of ——— dollars, over all his debts and liabilities, and exclusive of property exempt by law from execution.

Sworn to before me this ——— } (Name of surety.)
day of ———, 188—. }

(Name of Notary Public.)

COUNTY OF ———, SS.

(Name of other surety), one of the sureties to the foregoing bond, being duly sworn, says, that he is a resident and freeholder within this State, and that he is worth the sum of ——— dollars, over all his debts and liabilities. and exclusive of property exempt by law from execution.

Sworn to before me this ——— } (Name of surety.)
day of ———, 188—. }

(Name of Notary Public.)

COUNTY OF ———, SS.

I certify that on this ——— day of ———, 188—, before me personally appeared the within-named [names of sureties], known to me to be the individuals described in and who executed the within bond, and severally acknowledged that they executed the same.

(Name of Notary Public.)

FORM OF COMPOSITION DEED.

Whereas, (name of debtor), of the town of ———, does justly owe and is indebted unto us, his several creditors, in divers sums of money, but by reason of many losses, disappointments, and other damages happened unto the said (name of debtor), he has become unable to pay and satisfy us our full debts and just claims and demands, and therefore we, the said creditors, have resolved and agreed to undergo a certain loss and to accept of twenty-five cents for every dollar owing by the said (name of debtor) to us, the several and respective creditors aforesaid, to be paid in full satisfaction and discharge of our several and respective debts. *Now know all men by these presents,* that we, the several creditors of the said (name of debtor), do for ourselves severally and respectively, and for our several and respective heirs, executors and administrators, covenant, promise, compound and agree to and with the said (name of debtor) and between ourselves, that we will accept, receive and take of and from the said (name of debtor), for each and every dollar that the said (name of debtor) does owe and is indebted unto us, the said several and respective creditors, the sum of twenty-five cents, to be paid in the manner following; that is to say:

One-half of the amount in cash, to be paid by the said debtor unto us on the —— day of ——, 188—. The balance is to be secured by the promissory notes of the said debtor, to be dated and delivered at the time of the first payment, and payable three months after the date thereafter.

And we, the said creditors, do further covenant and agree, that neither we, the said several and respective creditors, nor either of us, shall or will, at any time or times hereafter, except upon default in the payment of said cash or the delivery or payment of said notes, sue or trouble the said (name of debtor) or his goods and chattels, for any debt or other thing now due and owing to us or any of us, *provided,* however, that should default be made by the said (name of debtor) in the payment of the said installments or the delivery of the said notes, these presents shall be void and of no effect.

And all and every of the grants, covenants, agreements and conditions herein contained, shall extend to and bind our several executors, administrators and assigns, as well as ourselves.

In witness whereof, we, the said several creditors of the said (name of debtor), have hereunto set our hands and seals this —— day of ——, 188—.

Sealed and delivered)
  in the presence of ∫   (Signed)   (Names of creditors.)   [Seal.]
    (Name of witnesses.)

CHAPTER XVII.

SHIPPING.

Sale of a Ship—Mortgage of—Bottomry Bonds—Respondentia Bonds—Liens on a Ship—Freight—When Freight is Earned—Damage to Cargo—Bills of Lading—Indorsement Of—Descriptions in—Delivery of Goods—Place Of—Bonded Warehouses—Charter-Parties—Lay-days and Demurrage—Perils of the Sea—Collision—Right of Way—Salvage—General Average—Rights of the Captain—Shipping Articles—Wages of Sailors—Pilots—Necessary Papers. MARINE INSURANCE: *Risks Insured Against—Actual Total Loss—Constructive Total Loss—Abandonment—Partial Loss—Seaworthiness—Deviation.*

By the provision of the Constitution of the United States, the Federal courts have jurisdiction of questions involving maritime matters and shipping interests generally. Actions of this nature must therefore be brought in the District and Circuit Courts of the United States.

Sale of a Ship. A ship is personal property and is usually sold by bill of sale. This should be recorded in the Custom House of the port where the ship is registered or enrolled.

Mortgage Of. A ship may be mortgaged by the

owner, and this mortgage should be recorded in the Custom House.

Bottomry Bonds.   A bottomry bond is a kind of mortgage peculiar to shipping.   It is a conveyance of the ship as security for advances made to the owner.

If the ship is lost, the creditor loses his money, and has no claim against the owner personally.

It is allowable, notwithstanding usury laws, for a loan made on such a bond to bear any rate of interest in excess of the legal rate.   This is called maritime interest.

Respondentia Bond.   The captain or master of a ship has the power in case of necessity to mortgage the cargo, no matter to whom it belongs.   This is done by an instrument known as respondentia bond.

The necessity to justify the master in doing this must be very great.   It is only done where the ship is far from home, and is disabled or in serious need of repairs to enable her to continue the voyage, and where the master is unable to communicate with the owners, and can raise the requisite funds in no other way.

If the cargo is lost, after all, the holder of the respondentia bond has, as in a bottomry bond, no personal claim.   The interest may be of any rate.

Liens on a Ship.   Material men, or those who repair a ship or furnish supplies, have a lien on it for the value of their services.   If the owner will not pay them, they can take possession of the ship and sell it. Stevedores and ship-brokers have no lien.

Freight. The compensation received by the ship-owner for transporting the cargo is called the freight. Sometimes the word "freight" is applied to the cargo itself, but this is not the sense in which it is used in connection with shipping.

When Freight is Earned. As soon as the cargo is delivered at the port of destination, the freight is earned, and the ship-owner has a lien on the goods and may retain them until it is paid.

If the goods are not delivered on account of loss by shipwreck or capture by pirates or an enemy, the shipper is not obliged to pay any freight.

Damage to Cargo. Any damage to the goods on their passage, as from water, if caused by the negligence of the ship-owner or the captain, must be deducted from the freight, or if the loss is more than the freight, the ship-owner must pay the difference.

If the loss occurred by reason of the nature of the goods themselves, as by leakage from the barrels or casks, etc., the loss is the shipper's, and he must pay the freight, even where loss is total.

Bills of Lading. Bills of lading are always given on receipt of the goods, and are signed by the master or shipping clerk. The shipper or consignor is given one copy, the master retains another, and a third is sent to the consignee.

The consignee is the one to whom the master looks for the payment of freight.

Indorsement Of. The transfer of a bill of lading by the consignee, which he does by indorsement, cuts off the right of the consignor to stop the goods in transit, which he would otherwise have in case of the consignee's insolvency.

Descriptions In. The descriptions in a bill of lading of the goods received are evidence of all the facts stated, and bind the ship-owner. It is therefore prudent to describe them as boxes, barrels or bales, "contents unknown."

Delivery of Goods. The master must deliver all the goods. He cannot compel the consignee to receive part of the consignment, and ask him to pay *pro rata* freight.

Place of. The goods need only, as a rule, be delivered at the wharf. It is not obligatory or usual for the master to send them to the consignee. Notice of arrival should be sent to the consignee, and it is his duty to come at once and take the goods away. Otherwise he may be charged storage.

Bonded Warehouses. If the consignee does not wish goods coming from a foreign country at once, and desires to delay payment of the Custom duties, he may have them stored in the United States bonded warehouses. He may have them at any time by paying these duties, or he may reship them without such payment.

Charter-Parties. Any person may hire or charter a ship, retaining the captain and crew, or agreeing to equip and man the vessel himself. This contract need not be in writing to be valid, but it usually is, and this written agreement is known as a "charter-party." A form is given at the end of this chapter, but the parties may agree upon any terms they please and insert whatever stipulations and covenants may be deemed desirable.

Lay-days and Demurrage. Where a ship is chartered for a voyage, the charterer or hirer is allowed a certain number of days to load and unload the cargo. These are known as lay-days. If he takes a longer time, this gives the ship-owner a claim for additional compensation, known as demurrage.

Perils of the Sea. The ship-owner or carrier agrees in the bill of lading to carry the goods safely and deliver them in good condition, "perils of the sea excepted." The owner is, therefore, liable for all loss of or injury to the goods, unless caused by the violence of the wind or the sea, wreck, stranding, capture by the public enemy, or pirates, or fire.

The owner of a vessel or boat, as barges, lighters, steam-boats, canal-boats, etc., engaged in inland navigation on the rivers and lakes, is liable to the shipper for loss by fire.

Collision. In case of the collision of two vessels, the one in fault, whose negligence caused the accident, must suffer its own loss and pay the loss of the other.

If they are both guilty of negligence the loss of each vessel is added and divided equally. The one which is injured the least must pay the other enough to make the loss equal.

The owner of a ship is not personally liable for injuries arising from collision. The amount of damages is limited to the value of the ship and the cargo.

Right of Way. When two vessels are approaching each other, the one going free must give way to the one close-hauled.

If they are both close-hauled each must go to the right.

Steam-boats may go to the right or left of sailing vessels. The latter need not change their course, as they have the right of way over steamers.

There also should be certain green and red lights carried at night.

Salvage. By salvage is meant the compensation which is given to persons or vessels that voluntarily assist in saving either ship or cargo, wrecked, or in danger of being wrecked.

If a ship is wrecked on the coast, wreckers living on shore may be salvors. On the high seas, a ship which saves another is a salvor, and in case of a "derelict" or abandoned ship, the amount of salvage is very large.

The amount of salvage to be given is fixed by the United States Court on application, and varies very much in different cases. Sometimes one-third or one-half of all the property saved is decreed as compensation.

General Average. In case a storm or other peril

endangers the ship, and it is found necessary to cut away the masts, or lighten the ship by throwing part of the cargo overboard in order to save the rest, the owners of the part saved must contribute to make up the loss of what was sacrificed.

To ascertain the percentage each is obliged to pay, the value of the whole cargo and ship is computed, and the amount of loss. The ratio of the loss to the whole value is the percentage required. The whole value is generally taken to be four-fifths of the value when the vessel last sailed.

The throwing over of any of the cargo is called jettison.

Rights of the Captain. The captain of a ship has entire control of the crew and the passengers. He has almost absolute rights. He is a general agent, and can bind the owners, and make them responsible for many of his acts and contracts. Under extraordinary circumstances he even has the right to sell or mortgage the ship.

Primage is a certain percentage of the freight, to which the captain is entitled by usage.

Shipping Articles. Every vessel bound from a home port to a foreign port, or if it be of fifty tons or more, to a port in another (not adjoining) State, must have on board shipping articles. These articles must describe the voyage for which the sailors ship, and the terms on which they ship. It must be signed by each sailor, and there is a fine or penalty of twenty dollars for each one who does not sign.

Wages of Sailors. The sailors have a lien on the ship for their wages, which takes precedence of all other liens.

The captain has no such lien.

If the captain discharges any sailor, abroad, with his own consent, he must pay the American Consul at that port, all the wages due, and three months' wages in addition.

If the sailor is discharged, abroad, without his consent, the captain is liable to a fine of $500, or six months' imprisonment, and the sailor can recover damages for his time lost and his expenses.

The Consul, however, may authorize the discharge of a sailor for disobedience and other faults.

Flogging is expressly forbidden by law.

Desertion causes the forfeiture of wages.

Pilots. Pilots must be regularly appointed. A ship coming into port is obliged to take the first pilot that offers, or else pay him half the regular pilotage fees. The captain is not responsible while the pilot is in charge, for the moment the pilot steps on board he supersedes the authority of the captain and has complete control.

Necessary Papers. Besides the shipping articles, all vessels must have registry and clearance papers, which should be deposited with the Collector of Customs of the port. There must also be a "manifest," containing a description of the cargo and the vessel, the names of consignees and passengers, etc.; also a list of the crew.

MARINE INSURANCE.

THE general rules applicable to fire and life insurance are most of them equally true of marine insurance, but there are certain points of great difference. The principles governing re-insurance, double insurance, insurable interest, alienation of the property, assignment of the policy, warranty and representations, are practically the same.

Risks Insured Against. The risks insured against are perils of the sea, fire, barratry, or the wrongful acts of officers or crew producing damage to the ship-owner, theft, robbery, piracy, capture, arrests and detentions.

Perils of the sea would include loss caused by the violence of the wind or sea, or by wreck, stranding, etc.

The insurers are also liable for loss by collision, for salvage, and for general average claims.

When war risks are taken, the rates of premium are much higher than the ordinary rates.

Actual Total Loss. Both ship and cargo may be insured, and there may be an actual total loss of either or both. The insurance company would in that case be liable up to the full value of the property, if the policy be an open one, or only to the amount of risk taken, if the policy be valued.

Constructive Total Loss. But the ship or the cargo may not be totally destroyed; a valuable part of it may be saved. Yet, if the ship is injured more than one-half its value, or more than one-half the cargo perishes, the owner may insist on regarding this as a total loss, and compel the company to take the por· tion saved, and pay him the full value or amount of risk.   This is called "constructive" total loss.

Abandonment.   The owner has the option in such a case either to keep the property saved and demand compensation of the insurers for the partial loss, or to turn it all over to them.   If he exercises this right, it is called "abandonment."   This abandonment should be made at once, as soon as the claim for the loss is presented; if not, the owner will be deemed to have waived the right.

If there is a provision in the policy that there shall be no abandonment, the owner must keep the property saved, and receive only the amount of the partial loss.

Partial Loss.   In case of ordinary partial loss, the insurers pay the shippers of the cargo the full amount of their loss.   But there is a peculiar rule in regard to loss or injuries to the ship.   The rule is expressed "one-third off, new for old."   The meaning is that the insurers are to pay for the partial loss two-thirds of the whole expense of making the repairs with new materials, and that the owner must pay the other third.   The theory is that the old materials destroyed were only worth two-thirds as much as the new.

Seaworthiness.   The violation of any express warranty in the policy, as, for instance, a statement of the time of the ship's sailing, makes the policy void.   Beside express warranties, there are warranties implied whether expressed or not. The most important is the warranty of that the ship is seaworthy. A ship to be seaworthy must be competent to encounter ordinary risks, and furnished with everything necessary for the voyage. If the ship-owners have neglected any of these things the policy is void. If the ship gets out of repair during the voyage, it is the duty of the captain to repair before going further, or the insurance is forfeited in case of loss.

Deviation. There is also a warranty, implied when not express, that the ship will pursue the course described in the policy without deviation. If there is a deviation as by stopping at a port not mentioned, the policy is void. This is on account of the change of risk. Absolute necessity will justify deviation. The insurance is not forfeited where there is a voluntary deviation for the purpose of saving life, though it is where the object is to save property only.

FORM OF BILL OF LADING.

SHIPPED in good order and condition, by [name of consignor], on board the bark called the *Victoria*, whereof Isaac Bell is master, now lying in the port of New York, and bound for the port of Charleston, S.C. [here insert the list of goods], being marked and numbered as in the margin, and are to be delivered in the like order and condition at the port of Charleston, the dangers of the seal only excepted unto [name of consignee], or to his assigns, with primage and average accustomed.

In Witness Whereof the master or purser of the said vessel hath affirmed to three bills of lading, all of this tenor and date, one of which being accomplished the others to stand void.

Dated in New York, the ——— day of ———, 18—.

(Signature of Master.)

FORM OF CHARTER-PARTY.

Articles of Agreement, made this ——— day of ———, 18—, by and between [name of owner], of the City of ———, party of the first part, and [name of charterer], of the same place, party of the second part, *Witnesseth*, that the said party of the first part has this day chartered and hired unto the said party of the second part the vessel [steamer, etc.] named Henry Clay, of ———, and of the burden of ——— tons, or thereabouts, with all the appurtenances, cables, anchors, chains, etc., which belong to said vessel, for the term of ——— months, from the ——— day of May, to be delivered at the port of ———.

For the use of the said vessel, the said party of the second part, agrees and binds himself to pay to the said party of the first part, the sum of ——— dollars, the payments to be made as follows: ——— dollars, on the delivery of the said vessel; ——— dollars on the ——— day of ———; and ——— dollars at the expiration of the said ——— months. And it is agreed that the said party of the second part shall be at all the expense of manning and furnishing said vessel for the time above stated, and shall return the same to the said party of the first part, at the port of ———, in as good condition as it now is, with the exception of the ordinary use and wear; and if the said party of the second part shall at any time refuse to fulfill on his part, the said party of the first part shall have the right to take possession of the said vessel, wherever the same be found.

In Witness Whereof, the said parties have hereunto set their hands and seals, the day and year above written

Sealed and delivered in }
    the presence of   }   (Signature.)   [Seal.]
      (Name of witnesses.)

CHAPTER XVIII.

DEEDS.

*What is Real Estate—Easements—Sale of Land—Search-
ing the Title—Liens—Requisites of Deeds—Consideration
—Description—Covenants— Who Can Make a Deed—
Married Women—Signing—Delivery—Kinds of Deeds
—Acknowledgment—Recording.* FORMS: *Short Form
—Acknowledgment—Full Warranty Deed—Quitclaim
Deed—Executor's Deed—Release of Dower—Right of
Way—Contract for Sale of Land.*

A DEED is an instrument in writing under seal by
which the title to property is conveyed from one person to another. A deed may convey personal as well
as real property, but the word "deed" is almost exclusively applied to conveyances of real estate.

What is Real Estate. Real estate includes land
and the buildings erected upon it. Land covered by
water, such as a pond, is real estate. Oyster beds
must be transferred by deed, as they are regarded as
real estate. Permanent fixtures in buildings are part
of the land, and are regarded as real estate. The
rents arising from land are not personal property until they are due, and are real estate up to that time.
A verbal assignment of future rent therefore is void,
as such an assignment must be made by deed.

Easements. An easement is a right possessed by one person, usually the owner of adjacent lands, in the land of another. Easements are sometimes called servitudes. The estate possessing the right is called the dominant tenement; the estate over which the easement lies is called the servient tenement.

The principal easements are the right of passing over or through another's land, or the right of way, the right to have a brook or stream of water kept pure and its current unchanged by the owners of land further up the stream, the right of flooding another's land by damming a stream and so forcing the water back, the right of taking soil, or timber, or water from another's land, the right of light and air and of preventing the adjacent land-owner from interfering with such light or air by building, even on his own land or in any other way.

Besides these easements there are many others. Some of them exist by implication, as where a man sells part of his land lying away from the road, and retains land lying on the road. The purchaser would have an implied right of way from necessity to pass over the seller's land to reach the road. Most easements, however, are created by deed. The mere right is conveyed in this way without any conveyance of land, but the deed is in other respects precisely like a deed of land in the ordinary understanding of that word. An easement may sometimes exist by prescription; that is, long usage, or exercise of the right for many years will make the easement a valid one, even though there was no deed in the first place.

Sale of Land. It is customary when land is sold for the parties to draw up and sign a written contract, by which the owner of the land agrees to sell, and to give the purchaser a deed at some time in the future, frequently thirty days.

This is called an executory contract of sale. It must be in writing, or otherwise the agreement or promise of either party is not binding upon him. If the agreement is merely verbal, either party may refuse to fulfill, the owner to sell, or the purchaser to buy. The advantage of a written contract is, that the owner can compel the purchaser to take the land and pay the contract price, or, if the owner should refuse, the purchaser can compel him to convey the land.

Searching the Title. The time between the execution of the contract and the delivery of the deed is given for the purpose of allowing the purchaser to examine or "search the title" of the land. By this is meant that he shall have the opportunity of searching the records of the county, in order to ascertain whether the seller actually has the title or ownership of the land, and what mortgages or other liens or encumbrances there may be upon it.

This examination should be made by a lawyer, or some one skilled in searching titles, and the purchaser is the one who employs him and pays the fees.

Liens. The liens to be looked for, after the searcher has assured himself that the deeds on record show the title to be in the seller, are mortgages, judgments and decrees of the State and Federal Courts, mechanic's liens, taxes, notices of the pendency of an action, sheriff's sales and assignments. If any of these are found unpaid or uncancelled, the purchaser can refuse to "take the title," that is, to pay the purchase money, and he can demand back whatever he has already paid, unless the owner discharges the liens by paying them.

If the title is free and clear, the contract must be carried out at the appointed time and place, by the payment of the money and the delivery of the deed. The seller is called the grantor, and the buyer, the grantee.

Requisites of Deeds. A deed should be written on paper or parchment. A seal is almost universally used, and is in most States necessary to the validity of the deed. The seal may be of wax, or may consist merely of paper affixed to the deed by some adhesive substance. In some, especially the Western States, the letters " L. S." after the name is sufficient. The letters are the initials of the Latin words, "locus sigilli," meaning the place of the seal.

Consideration. The deed should contain the names of the grantor and the grantee, and the date of execution. The receipt of a consideration must be acknowledged by the grantor in order to pass the title. It is not necessary to name the exact or true consideration.

The acknowledgment of the receipt of one dollar is a frequent occurrence, and is enough to pass the title.

It is not essential that the one dollar should actually be paid. A consideration different from the actual sum is often named in the deed for the purpose of preventing others from ascertaining what the sum was by an examination of the records.

Description. There must be a description of the land conveyed in the deed. It need not be extremely long or minute, but it should be clear and absolutely accurate. It is well to copy the description from the previous deed by which the property was conveyed to the present grantor, and to use the same form of words which have been used in describing the property. The language of the description is generally in the terms employed by the surveyor of the land. Sometimes it becomes necessary to have a resurvey made. This is often done where only part of the land is sold. It is necessary for the purpose of clearly defining the boundary lines of the estate.

Covenants. In almost all deeds there are certain agreements or covenants made by the grantor with the grantee. The usual covenants are the covenants of seizin and right to convey, against incumbrances, of further assurance, of quiet enjoyment, and of warranty. These covenants are not necessary to pass the title, but are desirable for the grantee to have in the deed. The general effect of them is that if the title should prove defective in any particular or there should be any unnoticed mortgages or liens upon the property, the grantor will be bound to make the title good by paying off the incumbrances, or compensating the grantee for any loss he may sustain. The grantee can compel the grantor to do this by an action at law.

Who can Make a Deed. A valid deed can only be made by a person of full age. An infant, under twenty-one years of age, cannot sell his real estate, except on application to some court and by its permission.

A deed made by an insane person may be set aside by suit.

Deeds obtained by force or fraud or threats may also be set aside in the same way.

Married Women. Married women can, in some States, make a valid deed of their own separate real estate. In some States they must obtain the husband's consent in writing, or he must sign the deed to make it good. In other States, a married woman may deed her property without her husband's consent, but subject to his rights of courtesy. It is desirable always that the husband should sign the deed of his wife's land as well as the wife herself.

The wife should sign a deed of land made by her husband in all States where dower is not abolished. This is for the purpose of "signing off" her rights to a life-interest in one-third of the land on her husband's death. It is unsafe to accept the deed of a married man unless his wife signs it. The wife is not obliged to deed away her rights, but she may consent of her own free will.

Signing. The deed must be signed by the grantor

or grantors at the end. This may be done in the presence of witnesses, who then sign their names as such. In some States witnesses are essential. In others, there may be witnesses, but the deed is valid without them. The seal is usually affixed immediately opposite the signature.

The grantor may be unable to sign in person, and the deed may then be signed by his agent or attorney. The agent's authority to do this can only be given by a power of attorney, a formal legal instrument under seal.

There should be no alteration or erasures in the deed after it has been signed.

The grantee does not sign the deed.

Delivery. The deed takes effect from its delivery to the grantee. The title does not pass until such delivery. The deed may be delivered by the grantor or his agent. Sometimes, after a deed has been duly executed, it is placed in the hands of a third person to be delivered to the grantee on the happening of some event, as, for example, the payment of the consideration. This is called an escrow. It has no effect as a deed until the condition is performed. A deed should not be made or delivered on Sunday.

Kinds of Deeds. A deed poll is a deed executed by the grantor alone, and he alone is bound by the covenants therein contained.

An indenture is a deed executed by both grantor and grantee, and both parties are bound by the covenants. A deed is often called an indenture, even when only the grantor signs it.   Covenants in a deed now bind any person who receives it.

A warranty deed is a deed containing a covenant of warranty.   The grantor thereby promises that if the grantee shall ever be dispossessed by any person who may prove to have a better legal right to the land, he will make the loss good.

A quitclaim deed is a grant of all the right, title and interest which the grantor has in the land, whatever it may be.

A release is a deed by which some claim of the grantor to land is released.   Dower is frequently released by a widow in this way.

A bargain and sale deed is the ordinary form of deed used in many States.

Grant is a term which formerly applied only to deeds conveying easements, but now embraces all kinds of conveyances.

Acknowledgment.   A deed should be acknowledged by the grantor to be his free act and deed before a Notary Public, or other official qualified to take an acknowledgement.   Judges, including Justices of the Peace, Mayors of Cities, and Commissioners of Deeds, are generally authorized to perform such an act.   The officer should add a certificate to the deed, stating the fact of acknowledgment, and should sign his name and official title.

Acknowledgment is not absolutely necessary to make a deed valid, but it is necessary in order to have it recorded.

In some States when a married woman executes a deed, her acknowledgment must be taken by the officer on an examination separate and apart from her husband. She must state that she signs without fear or compulsion of her husband.

The form of an acknowledgment differs in different States, and the parties should take care to employ the proper form.

Recording. After the execution and acknowledgment of a deed it should be recorded at once in the proper office. This office is generally the office of the County Clerk of the county where the land is situated, or the office of the Register or Recorder of Deeds. There are certain fees payable by the grantee before his deed will be recorded. The deed should be presented for record without delay, as a matter of precaution. In some States it must be recorded within a certain number of days or it is void. The object of the record is to give actual or constructive notice to all persons of the title or ownership of the land. The title may safely be considered to be in the person who appears on the record as the grantee of the last deed.

A subsequent grantee or mortgagee of the grantor in an unrecorded deed is entitled to the land if he gets his deed on record before the first grantee.

SHORT FORM OF DEED.

This indenture witnesseth, that, I, A. B., of the town of ——, party of the first part, in consideration of one dollar to me in hand paid by C. D., party of the second part, do bargain, sell and grant to C. D., his heirs and assigns forever, all that lot of land [here insert description].

Witness my hand and seal this 10th day of June, 1885.

Sealed and delivered }   (Signature of grantor.)   [Seal.]
  in the presence of }
    (Witnesses.)

ACKNOWLEDGMENT TO FOLLOW DEED.

State of New York, } ss.
County of Kings. }

On this 10th day of June, in the year of our Lord one thousand eight hundred and eighty-five, before me personally came [name of grantor, A. B.], to me known and known to me to be the individual described in, and who executed the within conveyance, and who acknowledged to me that he executed the same.

                (Signed.)   [Name.]
                            Notary Public,
                            Kings County.

FORM OF ACKNOWLEDGMENT, WITH ADDITIONAL CLAUSE AS TO WIFE.

State of New Jersey, } ss.
Hudson County. }

Be it remembered, that on this twelfth day of April, in the year one thousand eight hundred and eighty-two, before me, A. B., a Notary Public, of the State of New Jersey, personally appeared (names of the grantor and his wife), who, I am satisfied, are the grantors in the within Deed of Conveyance named; and I, having first made known to them the contents thereof, they did acknowledge that they signed, sealed and delivered the same as their voluntary act and deed, for the uses and purposes therein expressed.

And the said (name of wife), being by me privately examined, separate and apart from her said husband, did further acknowledge that she signed, sealed and delivered the same as her voluntary act and deed, *freely*, without any fear, threats, or compulsion of her said husband.

                          (Name of Notary Public.

FORM OF A FULL WARRANTY DEED.

This Indenture, made the first day of September, in the year one thousand eight hundred and eighty-four, *between* (name of grantor), party of the first part, and (name of grantee), party of the second part, *Witnesseth,* That the said party of the first part, for and in consideration of the sum of —— dollars, lawful money of the United States of America, to him in hand paid by the said party of the second part, at or before the ensealing and delivery of these presents, the receipt whereof is hereby acknowledged, and the said party of the second part, his heirs, executors and administrators, forever released and discharged from the same, by these presents, *Hath* granted, bargained, sold, aliened, remised, released, conveyed, and confirmed, and by these presents, *Doth* grant, bargain, sell, alien, remise, release, convey, and confirm, unto the said party of the second part, and to his heirs and assigns forever, *All*

[Here insert description.]

Together with all and singular, the tenements, hereditaments and appurtenances thereunto belonging or in any wise appertaining, and the reversion and reversions, remainder and remainders, rents, issues and profits thereof. *And also,* all the estate, right, title, interest, property, possession, claim and demand whatsoever, as well in law and in equity, of the said party of the first part, of, in and to the same, and every part and parcel thereof, with the appurtenances. *To have and to hold* the above granted, bargained and described premises, with the appurtenances, unto the said party of the second part, his heirs and assigns, to their own proper use, benefit and behoof, forever.

And the said party of the first part, for himself, his heirs, executors and administrators, doth covenant, grant and agree, to and with the said party of the second part, his heirs and assigns, that the said party of the first part, at the time of the sealing and delivery of these presents, is lawfully seized in his own right of a good, absolute and indefeasible estate of inheritance, in fee simple, of and in all and singular the

above granted, bargained and described premises, with the appurtenances, and hath good right, full power, and lawful authority
to grant, bargain, sell and convey the same in manner and form
aforesaid. *And* that the said party of the second part, his heirs
and assigns, shall and may at all times hereafter, peaceably and
quietly have, hold, use, occupy, possess and enjoy the above
granted premises, and every part and parcel thereof, with the
appurtenances, without any let, suit, trouble, molestation, eviction or disturbance of the said party of the first part, his heirs or
assigns, or of any other person or persons, lawfully claiming or to
claim the same. *And* that the same are now free, clear, discharged and unincumbered of and from all former and other
grants, titles, charges, estates, judgments, taxes, assessments and
incumbrances of what nature or kind soever. *And also*, that the
said party of the first part, and his heirs, and all and every other
person or persons whomsoever, lawfully and equitably deriving
any estate, right, title or interest of, in, or to the hereinbefore
granted premises, by, from, under, or in trust for them, shall and
will at any time or times hereafter, upon the reasonable request,
and at the proper costs and charges in the law, of the said party of
the second part, his heirs and assigns, make, do and execute, or
cause or procure to be made, done and executed, all and every
such further and other lawful and reasonable acts, conveyances
and assurances in the law, for the better and more effectually
vesting and confirming the premises hereby intended to be granted,
in and to the said party of the second part, his heirs and assigns,
or his counsel learned in the law, shall be reasonably devised, ad-
vised or required.

And the said party of the first part, and his heirs, the above
described and hereby granted and released premises, and every
part and parcel thereof, with the appurtenances, unto the said
party of the second part, his heirs and assigns, against the said
party of the first part, and his heirs, and against all and every
person or persons whomsoever, lawfully claiming or to claim the
same, shall and will *Warrant*, and by these presents forever *Defend.*

In witness whereof, the said party of the first part hath hereunto set his hand and seal the day and year first above written.

Sealed and delivered }
in the presence of }   (Signed) (Name of grantor.)   [Seal.]
[Names of witnesses.]

STATE OF ———, } ss.
COUNTY OF ———. }

On this first day of September, in the year of our Lord one thousand eight hundred aad eighty-four, before me personally came [name of grantor], to me known and known to me to be the person described in, and who executed the within conveyance and acknowledged that he executed the same.

[Name of Notary Public, etc.]

FORM OF A QUITCLAIM DEED.

This Indenture, made the — day of ———, in the year of our Lord one thousand eight hundred and ———, *Between* (name of grantor), party of the first part, and (name of grantee), party of the second part, *Witnesseth*, that the said party of the first part, for and in consideration of the sum of ——— dollars, lawful money of the United States of America, to him in hand paid by the said party of the second part, at or before the ensealing and delivery of these presents the receipt whereof is hereby acknowledged, has remised, released, and quitclaimed, and by these presents does remise, release, and quitclaim unto the said party of the second part, and to his heirs and assigns, forever, All that certain lot, piece or parcel of land situated, lying and being in the town of ——— and bounded and described as follows:

[Here insert the description of the property.]

Together with all and singular, the tenements, hereditaments and appurtenances thereunto belonging or in anywise appertaining, and the reversion and reversions, remainder and remainders, rents, issues and profits thereof. *And also*, a l the estate, right, title, interest, property, possesion, claim and demand whatsoever, as well in law as in equity, of the said party of the first part, of, in or to the above described premises, and every part and parcel thereof with the appurtenances. *To have and to hold* all and singular the above-mentioned and described premises, together with the appurtenances, unto the said party of the second part, his heirs and assigns forever.

In witness whereof, the said party of the first part has hereunto set his hand and seal the day and year first above written.

Sealed and delivered)
in the presence of }   (Signed) (Name of grantor.) [Seal.]
    [Name of witnesses.]

STATE OF ———,)
COUNTY OF ———. } ss.

On this ——— day of ———, in the year of our Lord, one thousand eight hundred and eighty ———, before me personally came [name of grantor], to me known, and known to me to be the individual described in, and who executed the within conveyance, who acknowledged to me that he executed the same.

        (Signed)   [Name of Notary Public.]

FORM OF EXECUTOR'S DEED.

This Indenture, made the ——— day of ———, in the year of our Lord, one thousand .eight hundred and eighty ———, *Between* A. B., as Executor of the Last Will and Testament of ———, deceased, and ———, party of the second part, Witnesseth, that the said party of the first part, by virtue of the power and authority to him given in and by the said last will and testament, and for and in consideration of the sum of ——— dollars, lawful money of the United States of America, to him in hand paid, at or before the ensealing and delivery of these presents, by the said party of the second part, the receipt whereof is hereby acknowledged, and the said party of the second part, his heirs, executors and administrators forever, released and discharged from the same, by these presents, has granted, bargained, sold, aliened, released, conveyed and confirmed, and by these presents, does grant, bargain, sell, alien, release, convey and confirm, unto the said party of the second part, his heirs and assigns forever, all that certain piece, parcel (farm), or tract of land, situate, lying and being in the (town), City of ———, State of ———, and bounded and described as follows:

[Here insert the description of the premises.]

Together with all and singular, the edifices, buildings, rights, members, privileges, advantages, hereditaments and appurtenances to the same belonging, or in anywise appertaining, and the reversion and reversions, remainder and remainders, rents, issues, and profits thereof. *And also*, all the estate, right, title, interest, claim and demand whatsoever, as well in law as in equity, which the said testator had in his lifetime, and at the time of his decease, and which the said parties of the first part has by virtue of the said last Will and Testament, or otherwise, of, in and to the same, and every part and parcel thereof with the appurtenances.

To have and to hold the said premises above mentioned and described, and hereby granted and conveyed, or intended so to be, with the appurtenances unto the said party of the second part, his heirs and assigns, to their own proper use, benefit and behoof, forever.

And the said party of the first part for himself, his heirs, executors and administrators, doth covenant, grant, promise and agree, to and with the said party of the second part, his heirs and assigns, that the said party of the second part, his heirs and assigns, shall and lawfully may from time to time, and at all times forever hereafter peaceably and quietly have, hold, use, occupy, possess and enjoy, all and singular the said hereditaments and premises hereby granted and conveyed or intended so to be, with their and every of their appurtenances, and receive and take the rents, issues and profits thereof, to and for their own use and benefit, without any lawful let, suit, hindrance, molestation, interruption or denial whatsoever, of, from or by him, the said party of the first part or his assigns; or of, from, or by any other person or persons whomsoever lawfully claiming, or who shall or may lawfully claim hereafter, by, from or under them, or by, from or under their right, title, interest or estate; and that the same are now free and clear, and freely and clearly discharged, acquitted and exonerated, and shall be well and sufficiently saved, defended, kept harmless, and indemnified by him, the said party of the first part, his successors and assigns, of, from and against all and all manner of former and other gifts, grants, bargains, sales, mortgages, judgments and all other charges and incumbrances whatsoever, had, made, committed, executed, or done by him, the said party of the first part, or by, through, or with his acts, deeds, means, consent, procurement or privity.

IN WITNESS WHEREOF, the said party of the first part has hereunto set his hand and seal the day and year first above written.

Sealed and delivered }   (Signed.) (Name of executor.) [Seal.]
  in the presence of }
    (Name of witness.)

FORM OF RELEASE OF DOWER.

Know all men by these presents, That I, Mary Brown, of the town of Kent, wife of John Brown [or widow of John Brown, late of said town, deceased], party of the first part, in consideration of one thousand dollars, to me paid by Charles Smith, of the said town of Kent, party of the second part, the receipt whereof is hereby acknowledged, have granted, remised, released, conveyed, and forever quitclaimed, and by these presents do grant, remise, release, and forever quitclaim unto the said Charles Smith, and to his heirs and assigns, forever, all the dower and thirds, and all other right, title, interest, property, claim and demand whatsoever, in law and in equity, of me, the said Mary Brown, of, in and to, *All* that certain piece, parcel or lot of land, situate, lying, and being in the town of Kent, and bounded and described as follows:

[Here insert description.]

So that neither I, the said Mary Brown, my heirs, executors, administrators and assigns, nor any other person or persons, for me, them, or any of them, shall have, claim or demand any dower, or thirds, or any other right, title, claim or demand, of, in, or to the same, or any part thereof, but thereof and therefrom shall be utterly barred and excluded forever.

In witness whereof, I have hereunto set my hand and seal, this sixth day of August, in the year one thousand eight hundred and eighty-one.

Sealed and delivered }   MARY BROWN. [Seal.]
    in presence of }

(Names of witnesses.)

(Acknowledgment.)

FORM OF CLAUSE GRANTING A RIGHT OF WAY.

All that certain lot of land, etc., together with a right of way in and over a certain strip of land along the east side of the barn on the above-described premises, for the said party of the second part, his heirs and assigns, at all times freely to pass and repass, on foot, or with animals, vehicles, or otherwise, to and fro, between the premises, hereby granted, and the Bedford road, the said strip of land and way being twenty feet wide.

FORM OF CONTRACT FOR THE SALE OF LAND.

Articles of agreement, made the ninth day of March, one thousand eight hundred and eighty-three, between A. B., of Dover, party of the first part, and C. D., of the same place, party of the second part, *Witnesseth*, That the said party of the first part, for and in consideration of the sum of one dollar to him in hand paid, has contracted and agreed to sell to the said party of the second part:

All that certain piece, parcel or lot of land, situate in the town of Dover, and County of Monmouth, and bounded and described as follows:

[Here insert description.]

And the said party of the first part agrees to execute and deliver to the said party of the second part a warranty deed for the said land, provided, and upon condition, nevertheless, that the said party of the second part, his heirs or assigns, pay to the said party of the first part, his heirs or assigns, for the said land, the sum of three thousand dollars, lawful money of the United States of America, payable as follows: The sum of three hundred dollars to be paid to A. B. on signing this agreement; the sum of two thousand seven hundred dollars, on the delivery of the deed, which is to be at the office of X. Y., attorney-at-law, at 12 o'clock on the ninth day of April, 1883. *And* the said party of the second part, for himself, his heirs, executors, and administrators, does covenant and agree to and with the said party of the first part, his heirs and assigns, that the said party of the second part will pay the said several sums as they become due, with the interest thereof. *And* it is further agreed between the parties to these presents, that if default be made in fulfilling this agreement, or any part thereof, on the part of the said party of the second part, then and in such case, the said party of the first part, his heirs and assigns, shall be at liberty to consider the contract as forfeited and annulled and to dispose of the said land to any other person, in the same manner, as if this contract had never been made.

In witness whereof, they have hereunto set their hands and seals the day and year above written.

Sealed and delivered }   A. B. [Seal.]
  in the presence of }   C. D. [Seal.]
    (Witnesses.)

CHAPTER XIX.

MORTGAGES OF REAL ESTATE.

Form of Mortgage—Sale and Mortgage—The Debt Secured—Purchase-Money Mortgage—Mortgage to Secure Future Advances—Mortgages of Indemnity—Legal Mortgages—Equitable Mortgages—Who May Mortgage—Wife Must Sign—Mortgages by Corporation—Acknowledgment — Recording — Object of Record—Priority of Mortgages—Assignment—Assignee Should Give Notice—Satisfaction—Assuming a Mortgage—Possession—Rights of the Mortgagor—Liabilities—Rights of Mortgagee—Mortgagee in Possession—Foreclosure—Effect Of—Deeds of Trust. FORMS: Short Form of Mortgage—Full Form—Insurance Clause—Tax Clause—Clause as to Future Advances—Assignment of Mortgage — Satisfaction-Piece —Bond to Accompany Mortgage—Deed of Trust.

A MORTGAGE is a conveyance of property for the purpose of securing a debt, with a condition that if the debt is paid, the conveyance is to become void. A mortgage of personal property is called a chattel mortgage. The word "mortgage" simply is popularly applied to mortgages of land, or real estate, as these are much more common and prevalent in actual use. The debtor who gives the mortgage on his land is called the mortgagor, and the creditor who receives 'nd holds it, is called the mortgagee.

Form of Mortgage. A mortgage in form is a deed of the land, conveying the title from the mortgagor to the mortgagee, but following the granting clause there is the condition mentioned, which indicates that the grant is not absolute, but only for the security of the debt. There is usually inserted a power of sale to enable the mortgagee to sell the land in case the debt should not be paid when it comes due.

The condition is called the defeasance. It may be, and almost always is, a part of the instrument. But it may be contained on a separate paper, in which case it should be under seal. A verbal defeasance is, however, valid.

Sale and Mortgage. If the intention of the parties in giving and taking a deed is merely to secure a loan, and there is an understanding that the debtor is to have his land back on repayment of that loan, the transaction is regarded, not as a sale, but as a mortgage. The importance of this is that if it be a mortgage, the debtor or mortgagor can redeem the land at any time by paying the money and interest, which in case of a sale he cannot do.

The Debt Secured. Any valid debt may be secured by mortgage. If the debt is void for any reason, such as usury, the mortgage is also void.

It is usual for the debtor at the time of executing the mortgage to also execute a bond or promissory note in favor of the creditor for the amount of the debt. A bond is preferable, as it is not negotiable like a note. The bond and mortgage are delivered to the mortgagee at the same time. If the note or bond is sold or assigned, the mortgage should also be assigned. If it is not, the purchaser is nevertheless entitled to it, and this whether he knows that the debt is so secured or not.

Purchase-Money Mortgages. When land is purchased by one who is unable for any reason to pay for it in full, it is an ordinary arrangement for the purchaser on receiving the deed to give back to the grantor a mortgage on the land conveyed for the unpaid balance of the consideration. This is known as a purchase-money mortgage. It is not necessary for the wife of the mortgagor to sign such a mortgage, as it takes precedence of her rights of dower.

Mortgage to Secure Future Advances. A mortgage may be made not only to secure an old debt or a contemporaneous loan, but also advances or loans of money to be made by the mortgagee to the mortgagor from time to time in the future. Such a mortgage has priority over other subsequent mortgages on the same land, not up to the face value, but to the amount of money actually advanced.

It is advisable for any person before loaning money on a second mortgage in cases where there is a first or prior mortgage of this kind, to get a statement from the first mortgagee of the amount he has hitherto advanced to the mortgagor, and to give such mortgagee notice of the execution of the second mortgage. The first mortgagee is bound by any statement he may make, and any advances of money made after such notice are postponed to the second mortgage as a lien on the land.

Mortgages of Indemnity.

Mortgages are frequently given, in cases where there is no debt existing, to secure or indemnify the mortgagee against some liability which he may possibly incur on behalf or for the benefit of the mortgagor. For instance, where a man has indorsed another's note for the latter's accommodation, or gone on his bond as surety, the latter may execute to the former a mortgage of indemnity. If the liability is incurred, as by the protest of the note, the mortgagee has a lien on the mortgaged land for all he is obliged to pay; if not incurred, the mortgage is of no effect.

Legal Mortgages.

A legal mortgage is one drawn up and executed in legal form. It must be written. It should contain the date of making, the names of the mortgagor and mortgagee, a description of the premises mortgaged, the amount of the consideration, the defeasance, and such covenants as may be agreed upon. The mortgage should be signed by the mortgagor, and sealed. In many States the letters L. S. are sufficient as far as a seal is concerned. It is not necessary for the mortagee to sign, but the mortgage must be delivered to him to make it effective.

Equitable Mortgages.

Beside the ordinary or legal mortgages, there is a class known as equitable mortgages. A legal instrument intended for a mortgage, but defective in form, is good as an equitable mortgage.

The lien of the vendor or seller of land for the con sideration-money before the deed is given, and in some States, as New York, *after* the deed is given, is an equitable mortgage.

So is a written agreement between the parties to make a mortgage, or a deposit of title deeds as security.

In all these cases the mortgagee has the right to demand a legal mortgage, or to foreclose his equitable mortgage, and recover the amount of his loan. It is not a safe security, however, as a legal mortgage, sub sequently made, takes precedence of it.

Who May Mortgage. Any person owning land in fee may mortgage it. Anyone having a life-estate or a lease may mortgage his interest. Infants under twenty-one cannot mortgage their land, except by permission of a court of equity. Married women now have the right to make a mortgage of their separate property. In some States it is only necessary for her alone to sign the mortgage. In other States she must obtain her husband's consent, and he must sign with her.

Wife Must Sign. When a married man makes a mortgage his wife should sign with him, in order to cut off her dower rights. If she does not sign, she is entitled to her dower in the entire property, which fact may seriously impair the value of the mortgage as security. If she does sign, she is entitled to her dower, subject to the mortgage, that is, to a life-estate in one-third of the surplus of the value of the land over the mortgage.

Mortgages by Corporation. The power of a corporation to make a mortgage is regulated by its charter or the general law under which it is organized. It is unsafe to accept such a mortgage without ascertaining whether it is valid under the law. The mortgage must generally, when permissible, be signed by the president of the corporation, and authorized by a vote of the directors or stockholders. Religious corporations can only mortgage by consent of court.

Acknowledgment. As between the mortgagor and mortgagee there is no need of any acknowledgment. The mortgage is good without it. But in order to entitle it to be recorded, it is necessary for the mortgagor to appear before a Notary Public, or Judge, or Magistrate, and acknowledge the execution of the mortgage.

In many States the wife of the mortgagor must make her acknowledgment on a private examination, separate and apart from her husband, and admit that she signs the mortgage without fear or compulsion of her husband.

Recording. The mortgage is then delivered to the County Clerk, or the Recorder or Register of Deeds of the county where the land is situated. This official then transcribes it on the records. It is important that this should be done by the mortgagee, as soon as possible after the delivery of the mortgage.

Object of Record. The object of recording is to give notice of the existence of the mortgage to anyone who might wish to purchase the land, or to take a mortgage upon it. The fact of record is constructive notice to all persons, whether they actually see the record or not. After the mortgage is recorded, it is returned to the mortgagee.

Priority of Mortgages. There may be several mortgages on the same premises. The first mortgage in point of time has priority over the others, and is entitled to be paid first in full. After the first is paid, then the second is entitled to be paid, then the third, and so on.

If the first mortgagee, however, neglects to put his mortgage on record, a second mortgagee, who takes a mortgage without any knowledge of the first, and duly records his own, is entitled to priority over the first. Mortgages have priority, not in order of time of execution, but in order of time of record.

Very frequently the second or third mortgagee gets little or nothing, as the value of the premises is only sufficient to pay the first, and his personal claim against the mortgagor is valueless on account of the latter's insolvency.

Assignment of Mortgage. The mortgagee may assign the mortgage, that is, sell it to any person he pleases. The assignee or purchaser then becomes entitled to all the rights of the original mortgagee. An assignment or sale of the debt alone, as the note or bond, passes the mortgage.

The mere delivery of the mortgage to the assignee is a valid assignment. The assignment is often indorsed on the mortgage itself.

By far the safest method, however, is for the mortgagee to execute a formal legal assignment to the assignee. This should contain a description of the premises, and of the mortgage, when made, and when and where recorded. It should be signed by the mortgagee, under seal, and be acknowledged in the same manner as a mortgage. It should then be recorded. If not recorded, a subsequent assignee of the mortgage, in case the mortgagee were dishonest enough to make such an assignment would, by putting his assignment on record, have the better right to the mortgage.

Assignee Should Give Notice. The assignee of the mortgage should at once give notice to the mortgagor that the mortgage has been assigned to him. The mortgagor is not bound by the constructive notice of the record. The object of this notice is to inform the mortgagor to pay the mortgage money or the interest to the assignee and not to the original mortgagee. If the mortgagor did not receive any such notice he might innocently and in good faith pay it to the latter. The loss would, in such a case, fall on the assignee, as he incurred it by his own neglect.

Satisfaction of Mortgage. By the satisfaction of a mortgage is meant its payment. The payment should be made to the mortgagee or his agent as soon as the mortgage is due. If not paid then, the mortgagee has the right to foreclose. But the money can be paid and the land redeemed at any time before the foreclosure sale.

The payment of the debt discharges the lien of the mortgage on the land. A tender of good legal money has the same effect, even if the mortgagee refuses to accept it. This tender does not effect the debt, except to stop the running of interest, but only the mortgage security.

It is the duty of the mortgagee on receiving the money to draw up and deliver to the mortgagor a satisfaction-piece, as it is called; an instrument acknowledging the receipt of the money and consenting that the mortgage be cancelled on the records. This paper is delivered to the County Clerk or Register, who records it, and marks the mortgage "discharged."

Assuming a Mortgage. The mortgagor is personally liable to the mortgagee for the debt, independent of the mortgage security. If the land is insufficient to pay it, he may sue the mortgagor personally for the balance.

But if the mortgagor has sold the land " subject to the mortgage," the mortgagee has no personal claim against the purchaser. He must foreclose the mortgage, sell the land and collect the deficiency of the mortgagor.

If the land, however, is sold with a clause in the deed to the effect that the purchaser assumes the

payment of the mortgage as part of the considera
tion, then the purchaser becomes liable to the mort
gagee personally. The mortgagor is also liable.

Possession. In most of the States the mortgagor
is entitled to retain possession of the property until
the foreclosure sale. In others the mortgagee has
the right to the immediate possession, or as soon as
the mortgage debt is due.

Rights of the Mortgagor. The mortgagor has
the title or ownership of the land. He may sell it,
rent it, devise it by will, or mortgage it a second time.
But this can only be done subject to the mortgage,
as the rights of the mortgagee cannot be impaired.
The interest of the mortgagor can be seized by the
sheriff on execution and sold for his debts. It is also
subject to dower.

This interest of the mortgagor in the land is called
the " equity of redemption," a phrase signifying that
he has a right in equity to redeem from the mortgagee by paying the debt. He may insure the
premises.

Liabilities. It is the duty of the mortgagor, not
of the mortgagee, to pay all taxes and assessments.
He must not injure or lessen in any way the value of the
mortgaged premises, so as to impair the security.
Such injury is called " waste," and may be stopped
by the mortgagee. The mortgagor is not liable to
the mortgagee for rent, no matter how long he remains in possession. But he is liable for interest on
the debt during that time.

Rights of Mortgagee. The mortgagee may foreclose the mortgage at maturity if the debt is not paid. He may insure the premises for his own benefit. If the insurance company has to pay, it can enforce the mortgage against the mortgagor.

The mortgagee may release any portion of the land from the lien of the mortgage by a sealed instrument, called a release. The mortgage can then only be foreclosed on the residue of the land.

If there are any subsequent mortgages, judgments or other liens on the land, or part of it, it is very dangerous to sign such a paper.

The statute of limitations may bar the mortgage debt, but not the mortgage. The mortgagee generally has the right to foreclose at any time.

Mortgagee in Possession. If the mortgagee takes possession of the land, he must take care of it, and make all necessary repairs. He has no right to make extensive repairs, however, and may be compelled to pay for them himself in case he does so. He should pay all taxes, assessments, insurance premiums, etc., and he can include all these expenses in the amount due to him on the mortgage. He is liable, and must account for all the rents and profits of the property while he was in possession, and credit them on the mortgage debt.

Foreclosure. The mortgagee may, under his power of sale, sell the premises for the payment of the mortgage debt. In some States this is done by advertising for a certain time, and selling the land at public auction.   This is called foreclosure by advertisement.

There may also be a foreclosure by suit or an action in equity.   These proceedings also terminate in a sale, under the direction of a referee appointed by the court.

Of the two methods, foreclosure by suit is preferable, as irregularities are waived by the judgment. In foreclosure by advertisement the proceedings must be strictly accurate, and any irregularity makes the sale void.

Effect of.   By foreclosure all the rights of the mortgagor, his wife if she signed the mortgage, and all persons claiming under him, such as a tenant, are entirely taken away.   The tenant of the mortgagor has no right to the unripe crops sown by him and growing upon the land at the time of foreclosure. They go to the mortgagee, or the purchaser, who is under no obligation to pay for them.

If there are any surplus moneys arising from the sale they go to the mortgagor and his heirs, unless there are other mortgages or liens on the property. In that case such liens are paid first out of the surplus before the mortgagor receives anything.

Deeds of Trust.   In Virginia and a few other States, deeds of trust are used instead of mortgages to secure debts.   The general character of the security is the same as a mortgage.

SHORT FORM OF MORTGAGE.

This Indenture, made the — day of ——, in the year 188—, be

tween John Doe, of ———, party of the first part, and Richard Roe, of ———, party of the second part, Witnesseth, that the said party of the first part, for and in consideration of the sum of ——— dollars, doth grant, bargain, and sell unto the party of the second part, his heirs and assigns, All [insert description of land].

These presents are upon the express condition, that if the said party of the first part, his heirs, or executors, or administrators, shall well and truly pay unto the said party of the second part, his executors, administrators, and assigns, the said sum of ——— dollars, with the interest thereon, on the — day of ——, 18S—, then these presents and the estate hereby granted shall cease and become null and void.

But in case default shall be made in the payment of the principal or interest, as above provided, then the party of the second part, his executors, administrators, and assigns, are hereby empowered, to sell the premises above described, with all of the appurtenances, or any part thereof, in the manner prescribed by law; and out of the moneys arising from such sale, to retain the said principal and interest, together with the costs and charges of making such sale, and the overplus, if any there be, shall be paid to the party of the first part, his heirs or assigns.

In witness whereof, the party of the first part has hereunto set his hand and seal, the day and year first above written.

In the presence)
of   }   John Doe. [Seal.]
(Witness.)

FORM OF MORTGAGE.

This Indenture, made the — day of ———, in the year one thousand eight hundred and eighty———, *Between* [name of mortgagor], of the town of ———, State of ———, and ——— (his wife), parties of the first part, and [name of mortgagee] of the same place, party of the second part:

Whereas, the said [name of mortgagor] is justly indebted to the said party of the second part, in the sum of (state amount of debt) dollars, lawful money of the United States of America secured to be paid by a certain bond or obligation, bearing even date with these presents, in the penal sum of (twice amount of debt) dollars, lawful money as aforesaid, conditioned for the payment of the said first-mentioned sum of (amount of debt) dollars, which said bond also contains an agreement, that should any default be made in the payment of the said interest or any part thereof, on any day whereon the same is made payable as above expressed, and should the same remain unpaid and in arrear for the space of —— days, that then and from thenceforth, that is to say, after the lapse of the said interest, the aforesaid principal sum of —————— dollars, with all arrearages of interest thereon, shall at the option of the said party of the second part, or his legal representatives, become and be due and payable immediately thereafter, although the time limited for the payment thereof may not then have expired, anything in the said bond contained to the contrary thereof in any wise notwithstanding; as by the said bond or obligation, and the condition thereof, and the said agreement therein contained, reference being thereunto had may more fully appear.

Now this Indenture Witnesseth, that the said parties of the first part, for the better securing the payment of the said sum of money mentioned in the condition of the said bond or obligation, with interest thereon, according to the true intent and meaning thereof, and also for and in consideration of the sum of one dollar to them in hand paid by the said party of the second part, at or before the ensealing and delivery of these presents, the receipt whereof is hereby acknowledged, *Have* granted, bargained, sold, aliened, released, conveyed and confirmed, and by these presents *Do* grant, bargain, sell, alien, release, convey and confirm, unto the said party of the second part, and to his heirs and assigns, forever, *All* that certain piece, parcel (farm), or lot of land situated —————, and bounded and described as follows:

[Here insert description.]

Together with all and singular, the tenements, hereditaments, and appurtenances thereunto belonging, or in any wise appertaining; and the reversion and reversions, remainder and remainders, rents, issues and profits thereof. *And also*, all the estate, right, title, interest, property, possession, claim and demand whatsoever, as well in law as in equity of the said parties of the first part, of, in, and to the same, and every part and parcel thereof with the appurtenances. *To have and to hold* the above granted and described premises, with the appurtenances, unto the said party of the second party, his heirs and assigns, to their own proper use and benefit forever. *Provided always*, and these presents are upon this express condition, that if the said parties of the first part, their heirs, executors or administrators, shall well and truly pay unto the said party of the second part, his executors, administrators or assigns, the said sum of money mentioned in the condition of the said bond or obligation, and the interest thereon, at the time and in the manner mentioned in the said condition, according to the true intent and meaning thereof, that then these presents and the estate hereby granted, shall cease, determine and be null and void. *And* the said [name of mortgagor —husband] for himself, his heirs, executors, and administrators, does covenant and agree to pay unto the said party of the second part, his executors, administrators, or assigns, the said sum of money and interest as mentioned above, and expressed in the condition of the said bond. *And* if default shall be made in the payment of the said sum of money above mentioned, or the interest that may grow due thereon, or of any part thereof, that then and from thenceforth it shall be lawful for the said party of the second part, his executors, administrators and assigns, to enter into and upon all and singular the premises hereby granted, or intended so to be, and to sell and dispose of the same, and all benefit and equity of redemption of the said parties of the first part, their heirs, executors, administrators, or assigns therein, at public auction, according to the act in such case made and provided. *And*, as the attorney of the said parties of the first part, for that purpose by these presents, duly authorized, constituted and appointed to make and deliver to the purchaser or purchasers thereof, a good and sufficient deed or deeds of conveyance in the law for the same, in fee simple, and out of the money arising from such sale, to retain the principal and interest which shall then be due on the said bond or obligation, together with the costs and charges of advertisement and sale of the said premises, rendering the overplus of the purchase money (if any there shall be) unto the said (name of mortgagor), one of the parties of the first part, his heirs, executors, administrators and assigns, and against all other persons claiming or to claim the premises, or any part thereof, from or under them or either of them.

In witness whereof, the parties of the first part, to these presents, have hereunto set their hands and seals the day and year first above written.

Sealed and delivered } (Signed) (Names of mortgagors) [Seal.]
   in the presence of
[Name of witness.]

In case the mortgagor agrees to keep the premises insured the following clause may be inserted:

FORM OF INSURANCE CLAUSE.

And the said [name of mortgagor] further covenants for himself, his heirs and assigns, that he will, during all the time, until the said money secured by these presents shall be fully paid or satisfied, keep the building erected on the said lot of land insured in and by some incorporated company of good standing, against loss or damage by fire, in at least the sum of —— dollars, and will assign the policy or policies of such insurance to the said party of the second part, or his legal representatives, so and in such manner and form that he and they shall at all time and times, until the full payment of the said moneys, have and hold the said policy or policies as a collateral and further security, for the payment thereof.

And, in default of so doing, that the said party of the second part, or his legal representatives, may make such insurance from year to year, in a sum not exceeding —— dollars, for the purposes aforesaid, and pay the premium or premiums therefor; which premium or premiums thus paid, and the interest thereon from the time of payment, the said [name of mortgagor] does covenant as aforesaid to pay to the said party of the second part, or his legal representatives, on demand, and that the same shall be deemed to be secured by these presents, and shall be collectible thereupon and thereby in like manner as the said moneys mentioned in the said bond or obligation.

FORM OF CLAUSE AS TO TAXES.

And it is agreed, by and between the parties to these presents, that the said party of the first part, his heirs, executors, administrators and assigns, will pay and discharge all taxes, assessments, or other charges that now are a lien or hereafter shall be levied, assessed or imposed, and become a lien upon the premises above described, or any part thereof, and in default thereof for the space of —————— after the same shall have become due and payable by law, the said party of the second part, his executors, administrators or assigns, may pay such taxes, assessments or other charges and expenses, and the amount so paid, and interest thereon from the time of such payment, shall forthwith be due and payable from the said party of the first part, his heirs, executors, administrators or assigns, to the said party of the second part, his executors, administrators or assigns, and shall be deemed to be secured by these presents, and shall be collectible in the same manner and upon the same conditions as the interest upon the principal sum hereinbefore mentioned

FORM OF CLAUSE IN MORTGAGE FOR SECURING FUTURE ADVANCES.

Whereas, the party of the first part is indebted to the party of the second part in the sum of —————— dollars, and the said party of of the second part has agreed to make further advances of money to the said party of the first part, *Now*, these presents are upon the condition, that if the party of the first part, his executors, administrators and assigns, shall well and truly pay, or cause to be paid to the party of the second part, his executors, administrators or assigns, upon demand, all the sums due and to become due to the party of the second part, then this conveyance shall be void; otherwise to remain in full force.

FORM OF ASSIGNMENT OF MORTGAGE.

Know all men by these presents, That I, (name of mortgagee), of the town of ———, State of ———, party of the first part, in consideration of the sum of ——— dollars, lawful money of the United States, to me in hand paid by (name of assignee), of the same place, party of the second part, at or before the ensealing and delivery of these presents, the receipt whereof is hereby acknowledged, have granted, bargained, sold, assigned, transferred and set over, and by these presents do grant, bargain, sell, assign, transfer and set over, unto the said party of the second part, a certain indenture of mortgage, bearing date the ——— day of ———, in the year one thousand eight hundred and ———, made by (name of mortgagor) to (name of mortgagee), and recorded in the office of the Clerk (or Register or Recorder) of the County of ———, in Book (or Liber) No. —, of Mortgages, page —, on the ——— day of ———, in the year one thousand eight hundred and ———.

Together with the bond or obligation therein described, and the money due and to grow due thereon, with the interest. *To have and to hold* the same unto the said party of the second part, his executors, administrators and assigns forever, subject only to the proviso in the said indenture of mortgage mentioned.

And I hereby make, constitute and appoint the said party of the second part my true and lawful attorney irrevocable, in my name or otherwise, but at his own proper costs and charges, to have, use and take, all lawful ways and means for the recovery of the said money and interest; and in case of payment to discharge the same as fully as I might or could do if these presents were not made.

In witness whereof, I have hereunto set my hand and seal the ——— day of ———, in the year one thousand eight hundred and ———.

Sealed and delivered)
  in the presence of ∫   (Signed.) (Name of mortgagee.) [Seal.]
  (Name of witness.)

[Add Acknowledgment.]

FORM OF SATISFACTION-PIECE OF MORTGAGE.

I, [name of mortgagee], of the City of ——, State of ——, *Do hereby Certify* that a certain Indenture of Mortgage, bearing date the —— day of ——, one thousand eight hundred and ——, made and executed by [name of mortgagor] to [name of mortgagee], to secure the payment of the sum of —— dollars, and the interest thereon from the said date, and recorded in the office of the Clerk (or Register or Recorder) of the County of ——, in Book (or Liber) No. — of Mortgages, page ——, on the —— day of ——, in the year one thousand eight hundred and ——, is *Paid.*

And I do hereby consent that the same be discharged of Record.

Dated the —— day of ——, 18—.

In presence of } (Signed) [Name of mortgagee.] [Seal.]

[Name of witness.]

STATE OF ——, } ss.
COUNTY OF——. }

On the —— day of ——, in the year one thousand eight hundred and ——, before me personally came [name of mortgagee], to me known, and known to me to be the individual described in, and who executed the foregoing instrument, and who acknowledged that he executed the same.

[Name of Notary Public.]

FORM OF BOND FOR THE PAYMENT OF MONEY.

KNOW ALL MEN by these Presents, That I (or we), ——, of the city (or town) of ——, County of ——, State of ——, am (or are) held and firmly bound unto —— in the penal sum of [name double the amount of loan] dollars, lawful money of the United States of America, to be paid to the said ——, his (or their) executors, administrators or assigns: *For which payment,* well and truly to be made, I (or we) hereby bind myself (or our selves), my (or our) heirs, executors and administrators, firmly by these presents. Sealed with my Seal.

Dated the ——— day of ———, one thousand eight hundred and eighty ———.

The condition of the above obligation is such, that if the above bounden [naming debtor], his (or their) heirs, executors or adminisrators, shall well and truly pay, or cause to be paid, unto the above-named [naming creditor], his executors, administrators or assigns, the just and full sum of ——— dollars, on the ——— day of ———, which will be in the year one thousand eight hundred and eighty ———, with interest thereon, to be computed from the date hereof, at the rate of —— per cent., payable yearly (or any other period), without any fraud or other delay, then the above obligation to be void, otherwise to remain in full force and virtue.

Sealed and delivered in the presence of   (Signed) [Name of party.] [Seal.]
[Name of witnesses.]

A clause, providing that if any interest is not paid when the installment becomes due, then the whole sum is to become due and payable, is often inserted.

It is very advisable for the creditor to have this clause put in the bond.

FORM OF INTEREST CLAUSE.

And it is hereby expressly agreed, that should any default be made in the payment of the said interest, or of any part thereof, on any day whereon the sum is made payable as above expressed, and should the same remain unpaid and in arrear for the space of (number of days), then and from thenceforth, that is to say, after the lapse of the said (amount due), the aforesaid principal sum of (amount of bond), with all arrearage of interest thereon, shall, at the option of the said (name of creditor), or his legal representatives, become and be due and payable immediately threafter, although the period first above limited for the payment thereof may not then have expired, anything hereinbefore contained to the contrary thereof in any wise notwithstanding.

[Insert this before the signature.]

FORM OF DEED OF TRUST TO SECURE A DEBT.

This *Deed*, made the — day of ——, in the year 18—, between A. B., of the one part, and C. D. (the trustee), of the other part, *witnesseth*, that the said A. B. doth grant unto said C. D. the following property :

[Here insert description.]

In trust to secure a promissory note of five hundred dollars made by me in favor of said C. D., and dated the — day of ——, 18—, and payable three months after the date thereof.

Witness the following signatures and seals.

(Signatures and seals.)

CHAPTER XX.

CHATTEL MORTGAGES.

Form of Chattel Mortgage—Pledge of Chattels—What May be Mortgaged—Description of the Chattels—Possession—Power of Sale—Stock-in-Trade—Right of Mortgagor to Redeem—No Right to Remove Chattels—No Right to Sell Free of Mortgage—Assignment—Filing or Recording—Place of Filing—Acknowledgment —Affidavit to Accompany Mortgage—How Long Mortgage Remains Good—Renewal by Re-filing—Statement on Re-filing—Affidavit to Renew—Importance—Summary—Forms.

MORTGAGES of personal property are now frequently resorted to as security for debts and loans.   They are not as useful, nor do they afford such good security as mortgages of real estate, as chattels are more or less perishable in their nature, but in absence of anything better, they are desirable, and it is of great importance to understand the rules of law in regard to them.

Form of Chattel Mortgage.   In form a chattel mortgage is a bill of sale or conveyance of the chattel to the creditor, with a right of redemption to the debtor.   On the payment of the debt, the sale becomes void, and the title revests in the mortgagor.   A bill of sale, if given to secure a debt, is nothing more than a chattel mortgage, even though the right to redeem is not expressed. The creditor cannot claim the goods as owner, but only as mortgagee.

Pledge of Chattels. The difference between a chattel mortgage and a pledge is, that in a pledge the creditor takes possession of the chattels at once, and holds them until the debt is paid, while the mortgagee of chattels does not take possession, and has generally no right of possession until the mortgage debt is due. In the meantime the chattels remain in the possession and control of the debtor or mortgagor.

What May Be Mortgaged. Any personal property owned by the debtor may be mortgaged to secure the debt; furniture, fixtures, live stock, crops, ripe and unripe, merchandise, stock-in-trade, machinery, etc. It is not necessary for the wife of the mortgagor to join with her husband in executing the mortgage, as is the case with mortgages on real estate.

Description of the Chattels. The chattels mortgaged should be described clearly in the mortgage itself, or in a schedule referred to in the mortgage and annexed to it. The description should be unambiguous and should leave no room for doubt as to what the chattels are. It is well to mention their location also.

Possession. It is customary and prudent to insert in the chattel mortgage a provision to the effect that the debtor or mortgagor shall remain in possession until default is made in the payment of the debt, that is, until it is due. In some States such a provision is absolutely necessary in order to enable the mortgagor to retain possession of the goods.

Power of Sale. The mortgage almost invariably contains a power of sale conferred by the mortgagor on the mortgagee, whereby the latter is entitled, as soon as the mortgage debt is due, to take possession of the chattels and sell them to pay the debt, If there is a surplus it must be paid over to the debtor. If there is a deficiency—that is, if the chattels sell for less than the debt—the creditor (mortgagee) has a claim against the debtor (mortgagor), for the balance.

Stock in Trade. A provision is often inserted in a chattel mortgage, where a stock of goods in a store is mortgaged, that the mortgagor (debtor) may remain in possession, and have the power to sell the goods at retail or otherwise, and replace them with other similar goods, which shall be covered by the mortgage.

This agreement, though good between the debtor and this creditor, is void as to other creditors, and the latter can levy on the subsequently acquired goods for their debts.

There is, however, some difference between the law of the various States on this subject, as will be seen by the summary.

Right of Mortgagor to Redeem. The mortgagor has the right at any time after default in payment of the debt and before the sale to redeem the chattels by paying the debt, with the interest, all valid charges, and costs.

No Right to Remove Chattels. The mortgagor who retains possession of the chattels has usually no right to take them out of the county without the consent of the mortgagee. The penalty is often very severe. In some States it is made a felony punishable by fine and imprisonment.

No Right to Sell Free of Mortgage. The mortgagor of goods who assumes to sell them for the full value, without mentioning the mortgage, is guilty of fraud. All the purchaser gets in this case, or in any case, is the right to redeem by paying the debt. This act of the mortgagor is a crime in some States.

Assignment. A chattel mortgage may be assigned by the mortgagee to any person. The assignee will then have all the rights of the mortgagee. It might be well, however, for the mortgagee to indorse on the mortgage a power of attorney for the assignee to foreclose.

The assignment may be oral, as by merely delivering the mortgage, or it may be in writing.

Any assignment of the debt, as a transfer of the promissory note, bond, etc., carries with it the mortgage security.

Filing or Recording. A chattel mortgage is good as between the parties to it, whether it is filed or recorded or not.

It does not become a valid lien as to third persons,

however, such as other creditors, or purchasers of the chattels, unless it is filed or recorded according to law in the proper place.

Some States require that the chattel mortgage itself, or a true copy of it, be *filed*. In other States the mortgage is *recorded;* that is, transcribed into the records.

Place of Filing. The proper place for such filing or recording is the office either of the County Clerk, the Town Clerk, or the Register. If the mortgagor lives in one county and the property is situated in another, the mortgage must be filed in both counties.

Acknowledgment. The mortgage must be acknowledged in proper form before a Notary Public, etc., before it is entitled to be recorded or filed. The acknowledgment is the same in form as in the case of a real estate mortgage or a deed.

Affidavit to Accompany Mortgage. Some States require that to entitle a chattel mortgage to be filed, it must be accompanied by an affidavit made by both parties, or by the mortgagor alone, to the effect that the mortgage is made in good faith, and without any design to hinder, delay or defraud creditors.

How Long the Mortgage Remains Good. After filing, the mortgage remains good only for a certain time, which varies very much in the different States, but usually one or two years. In some States it is good for an indefinite period.

Renewal by Re-filing. At the expiration of the time for which the mortgage is allowed to be good, it may be renewed in various ways. One method is to re-file a copy of the mortgage, only changing the dates. It is then good for another year, or two, or more, as the case may be.

Statement on Re-filing. A statement of the amount paid on the debt, if anything, and the amount still due, must be made on re-filing the mortgage.

Affidavit to Renew. In some States, the only thing necessary to renew the mortgage is to file an affidavit of the mortgagee, stating his interest in the property, and the amount still due to him on the mortgage.

Importance of Filing or Recording. The person who takes a mortgage should put it on file at once. Otherwise, if the owner or mortgagor of the chattels should sell them, or mortgage them to one who puts his mortgage on record before the first mortgage, the latter would lose his rights to the chattels, or in the second case would only be entitled to the position of the holder of a second mortgage.

SUMMARY OF THE LAWS OF CHATTEL MORTGAGES.

ALABAMA.—Chattel mortgages are void as against creditors and purchasers without notice unless recorded in the county where the mortgagor resides, and also in the county where the property is, if it is in a different county. If the property is removed into another county, the mortgage must be recorded in that county within six months.

ARIZONA.—Chattel mortgages must be recorded unless the mortgagee receives possession of the property.

ARKANSAS.—They may be filed and not recorded at option of mortgagee. Liens from the time of filing. When not recorded they become void at the end of a year, unless an affidavit is filed by the mortgagee, showing the amount of money still due. If the mortgagor be allowed to remain in possession with power of disposition, as to sell, the mortgage is void.

CALIFORNIA.—Mortgage must be accompanied by an affidavit of all the parties that it is made in good faith and without any design to hinder, delay or defraud creditors. It must be acknowledged and recorded in the county where the mortgagor resides, and also in the county where it is situated.

COLORADO.—Must not be given for more than two years, and after it is due the mortgagee must not delay in taking possession, or his lien will be lost as to third parties. Any mortgagor who sells such chattels without informing the purchaser of the mortgage, may be compelled to pay the purchaser twice the value of the chattels. It is also larceny.

CONNECTICUT.—Mortgage to be good must be recorded within a reasonable time in the Town Clerk's office.

DAKOTA.—Must be filed in the office of the Register of Deeds of the county. Good for three years. May be renewed by refiling a copy together with an affidavit stating the amount due on the mortgage. This is good for three years more. A chattel mortgage must be signed by the mortgagor in the presence of two witnesses who must also sign as such.

DELAWARE.—Must be recorded within ten days after their acknowledgment. Good for three years as a lien. Must then be renewed. The mortgagor cannot remove the property from the county.

FLORIDA.—Mortgaged chattels must be delivered to the mortgagee.

GEORGIA.—Must be filed within thirty days after execution.

IDAHO.—Mortgage must state the residence of the mortgagor and the mortgagee. There must be an affidavit attached to the mortgage when it is recorded to the effect that it was made without any design to hinder, delay or defraud creditors.

ILLINOIS.—Mortgage is good for two years. It cannot be then renewed, but a new mortgage must be given to continue the lien.

A mortgage of stock-in-trade with power to sell and replace the stock from time to time is good between the parties or if the mortgagee takes possession ; but it can be set aside by creditors.

INDIANA.—Chattel mortgages are usually made in the form of an absolute bill of sale with a defeating clause. They must be recorded within ten days after execution in the Recorder's office of the county.

IOWA.—Mortgage good for ten years. In the absence of any provision to the contrary the mortgagee is entitled to immediate possession.

KANSAS.—The mortgage, or a true copy thereof, must be filed in the office of the Register of Deeds. Such mortgage shall be void as against creditors of the mortgagor or purchasers of the property unless before the expiration of the year and every year thereafter, the mortgagee files an affidavit to be attached to the original mortgage, stating the amount still remaining due and unpaid.

KENTUCKY.—Usual provisions in regard to recording. Mortgages of stock-in-trade are good against all persons as to existing stock, and good between the parties as to future additions; but not as to other creditors of the mortgagor.

LOUISIANA.—There are no chattel mortgages. Personal property may be pledged or pawned, but the mortgagee must always take possession.

MAINE.—Mortgage must be recorded in the Town Clerk's office where mortgagor resides. No renewal is required. The mortgagor has no right to the possession unless so stipulated.

MARYLAND.—Are liens for twenty years. Must be recorded within twenty days. An affidavit must be filed with the mortgage in these words: "The consideration in said mortgage is true and *bona fide*, as therein set forth."

MASSACHUSETTS.—Chattel mortgages need not be under seal or acknowledged. Must be recorded in city or town where the mortgagor reside, within fifteen days from execution; otherwise not valid as against creditors.

MICHIGAN.—The mortgage or a true copy must be filed in the office of the Township Clerk or City Clerk. Affidavit must be filed every year by mortgagee, stating the amount remaining due. Otherwise it becomes void.

MINNESOTA.—Must be filed in the office of the Town Clerk. Valid lien for two years.   Affidavit of mortgage as to amount remaining due must be filed every year thereafter.   A chattel mortgage containing a clause permitting mortgagor to retain possession and sell is void as against creditors and purchaser.

MISSISSIPPI.—Usual rules as to recording.   Mortgage may be executed on growing crops.

MISSOURI.—Usual provisions as to recording.   Mortgages upon stock-in-trade are void as to other creditors.

NEBRASKA.—Mortgage is good for five years and then ceases to be valid as against creditors and purchasers, although remaining good as between the parties.   A mortgage of chattels with possession and power of sale by the mortgagor, is void as to creditors. It is felony for the mortgagor to remove the property out of the jurisdiction of the District Court of the county where the property was when mortgaged, without the consent of the mortgagee.

NEVADA.—No mortgage of personal property shall be valid, except between the parties, unless possession be given to the mortgagee, except mortgages on growing crops.

NEW HAMPSHIRE.—Mortgage must be recorded in the Town Clerk's office.   It will not be valid as to creditors unless both parties subscribe and make oath to the following affidavit, which must be made on the mortgage and recorded with it:

"We severally swear that the foregoing mortgage is made for the purpose of securing the debt specified in the condition thereof, and for no other purpose whatever, and that said debt was not created for the purpose of enabling the mortgagor to execute said mortgage, but is a just debt, honestly due, and owing from the mortgagor to the mortgagee."

The mortgagee may sell the property at auction at any time within thirty days after the mortgage is due, posting notices of sale in two public places and giving written notice to mortgagor at least four days before the sale.

NEW JERSEY.—Usual provisions as to recording with the Clerk

or Register of the county. It is prudent to annex to the mortgage an affidavit made by the holder of the mortgage, stating the considerations of said mortgage and the amount due.

NEW MEXICO.—Must be filed with Recorder of the county. Good for one year. May then be renewed by filing an affidavit of the mortgagee showing the amount still due. This must be done every year or it is void as against creditors and purchasers.

NEW YORK.—Must be filed in Town Clerk's office, except when the office of the County Clerk is situated in the town or city. The mortgage is then filed in that office. In New York City, the office of the Register is the proper place. Must be renewed every year by filing a copy with a statement of the amount due. No seal necessary. Mortgagor who sells or secretes the mortgaged property is liable to imprisonment in county jail for one year, or to a fine of three times the value of the property so disposed of, or both.

NORTH CAROLINA.—A form is prescribed by statute for chattel mortgages not exceeding three hundred dollars ; the probate and registration fees are less than on ordinary chattel mortgages. All mortgages must be registered in the county where mortgagor resides. No statute requiring renewal. The following is the short form referred to:

" I, of the County of ——, in the State of North Carolina, am indebted to ——, of —— County, in said State, in the sum of —— dollars, for which he holds my note, to be due the — day of ——, A. D., 18—, and to secure the payment of the same I do hereby convey to him these articles of personal property, to-wit: (insert description); but on this special trust that if I fail to pay said debt and interest on or before the — day of——, A. D., 18—, then he may sell said property or so much thereof as may be necessary, by public auction for cash, first giving twenty days' notice at three public places, and apply the proceeds of such sale to the discharge of said debt and interest on the same, and pay any surplus to me.

Given under my hand and seal this — day of——, A. D., 18—.

(Signature.) [Seal.]

OHIO.—The chattel mortgage, or a true copy, should be deposited with the Clerk of the township; before such filing the mortgagee must make and sign his affidavit on the mortgage as to the amount of his claim and that it is just and unpaid. Mortgages must be renewed at the expiration of each year by filing a copy, together with a sworn statement of the mortgagee as to the amount unpaid.

Mortgage of stock-in-trade, with power to sell for mortgagor's own benefit, void as to creditors acquiring liens, but power to sell and pay proceeds over to mortgagee is good.

OREGON.—Mortgage or a copy must be filed with County Clerk. Good as against creditors, etc., only for one year. May be renewed before the expiration of the year by filing an affidavit showing the amount still due the mortgagee. If the mortgage is for less than five hundred dollars, the property may be sold by the Sheriff or any Constable, upon the written request of the mortgagee.

PENNSYLVANIA.—Not in general use.

RHODE ISLAND.—Must be recorded in the office of the Town Clerk. May be foreclosed by sale within sixty days after mortgage becomes due.

SOUTH CAROLINA.—Must be recorded within forty days after execution. Mortgages of stock of goods with power to sell given to mortgagor, and to replace them by new purchases, are valid.

TENNESSEE. Usual provisions as to registration. Mortgage of stock-in-trade, with power of sale, is fraudulent and void.

TEXAS.—Must be filed in the office of the County Clerk. If the mortgagor removes the property from the county, the mortgagee becomes entitled to the possession of the property and immediate sale whether his debt is due or not.

UTAH.—Mortgage must be accompanied by an affidavit of the parties to the effect that it is made in good faith, and that it is not intended to hinder or delay the creditors of the mortgagor. These must be filed in the county where the mortgagor resides, and the mortgage is good one year from its date. Any mortgagor selling or disposing of mortgaged property without the written consent of the mortgagee, is guilty of obtaining money under false pretenses, and may be fined and imprisoned.

VERMONT.—Must be recorded in the office of the Clerk of the city or town where the mortgagor resides. With it must be appended and recorded the affidavit of both parties, as follows: "We severally swear that the foregoing mortgage is made for the purpose of securing the debt specified in the conditions thereof, and for no other purpose whatever, and that the same is a just debt, honestly due and owing from the mortgagor."

No mortgagor can execute a second mortgage upon the same chattels, unless the fact of the existence of the first mortgage is set forth in the second mortgage. A violation of this is punishable with a heavy fine. No provision as to renewal.

VIRGINIA.—Must be recorded with Clerk of County Courts, or wherever deeds and wills are recorded. Mortgages of stock-in-trade with power to sell, are void.

WASHINGTON TERRITORY.—Mortgages must be accompanied by the affidavit of the mortgagor that it was made in good faith and without design to hinder, delay or defraud creditors.

In a mortgage of property exempt from execution the wife must join.

The mortgaged property may be taken into possession by the mortgagee, when the debt is due, or, if it is not due, when he has reasonable ground to believe that his debt is insecure, and that by leaving the property in the hands of the mortgagor, he is in danger of losing the debt.

Chattel mortgages are binding until six years after they become due.

Stock-in-trade may be mortgaged, but the mortgagor can not sell, if the mortgagee prevents him, and goods subsequently purchased would not be covered by the mortgage.

WEST VIRGINIA.—Chattel mortgages are seldom, if ever, used. Deeds of trust take their place, and the trustee will sell the property when required by the creditor, after the debt is due.

WISCONSIN.—The mortgage, or copy of it, must be filed with

the Clerk of the town, city or village. Good for two years. May be renewed at the expiration of that time and every two years thereafter, by the filing of an affidavit by the mortgagee, stating his interest in the property and the amount due him.

Mortgage of stock in trade with power of sale is void as against creditors.

Chattel mortgages in this State usually contain a provision that the mortgagee may take possession of the chattels whenever he feels himself insecure. He may therefore do so whether his grounds are reasonable or not.

WYOMING.—Mortgages must be recorded in the office of the County Clerk of the county where the property is situated.

The mortgage is valid for the term for which it was given and for two months afterward. May then be renewed and every year thereafter by filing the affidavit of the mortgagor as to the amount of his claim.

SHORT FORM OF CHATTEL MORTGAGE.

Know all men by these presents, that I [name of mortgagor], of the town of ——, County of ——, being indebted to [name of mortgagee], in the sum of —— dollars, with interest from this date, for the security of said sum, I do hereby mortgage, sell and assign to the said [name of mortgage] all the goods and chattels of every kind and description, now in the dwelling-house situated —— in the town of ·——, and I do hereby authorize and empower the said [name of mortgagee] to take possession of said goods and chattels, on default in the payment of the said indebtedness on and after the — day of ——, 18--, and to sell the same, and to apply the proceeds of such sale to the payment of said debt and interest, the surplus (if any) to be paid over to me.

In witness whereof I have hereunto set my hand and seal this — day of ——, 18—.

Etc

FORM OF CHATTEL MORTGAGE.

To all to whom these presents may come, know ye that I, ——, of the town (or city) of ——, in the County of ——, and State of ———, party of the first part, for securing the payment of the money hereinafter mentioned, and in consideration of the sum of one dollar, to me duly paid by ———, of the same place (or if of another place, of such place), party of the second part, at or before the ensealing and delivery of these presents, the receipt whereof is hereby acknowledged, have bargained and sold, and by these presents do grant, bargain and sell unto the said party of the second part, the goods and chattels enumerated in the schedule hereunto annexed, and now in [name the place where they are]. *To have and to hold*, all and singular the goods and chattels above bargained and sold, unto the said party of the second part, his executors, administrators and assigns forever. And I, the said party of the first part, for myself, my heirs, executors and administrators, all and singular, the said goods and chattels, above bargained and sold unto the said party of the second part, his heirs, executors, administrators and assigns, against me, the said party of the first part, and against all and every person or persons whomsoever shall and will warrant, and forever defend.

Upon condition, that if I, the said party of the first part, shall and do well and truly pay unto the said party of the second part, his executors, administrators or assigns, the just and full sum of ——— dollars, in ——— days (or months) after the date hereof, in which said sum I am now justly indebted to him for money loaned and advanced by him to me, then these presents shall be void.

And I, the said party of the first part, for myself, my executors, administrators and assigns, do covenant and agree to and with the said party of the second part, his executors, administrators and assigns, that in case default shall be made in the payment of the said sum above mentioned, then it shall and may be lawful for , and I, the said party of the first part, do hereby authorize and empower the said party of the second part, his executors, administrators and assigns, with the aid and assistance of any person or persons, to enter any dwelling-house, store, and other premises, and such other place or places as the said goods and chattels are or may be placed, and take and carry away the said goods and chattels, and to sell and dispose of the same for the best price they can obtain; and out of the money arising therefrom to retain and pay the said sum above mentioned, and all charges touching the same; rendering the surplus (if any) unto me or to my executors, adminstrators or assigns. And until default be made in the payment of the said sum of money, I am to remain and continue in the quiet and peaceable possession of the said goods and chattels, and the full and free enjoyment of the same.

In witness whereof, I, the said party of the first part, have here. unto set my hand and seal the ———— day of ————, one thousand, eight hundred and ————.

Sealed and delivered ⎰
  in the presence of ⎱
      (Witnesses.)   [Signed.]   (Name.)   [Seal.]

SCHEDULE.

(Here insert description of all the articles covered by the mortgage.)

FORM OF STATEMENT OF MORTGAGEE ON RE-FILING A CHATTEL MORTGAGE.

I, ————, the mortgagee within named; do certify and state that there remains due and unpaid on the mortgage of which the foregoing (or within) is a true copy, the sum of ———— dollars, and interest thereon from the ———— day of ————, 18—, which sum is the amount of my interest in the property described in said mortgage claimed by me by virtue thereof.

Dated this ———— day of ————, 18—.

                  (Signed.)   Name.

FORM OF POWER OF ATTORNEY TO FORECLOSE A CHATTEL MORTGAGE.

(To be indorsed on mortgage.)

I, ————, do hereby nominate and appoint ————, as and for my true and lawful attorney, for me and in my name to take possession of the goods and chattels described in the within mortgage, and to foreclose the said mortgage by a sale of said goods and chattels described in the within mortgage, and to foreclose the said mortgage by a sale of said goods and chattels, in conformity with the power therein contained, and I authorize my said attorney to do all acts for me and in my behalf, which I, under the said power and under said mortgage, could lawfully do, and for that purpose to procure the aid and assistance of any person or persons.

And I also covenant with the said ——, that the sum of —— dollars and interest thereon from the —— day of ——, 18—, is now justly owing to me on the said mortgage, that I am the lawful owner and holder thereof, and that I will indemnify and hold him harmless for any acts done by him in carrying out and executing the power hereinbefore granted to him.

Dated the —— day of ——, 18—.

[Signed.]   (Name.)   [Seal.]

FORM OF NOTICE OF SALE UNDER A CHATTEL MORTGAGE.

By virtue of a chattel mortgage, executed by —— to ——, dated on the —— day of ——, 18—, and which was duly filed in the office of the Clerk of the town of ——, I will expose for sale at public auction at ——, in the said town of ——, on the —— day of ——, 18—, at — o'clock in the forenoon of that day, the following goods and chattels, to-wit:

[Here insert list of articles mentioned in the schedule.]

Dated the —— day of ——, 18—.

[Signed.]   (Name.)

Auctioneer.

CHAPTER XXI.

LANDLORD AND TENANT.

Verbal Leases—Written Leases—Covenants—Covenant to Pay Rent—Not to Assign—As to Fire—Use of Premises—Essentials of a Lease—When Leases are Voidable —Verbal Promises—Right of the Tenant to Demand Possession—To Easements—To Make Ordinary Repairs —To Crops—To Cut Wood—To Assign Lease—To Sub-let—To Take Away Fixtures—Permanent Fixtures —Trade Fixtures—Must be Removed During Term— Eviction—Implied Eviction—Rights of Landlord to Rent—Summary Proceedings—To Pay Taxes—To Insure—No Obligation to Repair—Covenant to Repair. FORMS: *Lease—Covenant of Renewal—Covenant for Repairs—Covenant to Pay Taxes—Short Form of Monthly Hiring—Clause for the Security of the Rent— Assignment of a Lease.*

A LANDLORD is the owner of land who lets it to another for hire, for a definite period of time. A tenant is one who rents or hires land and occupies it under a lease. A lease is a contract of hiring, either verbal or in writing.

Verbal Leases. A verbal lease of land for the period of one year is good and binding on both parties. But if the land is to be let for more than one year, there must be a written lease under seal in order to bind either party. If a tenant goes into possession under a verbal lease for a longer period, he is liable for rent to the landlord for " use and occupation." He is not obliged, however, to pay the rent stipulated by the contract, but only what the land was reasonably worth, which may often be much less.

The landlord in the same way is not bound by his unwritten promise to let for more than one year. He may terminate the tenancy at any time by giving the tenant notice, and if the tenant refuses to go, he may be ejected summarily by certain officers of the law. Any promises by either party, as to repair, are void and cannot be enforced. If a tenant at the end of the year holds over and continues to pay the same rent as before, he is deemed to have elected to take the premises for another year on the same terms.

Written Leases—Covenants. Where the lease is written and under seal, it generally contains various promises on the part of both landlord and tenant. These are called covenants. The landlord often covenants that he will pay all taxes and assessments and keep the premises in repair.

Covenant to Pay Rent. The usual covenant of the tenant is that he will pay the rent punctually, and that if he does not, the landlord may re-enter and eject the tenant, at any time after default. This is both a covenant and a " condition," as it has the effect of terminating the lease itself in case the rent is not paid, and also gives the landlord the right to sue the tenant for breach of contract. If this covenant is not express, it may be implied from the fact of the lease.

Covenant Not to Assign. There are sometimes other covenants by the tenant to the effect that he will not assign his lease or sub-let the premises without the written consent of the landlord; or that before the expiration of the term he will allow the landlord to put a sign or placard, "To Let," on the house. A violation of this first covenant gives the landlord the right to eject both the tenant and his assignee, and resume possession of his land

Covenant as to Fire, Etc. It is also provided frequently that if the premises are destroyed by fire the tenant shall not be bound to pay rent after that event. Without such a provision rent may still be exacted by the landlord up to the end of the term. In New York and some other States there is a statute which relieves the tenant from this obligation, when the premises are so destroyed or injured as to be unfit for occupation. It is safer, however, for the tenant to make this an express provision, as it avoids all possibility of dispute.

Use of Premises. The tenant may also covenant that he will not use the premises for business purposes or carry on any dangerous trade or occupation on them.

Essentials of a Lease. The necessary elements of a written lease are: (1) The names of the parties; (2) the consideration or rent; (3) the description of the premises; (4) the length of the term of the lease;

(5) the covenants; (6) the conditions; (7) the warranty; (8) the date; (9) the seal.

Both parties should sign the lease.

When Leases are Voidable. Fraud or misrepresentations by the landlord as to the condition of the premises vitiate the lease. The tenant can abandon them, and is not bound to pay rent. Concealment of certain facts, as that there has been small-pox in the house is fraud: though, as a rule, the landlord does not impliedly warrant the condition of the premises. The tenant must take them as he finds them, unless he has an express warranty.

Verbal Promise. A lease, like any contract under seal, can only be altered by a writing under seal. If the tenant during the term promises orally to pay a higher rent he is not bound to do so. Such a contract is without consideration. All he is legally obliged to do is to pay the rent mentioned in the lease. Such a promise to be of any force must be in writing under seal.

Rights of the Tenant to Demand Possession. The tenant has the right to demand possession on the day when his term is to commence. If the landlord refuses for any reason, or demands a larger rent, the other party can compel him to deliver him the premises at the agreed rent. He may also recover damages for breach of contract.

To Easements. He has the right to all accessories or easements, as a right of way over a neighbor's land, if that easement belongs to the landlord's estate.

To Make Ordinary Repairs. He may make ordinary repairs to keep the premises "wind and water-tight," but he cannot make extensive alterations without the landlord's consent.

To Crops. A tenant may take away the crops that are ripe on the expiration of the term of the lease, but not those that are unripe or will not mature for some time. If a mortgage made by the landlord is foreclosed and the land sold, he has no right to the unripe crops then on the land. They go to the purchaser.

To Cut Wood. If the premises rented are farming land, the tenant may cut wood for fences and fuel to a reasonable amount, but he cannot cut down fruit or ornamental trees. Such conduct is called "waste," and renders the tenant liable, not only for actual damages, but very frequently to heavy penalties. In New York the landlord can recover three times the amount of the real damage.

To Assign Lease. In the absence of a stipulation to the contrary in a lease, the tenant may assign his lease for the balance of the term to another, and he is no longer obliged to pay rent, though, of course, he is liable for any back rent still unpaid. The landlord must look to the assignee. If the assignee is irresponsible, that is the landlord's misfortune, for the tenant may assign to a beggar merely for the purpose of getting rid of the obligation to pay rent.

This makes it very important to insert a covenant against assignment in the lease.

To Sub-let. The tenant may also under-let for any rent he pleases. This sub-tenant is liable to the tenant for his rent, and the landlord has no claim against him. This under-letting may be for the whole or any part of the premises, and for the entire balance, or any part of the balance of the term.

To Take Away Fixtures. A fixture is any article of personal property attached in some way to the house or the land, as gas-fixtures, boilers, machinery, furniture, partitions, etc. The tenant who puts these up can usually take them down and remove them, provided he does not injure the premises, but restores them to as good condition as they were before he put the fixtures up.

Permanent Fixtures. If he should erect a house, however, or some other permanent structure, on the land without the consent of the landlord or owner, he could not remove them. They would become the property of the latter. If he does it with the consent of the landlord, and it is agreed that the tenant shall own the erections and have the right to take them away, the landlord cannot prevent him from doing so. It is much better to have this arrangement in writing and signed by the landlord.

Trade Fixtures. Fixtures, if made by the tenant for the purpose of his *trade, business or manufacture,* may be removed by him even without the landlord's consent. These fixtures may be of quite a durable nature, as sheds erected by the lessee of a hotel.

Must be Removed During Term. The tenant must in all cases take down his fixtures before the expiration of the term of his lease; at all events, before he gives up possession. Otherwise, it will be considered that he .dedicates or gives them to the landlord. He cannot subsequently remove them.

Eviction. If the landlord actually ejects the tenant from the premises, either by force or threats, the latter is, of course, no longer liable for rent. He may, at his option, regard the lease at an end, or he may compel the landlord to give him possession again by a law-suit, or he may recover damages for breach of contract, or, as it is called, covenant.

Implied Eviction. There are some acts of the landlord beside actual ejection, which will justify the tenant in quitting the premises of his own accord and refusing to pay rent any longer. This is where the landlord does something which makes the premises untenantable or uncomfortable, as by setting up an unhealthy or dangerous or disagreable business in close proximity—a bone factory, for instance, or a quarry where blasting is carried on.

Rights of the Landlord—To Rent. The landlord has the right to demand and receive the rent whenever it becomes due. He may enter the premises without the tenant's consent for this purpose, and will not be guilty of trespass. The lease usually specifies when and how often the rent is payable, whether yearly, half-yearly, or monthly.

Summary Proceedings. If the tenant does not pay promptly the landlord may eject him in most of the States by summary proceedings before a Justice of the Peace, and by serving a notice of two or three days to quit. The landlord himself, however, cannot use force in case the tenant refuses to leave, and will be guilty of assault if he does.

To Pay Taxes. It is the duty of the landlord, and not the tenant, to pay the taxes. The landlord sometimes covenants in the lease that he will do this, so as to save the premises from being sold away from the tenant for arrears.

To Insure. The landlord frequently agrees to keep the premises insured. The tenant may, however, take out a policy to protect his interests.

No Obligation to Repair. The landlord is under no duty to repair the premises unless he specially contracts or covenants to do so in the lease. The tenant takes the premises as he finds them, and it is his duty to keep them so—not the landlord's. If he took the premises in good condition, he must keep them "wind and water-tight," and to do this he is obliged to make whatever slight repairs are necessary. He is not obliged to make extensive repairs.

Covenant to Repair. It is usual, almost universal, for the landlord to promise in the lease to make necessary repairs. And if the tenant wishes to throw this duty on the landlord, he should see to it that this clause is inserted in the lease.

FORM OF LEASE WITH COVENANTS.

This Indenture, made the —— day of ——, 188—, between [name of lessor], of the city of ——, party of the first part, and [name of tenant], of the same place, party of the second part. *Witnesseth*, That the said party of the first part hath letten, and by these presents doth grant, demise, and to farm let, unto the said party of the second part, the premises known as No. —— —— street, in the city of ——, with the appurtenances, for the term of —— years, from the —— day of ——, one thousand eight hundred and eighty ——, at the yearly rent or sum of —— dollars, to be paid in equal monthly payments, in advance, on the first day of each and every month during said term. *And* it is agreed that if any rent shall be due and unpaid, or if default shall be made in any of the covenants herein contained, then it shall be lawful for the said party of the first part to re-enter the said premises, and to remove all persons therefrom. *And* the said party of the second part hereby covenants to pay for the said party of the first part the said yearly rent as herein specified. *And* the said party of the second part further covenants that he will not assign this lease, nor any interest therein, or let, nor under-let, the whole or any part of the said premises, nor make any alterations therein, without the written consent of the said party of the first part, under the penalty of forfeiture and damages; and that he will not occupy or use the said premises, nor permit the same to be occupied or used, for any business deemed extra hazardous, on account of fire or otherwise, without the like consent, under the like penalty. *And* the said party of the second part further covenants that he will permit the said party of the first part, or his agent, to show the premises to persons wishing to hire or purchase, and will permit the usual notice of "to let," or "for sale," to be placed upon the walls or doors of said premises, and remain thereon without hindrance or molestation.

And at the expiration of the said term, the said party of the second part will quit and surrender the premises hereby demised in as good state and condition as reasonable use and wear thereof will permit, damage by the elements excepted. *And* the said party of the first party doth covenant that the said party of the second part, on paying the said yearly rent and performing the covenants aforesaid, shall and may peaceably and quietly have, hold and enjoy the said demised premises for the term aforesaid. And it is further understood and agreed that the covenants and agreements contained in the within lease are binding on the parties hereto and their legal representatives.

In witness whereof the parties to these presents have hereunto set their hands and seals, the day and year first above written.

Sealed and delivered in ⎱ (Signed) [Name of landlord.] [Seal.]
   the presence of ⎰ [Name of tenant.] [Seal.]
[Name of witness.]

The following covenants may be inserted in the lease if desirable:

FORM OF COVENANTS OF RENEWAL.

And the said party of the first part, for and in consideration of the premises, hereby promises and agrees, to and with the said party of the second part, to make and execute unto him a new lease, similar in all respects to this, and to run for the same period of ———— years, of the premises aforesaid, upon receiving from the party of the second part a notice in writing, claiming such renewal, at any time within three months prior to the expiration of the term granted by these presents.

FORM OF COVENANT FOR REPAIRS.

"And the said party of the first part, for and in consideration of the premises, hereby promises and agrees, to and with the said party of the second part, to put and keep the said premises in good tenantable order and repair, at his own cost and expense, during the whole of the term hereby demised."

FORM OF COVENANT TO PAY TAXES AND ASSESSMENTS.

"And the said party of the second part hereby covenants to bear

pay and discharge all such taxes, duties and assessments, whatsoever, as shall or may, during the said term hereby granted, be
charged, assessed, or imposed upon the said demised premises."

SHORT FORM OF MONTHLY HIRING.

PHILADELPHIA, April 1, 1886.

This certifies that I have hired and taken from (the landlord)
the premises situated ———, and known as ——— for the term,
of one month, from April 1, 1886, at the monthly rental of ——
dollars, payable in advance.

Signed [name of tenant.]

FORM OF A CLAUSE FOR THE SECURITY OF THE RENT.

(This may be indorsed on the lease.)

In consideration of the letting of the premises within mentioned
to the within named (name of tenant), and the sum of one dollar
to me paid by the said party of the first part, I, (name of surety),
do hereby covenant and agree, to and with the party of the first
part above named, and his legal representatives, that if default
shall at any time be made by the said (name of tenant), in the
payment of the rent or performance of the covenants contained in
the within lease on his part to be paid and performed, that I,
(name of surety), will well and truly pay the said rent, or any
arrears thereof, that may remain due unto the said party of the
first part, and also all damages, that may arise in consequence
of the non-performance of said covenants or either of them, without requiring notice of any such default from the said party of
the first part.

Witness my hand and seal this — day of —— in the year 188—.
Witness ——— ⎱
                    ⎰   [Signed.]   (Name of surety.)   [Seal.]
(Name of witnesses.)

FORM OF ASSIGNMENT OF LEASE.

Know all men by these presents, that I, (name of tenant), of the
town of ———, for and in consideration of the sum of —— dollars, lawful money of the United States, to me duly paid by (name

of assignee), of the same place, have sold, and by these presents do grant, convey, assign, transfer and set over, unto the said (name of assignee), a certain indenture of lease bearing date the — day ——, in the year 188—, made by (name of original landlord) to (name of tenant), of premises known as ——, in the town of ——, with all and singular the premises therein mentioned and described, and the buildings thereon, together with the appurtenances. *To have and to hold* the same unto the said (name of assignee) and his assigns, from the — day of ——, 188—, for and during all the rest, residue, and remainder yet to come of and in the term of —— years mentioned in the said indenture of lease, subject, nevertheless, to the rents, covenants, conditions and provisions therein also mentioned. *And* I do hereby covenant, grant, promise and agree, to and with the said (name of assignee), that the said assigned premises now are free and clear of, and from all former and other gifts, grants, bargains, sales, leases, judgments, executions, back rents, taxes, assessments, and incumbrances whatsoever.

In witness whereof, I have hereunto set my hand and seal this — day of ——, 188—.

Sealed and delivered }
  in the presence of }   [Signed.] (Name of tenant.) [Seal.]
  [Name of witness.]

CHAPTER XXII.

WILLS.

Who Can Make a Will—Infants and Insane not—Married Women—Must be in Writing—Signing—In Presence of Witnesses—Seal—Witnesses—Legatee as a Witness—Holographic Wills—Nuncupative Wills—Codicil—Revocation—Place of Making Will—Construction—Undue Influence—Probate—Devises and Legacies—Legacies General and Specific—Abatement of Legacies—Lapsed Legacies—Conditional Legacies—In Lieu of Dower—Bequest Charged with Debt—Time of Payment—Life-Interests.

A WILL is a disposition or gift of property, usually in writing, by the owner, to take effect at his death. The person making the will is called the testator, or if a woman, the testatrix. The persons to whom personal property is willed are known as legatees, the donees of real estate are designated devisees.

Who Can Make a Will. All persons of sound mind and memory and of the requisite age may make a will. The age at which a person is competent to dispose of his property in this way varies greatly in the several States, but it is usually twenty-one. In many States persons must be older in order to make a will of real estate than is required to make a will of personal property. Women are often allowed to make a will at an earlier age than men.

Aliens, that is, citizens of another country resident in the United States, may make wills, but they cannot devise land in many States. As a rule, an alien cannot inherit or take real estate by will.

Persons of unsound mind, idiots, imbeciles, the insane from disease, even those afflicted with monomania with lucid intervals, are incompetent to make a will, and the instrument if drawn up is void. The will of a deaf and dumb, or a blind person, is valid; so is that of a person addicted to drunkenness, unless the will was made while he was not in possession of all his faculties. The tests of sufficient mental capacity are that the testator shall be able to understand the nature and amount of his property, the claims of others on his bounty, and to make up his mind as to the disposition of the property without prompting.

Married Women. An unmarried woman can make a will with the same freedom as a man. Generally a married woman has the same right, but in some States there are certain restrictions; as, for instance, that she cannot will more than half her property away from her husband, or deprive him of his rights in her land as tenant by curtesy. In many States, as in New York, she may dispose of all her separate estate by will and deprive her husband of curtesy.

Must be in Writing. Wills must be in writing. A verbal will, except under certain peculiar circumstances, is of no effect and void.

It is not necessary that the testator should himself write the body of the will, nor is any special form essential.   In Maryland a letter has been admitted to probate as a will.

Signing.   The testator must sign his name to the will in order to give it validity.   If he is unable to write, he may make his mark.   If he is unable to read, the will must be read to him before he executes it.

In most States the will may be signed for the testator by some other person, by his express directions and in his presence.   The will is then as valid as if signed by the testator himself.

In some States it is only necessary that the will be signed by the testator in any part of it; in others it must be subscribed at the end.

In Presence of Witnesses.   The signature must be written by the testator in the presence of the witnesses, or if made elsewhere, he must acknowledge to them that it is his signature.·   At the same time the testator must declare that the instrument is his will.   This is known as the publication of the will.   No particular form of words is necessary.

Seal.   A seal is not necessary on a will, but it may be used, and frequently is, for the purpose of evincing deliberation and reflection.

Witnesses.   There must always be a certain number of witnesses to a will.   In some States the number required is two, in others three, and in one **State** as many as five are necessary.

They must be credible and respectable persons. Any person competent to be a witness in court may be a witness to a will. A minor may be a witness,

No attestation clause is strictly necessary, but it is very desirable to insert such a clause, stating the facts of its execution. It leads to a strong presumption that everything was done correctly.

The testator in some States must request the witnesses to sign as such, and they should sign their names in his presence, and, desirably, in the presence of each other.

Legatee as a Witness. If any person, such as a legatee or devisee, interested in the will, signs it as witness, he cannot take the legacy or devise, unless there are enough witnesses besides him to prove the will. Husband and wife may be witnesses to each other's wills, subject to this rule.

Holographic Wills. Wills which are wholly in the handwriting of the testator, are in a few States valid without witnesses, if found among the valuable papers of the testator after his death, or in the possession of some person to whom it was delivered by the testator for safe keeping.

Nuncupative Wills. A nuncupative or verbal will can usually only be made by sailors and soldiers in actual service. Some States allow them to be made by any person in his last sickness in his usual habitation, or while absent from home on a journey when taken suddenly ill.

Such verbal disposition of property must be made

in the presence of at least as many witnessess as is required for a written will, and generally more. The testator must request the persons present to bear witness that the words spoken are his last will.

A verbal will, even where allowed, cannot dispose of real estate.

It is important to put the words of the testator in writing as soon as practicable, and if this is not done within a certain time, as six or ten days, the will cannot as a rule be proved after six months from death. .

Codicil. A codicil to a will is an alteration of the will subsequent to its execution. A mere interlineation, or erasure, or obliteration, or even an added clause, is absolutely void, and not a codicil. The codicil to be valid must be executed with the same formalities, as to signing, publication and witnesses, as the will itself.

Revocation. The testator has complete control over his will up to the time of his death, and may alter or revoke it at pleasure, either in whole or in part. Obliteration, or erasure is not a revocation of the parts obliterated, or erased, unless the whole will is so obliterated, as to show an intention to revoke it all. Total destruction of the will, as by burning or tearing, is a revocation. Revocation may also be effected by a clause in a subsequent will, or a codicil. In fact the mere making of a subsequent will would often imply a revocation, even if the old will is not destroyed.

The marriage of a woman in itself revokes a will

made by her previous to the marriage. The marriage of a man, and the birth of a child revokes his will made before marriage.

Place of Making Will. A will of personal property, executed in accordance with the regulations of the law of the place where the testator lives, is good everywhere, no matter where the property is. A will of real estate, wherever made, must be executed with the formalities required by the law of the State where the land is situated.

Construction of Will. In the construction of wills the intention of the testator will be the guiding consideration. There must be no ambiguity, however, on the face of the will, either as to the property, or the persons to whom it is given. Great care should be taken in drawing the will to make the language clear and unmistakable.

Undue Influence and Fraud. Wills, or legacies and devises in wills, are often declared to be void, because of undue influence exerted on the mind of the testator. If the testator is in possession of all his faculties and is induced by urgent persuasion to leave some person a legacy, this is not undue influence, and the legacy is good. Undue influence is a valid reason for declaring the will void where the testator is a person of weak understanding or of feeble health.

Bequests obtained by threats or fraud are void.

Probate of Will. The will should be presented as soon as possible after the death of the testator to the Surrogate or Probate Court, or to some similar court for probate or proof. By this is meant that the will must be proved by the testimony of the witnesses to have been executed according to law by the testator. If the witnesses are dead, or absent, and cannot be found, their handwriting may be established by the evidence of any persons familiar with it. If the proof offered is satisfactory, the Surrogate or Judge admits it to probate, and orders it to be recorded in the office of the court to be open for the inspection of any one who pleases.

Devise and Legacy. A devise, as has been said, is a gift of land by will, and a legacy a gift of personal property. Both are often included in the word "bequest." A bequest to "children" in a will, means *all* the children, even a posthumous child; but not such as are illegitimate, unless specially expressed to be in their favor.

Legacies General and Specific. A general legacy is a gift of a sum of money, generally without specifying any particular fund or securities, as, for instance, "I bequeath to A. C. $1,000." A specific legacy is a gift of certain specific property designated by the testator, as a watch, or a certain bond for $1,000.

Abatement of Legacies. The value of the distinction between general and specific legacies lies in the fact that if there is not enough money belonging to the testator in the hands of the executor to pay *all* the legacies in full, the specific legacies are first paid in full. The general legatees take only the balance in shares proportional to the amount of their several legacies. This is called "abatement."

Lapsed Legacies. If the testator leaves a legacy to a person who dies before the testator, the legacy is said to be "lapse," that is, it is not to be paid to that person's representatives, but remains part of the estate, and goes to the residuary legatee, if there is one, or to the next of kin.

There is an exception to this rule. In case the legatee who dies is a child or descendant of the testator, and leaves a child or children of his own, the legacy does not lapse, but goes to such child or children.

Conditional Legacies. A legacy or devise is often given upon the condition that the legatee or devisee will do or omit to do a certain thing. In order to be entitled to receive the bequest, all the conditions must be fulfilled by the person to whom it is bequeathed. There are two kinds of conditions—conditions precedent and conditions subsequent. In the first case, the title vests only when the condition is performed, while in the latter case, the title vests at once subject to being divested by the performance or non-performance of the condition.

A bequest to a son on condition that he shall marry some particular person is a condition precedent, and he cannot get the legacy until he marries that person. But a bequest to a son, and if he ever marries a person named, then the property to go over to another son, is a condition subsequent, and he is entitled to the bequest at once, subject to losing it in case of marriage with that person.

Conditions in general restraint of marriage are usually void, but the testator has the right, on making a bequest to his wife, to provide that she shall lose it in case she marries again. This is a condition subsequent.

In Lieu of Dower. A bequest is often made by the testator to his wife " in lieu of dower." No act of the husband can ever deprive his widow of dower without her consent. Consequently she is not obliged to take this bequest. She has her election or choice to take either the bequest or the dower. But she cannot take both. If she conclude to take the bequest, she must release her dower rights.

Bequest Charged With Debt. If a legacy or devise is made, charged with the payment of a debt, the legatee or devisee may refuse to accept it. But if he does, not only is the bequest liable for such payment, but the legatee, etc., himself is personally responsible, and may be sued for any deficiency between the debt and the amount of the bequest. It is dangerous to take such a legacy or devise until its value is ascertained to be at least equal to the debt.

Time of Payment. If any time of payment is mentioned in the will, the legacy cannot be demanded before that time. If no time is mentioned, legacies are payable a year after the death of the testator. In no case do they bear interest before they are due, unless so stated in the will.

Life-Interests. The testator frequently makes a bequest of property to some person for life, and on the death of that person to another person absolutely. The first person has the interest or use of the estate during life, but no right to the principal. As a general rule only two such life-estates can be created by the testator before the title vests absolutely. For instance, he can leave the estate to A, for life, and on A's death to B, for life, and on B's death to C. This is valid, but a provision creating a greater number of life-estates is void.

The following is a summary of the laws of the several States in regard to the execution of wills:

ALABAMA.—Any person twenty-one years of age can make a will of real estate. Persons of the age of eighteen can make a will of personal property. Only $500 worth of property can be bequeathed by a nuncupative will. All wills (except nuncupative) must be in writing, signed by the testator, or by some person in his presence at his direction. The will must be attested by at least two witnesses, who must subscribe their names in the testator's presence. Wills are recorded in the office of the Judge of the Probate Court.

ARIZONA.—All persons of the age of twenty-one can dispose of their property, real or personal, by will. Wills must be in writing, signed by the testator, or by some person, in his presence, at his direction. Wills must be attested by two or more witnesses, who must subscribe their names in the presence of the testator and of each other. Nuncupative wills cannot dispose of property worth over $300, and must be proved by two witnesses.

ARKANSAS.—Persons over twenty-one years of age can dispose of real estate by will, and persons over eighteen of personal property. Wills must be subscribed by the testator, at the end, or by some person at his request. This must be done in the presence of all the witnesses, or the subscription must be acknowledged to them by the testator, who must also declare the paper to be his last will and testament.   There must be at least two attesting witnesses, who must sign their names at the end, at the request of the testator, as witnesses.   Where the whole will is in the hand-writing of the testator, it can be proved by the evidence of three witnesses to the handwriting and signature, without any subscription as witnesses.   Nuncupative wills can dispose of only $500. Wills are recorded in the office of the Probate Court.

CALIFORNIA.—All persons eighteen years of age, including married women without their husband's consent, may make wills of all their property real and personal.   Wills must be in writing signed by the testator or some person in his presence and by his direction.   They must be attested by two witnesses who must subscribe their names as witnesses in the presence of the testator and of each other.   A nuncupative will cannot dispose of more than $1,000; it must be proved by two witnesses, and reduced to writing within thirty days.   A will entirely in the handwriting of the testator is valid.

COLORADO.—Males of the age of twenty-one years and females of the age of eighteen may dispose of all their property by will.   Any person seventeen years of age may make a will of personal property.   A married man cannot deprive his wife of over half his property, and a married woman, without her husband's consent in writing, cannot will more than one-half of her property away from her husband.   Wills devising lands must be in writing, and signed by the testator, or by some person in his presence at his request.   There must be two attesting witnesses who must sign in the presence of the testator.   Wills are recorded in the County Courts.

CONNECTICUT.—Persons eighteen years of age can dispose of all their property, real and personal, by will.   Married women may make wills subject to the rights of their husbands to curtesy in their land.   All wills must be in writing subscribed by the testator.   There must be three attesting witnesses, who must subscribe their names in his presence and in the presence of each other. Wills must be offered for probate within ten years after death. They are recorded in the Probate Court.

DAKOTA. All person of .the age of eighteen years can make wills of all their property, real and personal. Wills must be in writing subscribed by the testator at the end, or by some person in his presence and by his direction. This subscription must be done in the presence of two witnesses, or be acknowledged by the testator to them. He must declare the instrument to be his will. The witnesses must subscribe their names as such at the request of the testator and in his presence. They should write their place of residence after their names. A married woman may will her property without her husband's consent. Wills are recorded in the office of the Probate Judge.

DELAWARE.—Persons of the age of twenty-one years may make wills of all their property. Married women may make wills with the consent of their husbands in writing under seal in the presence of two witnesses. Wills must be in writing signed by the testator or by some person in his presence and by his direction, There must be two or more attesting witnesses who must subscribe the will. Wills are recorded in the office of the Register of Wills.

DISTRICT OF COLUMBIA.—Males of the age of twenty-one years and females of the age of eighteen may make wills of land. Wills must be in writing, signed by the testator, or by some person in his presence by his direction. They must be attested and subscribed in the presence of the testator by three or four witnesses.

FLORIDA.—Persons of the age of twenty-one years may dispose of their land and personal property by will. Wills must be signed by the testator, or by some person in his presence and by his direction. They must be at tested and subscribed in the presence of the testator by three or more witnesses. A nuncupative will must be reduced to writing within six days and sworn to before some judicial officer; otherwise it cannot be proved after six months.

GEORGIA.—Persons must be of the age of twenty-one years in order to make a will. All wills must be signed by the testator, or by some person in his presence by his direction. They must be attested and subscribed in the presence of the testator by three or more witnesses. Wills are recorded in the office of the Court of Ordinary.

IDAHO.— All persons over the age of twenty-one years may dispose of all his property by will, except that the widow is entitled to one-half of the common property. Persons over eighteen can make a will of personal property. Wills must be in writing signed by the testator, or by some person in his presence by his direction. They must be attested by two or more witnesses at the request of the testator in his presence and in the presence of each other. Wills are recorded in the Probate Clerk's office.

ILLINOIS.—Males of the age of twenty-one, and females of the age of eighteen may make a will. The will must be signed by the testator, or by some person in his presence at his direction. It must be attested and subscribed in his presence by two or more witnesses. Wills are recorded in the Probate Court.

INDIANA.—All persons over the age twenty-one may make a will of all their property. Wills must be signed by the testator, or by some person in his presence by his direction. There must be two witnesses who must subscribe their names in his presence. Wills are recorded in the office of the County Clerk.

IOWA.—Persons must be twenty-one years of age in order to make a will. Wills must be signed by the testator or by some person in his presence by his direction.

There must be two subscribing witnesses. A verbal will of personal property may be made, if in the presence of two witnesses. Wills are recorded in the office of the Clerk of the Circuit Court.

KANSAS.—Persons of the age of ——— years may make a will. All wills must be signed by the testator. There must be at least two subscribing witnesses. Any person may make a will in writing and inclose it in a sealed wrapper with the name of the testator indorsed upon it. This may then be deposited in the office of the Judge of the Probate Court. It may be recalled at any time by the testator during his life.

KENTUCKY.—Persons over twenty-one years of age may make

a will. A married woman can dispose of her separate estate by will. Wills must be in writing subscribed by the testator or by some person in his presence by his direction. The subscription must be made or acknowledged in the presence of two witnesses, who subscribe their names as such in the presence of the testator. If the whole will is in the handwriting of the testator, it need not be witnessed. Wills are recorded in the County Clerk's office.

LOUISIANA.—The testator cannot deprive certain persons called his "forced heirs," of more than a certain portion of his estate. If he has one child, he cannot dispose of more than two-thirds of his estate; if he leaves two children, not more than one-half; if he leaves three or more children, not more than one-third; if he leaves no children, but a father or mother, not more than two-thirds. There are four forms of wills. A will entirely in the testator's handwriting needs no witnesses. Other wills generally require five witnesses. The provisions of the Civil Code in regard to wills are very minute, and should be consulted carefully before drawing up a will.

MAINE.—A will must be signed by the testator or by some person for him at his request in his presence. It must be attested by three witnessess, who must sign it. Nuncupative wills are only valid when made in last sickness, and must be reduced to writing within six days, or they cannot be proved after six months. Such a will cannot dispose of more than $100, unless witnessed by three witnesses requested to act as such.

MARYLAND.—Males of twenty-one and females of eighteen may make a valid will of real estate. Wills must be in writing, signed by the testator, or by some other person in his presence by his direction. They must be attested and subscribed in the testator's presence by three or four witnesses. Wills of personal property are valid without witnesses. Wills are recorded by the Register of Wills. The Register will receive the wills of living persons for safe keeping for a fee of fifty cents.

MASSACHUSETTS.—All persons of full age (twenty-one years) may dispose of all his property by will. The will must be signed by the testator, or by some person in his presence by his direction.

It must be attested and subscribed by three or more witnesses in the presence of the testator. A bequest to a subscribing witness where there are not three others, is void. A married woman may make a will of her separate property, but cannot deprive her husband of his right to curtesy in her land, or of' more than one-half of her personal property, without his consent in writing. Wills are recorded in the registry of probate.

MICHIGAN.—All persons of full age (twenty-one) may make a will. A will must be signed by the testator or by some person in his presence by his direction. It must be attested and subscribed by two or more witnesses in the presence of the testator. Nuncupative wills cannot dispose of more than $300, unless proved by at least two witnesses. Wills are recorded in the Probate Court.

MINNESOTA.—Persons of full age (twenty-one), including married women, may make wills. Every will must be signed by the testator, or by some person in his presence, by his direction, at the end. It must be attested and subscribed by two or more witnesses in the presence of the testator. Wills are recorded in the office of the Probate Court.

MISSISSIPPI.—Any person twenty-one years of age can make a will. If the will is wholly in the handwriting of the testator, no witnesses are required. Every other requires at least two witnesses. Nuncupative wills can only be made during the last sickness of deceased, at his home or residence, for last ten days, except in case of soldiers and marines at sea. Such a will cannot dispose of more than one hundred dollars' worth of property, unless two witnessess prove that deceased called on some person present to bear witness that such was his will. Wills are recorded in the office of the Clerk of the Chancery Court.

MISSOURI.—Persons over twenty-one may make wills of real estate; persons over eighteen, of personal property. Married women over eighteen may make wills, even of real estate. Wills must be signed by the testator, and attested at his request and in his presence by at least two witnesses. Wills are recorded in the office of the Recorder of Deeds.

MONTANA.—All persons over eighteen years of age may make

wills. Every will must be signed at the end by the testator, or by some person in his presence and by his direction. It must be attested and subscribed in his presence by two or more witnesses. A married woman may make a will of her separate property. Nuncupative wills cannot dispose of more than $1,000, and must be proved by two witnesses, one of whom was asked by deceased to bear witness that such was his will. Such wills are only allowed in case of persons at sea or in actual military service in expectation of immediate death.

NEBRASKA.—Wills must be in writing, signed by testator, or by some person in his presence by his direction. They must be attested and subscribed in his presence by two or more witnesses. Wills are recorded in the office of the County Clerk.

NEVADA.—All persons over eighteen years of age may make wills of all their property. A married woman may dispose of her separate property by will without her husband's consent. She may will her share of the common property with her husband's written consent annexed to the will. All wills must be in writing, signed and sealed by the testator, or by his direction. They must be attested by two witnesses in his presence. Nuncupative wills cannot be made where the estate exceeds $1,000 in value. Such wills must be proved by two witnesses within three months. Wills are recorded in the Probate Court.

NEW HAMPSHIRE.—Persons over the age of twenty-one years are competent to make wills. A will must be signed and sealed by the testator, or by some person in his presence by his direction. It must be attested and subscribed in his presence by three or more witnesses. Married women may make wills. Nuncupative wills can only be made by the testator in his last sickness and in his home. There must be three witnesses, who must be requested to bear witness that such is his will. It must be reduced to writing within six days and proved within six months. Wills are recorded in the office of the Register of Probate.

NEW JERSEY.—Any person over twenty-one may make a will. A married woman may will her separate estate, but cannot take away her husband's interest in her real estate. Every will must be signed by the testator, or the writing acknowledged by him in the presence of two witnesses. He must declare at the same time that the paper is his will, and the witnesses must subscribe their names as such in his presence and in the presence of each other. Wills are recorded in the Surrogate's office.

NEW MEXICO.—Males over fourteen and females over twelve may make wills. Wills may be either written or verbal. If in writing, they must be signed by the testator and attested by three witnesses. If the testator is unable to write, some other person may sign at his request. Verbal wills must be proved by five witnesses.

NEW YORK.—All persons over twenty-one may make a will of real estate. Males over eighteen and females over sixteen may dispose of personal property by will. Every will must be in writing and subscribed by the testator at the end. This subscription must be made in the presence of at least two witnesses, or acknowledged by him to be his signature to each of such witnesses. He must declare that the instrument is his will in their presence, and request them to sign as witnesses. The witnesses must sign their names and residences at the end of the will in the presence of the testator. If they do not write their residences they are each liable to a penalty of $50. Wills are recorded in the Surrogate's office.

NORTH CAROLINA.—A will entirely in the handwriting of the testator does not require witnesses. All other wills must have two subscribing witnesses. Nuncupative wills cannot dispose of more than $200, unless made by the testator in his last sickness in his home, or on a journey. There must be two witnesses who must have been requested to bear witness. Such a will must be put in writing within ten days, or it cannot be proved after six months. Wills are recorded in the Probate Court.

OHIO.—Any persons of full age (21) may make a will. The will must be signed at the end by the testator, or by some other person in his presence, by his direction. This must be done in the presence of two witnesses or acknowledged to them. The witnesses must attest and subscribe the will in the presence of the testator. Any bequests to charitable or religious bodies are void as against children, unless the will was executed at least one year prior to the decease of the testator.

OREGON.—Persons over twenty-one may dispose of real estate by will; persons over eighteen, of personal property. Every will must be signed by the testator, or by some person in his presence, by his direction. There must be two witnesses, who must subscribe the will in the presence of the testator.

PENNSYLVANIA.—Any person over twenty-one may make a will. Wills must be in writing and signed by the testator at the end, or by some person in his presence, by his direction. There must be two witnesses who need not subscribe the will, though it is desirable they should. Married women must acknowledge their wills before the witnesses; the husband cannot be a witness to his wife's will. A bequest to charity to be valid, must be made by a will executed at least one month before the death of the testator. Nuncupative wills may be made by marines and soldiers in actual service, or by persons in their last sickness in their own home, or when taken sick while traveling.

RHODE ISLAND.—Any person over twenty-one may make a will of real estate, and any person over eighteen a will of personal property. Wills must be in writing, signed by the testator, or by some person in his presence, by his direction. They must be attested and subscribed by two or more witnesses, in the presence of the testator. Wills are recorded in the Town Clerk's office.

SOUTH CAROLINA.—All wills must be in writing and signed by the testator, in the presence of three or more subscribing witnesses. They are records in the office of the Probate Court.

TENNESSEE.—Any person, including a married woman of full age, may make a will. Wills must be signed by the testator or by some person in his presence, by his direction. If the will disposes of real estate, it must be subscribed in his presence by two or more witnesses. A will of personal property only needs no witnesses. A will entirely in the handwriting of the testator, even if it devises lands, is valid, without witnesses, provided it can be proved by three persons that the handwriting is his. Nuncupative

wills of more than $250 are not good unless proved by two wit-
nesses present at the time of the making of such will, unless they
were requested by the testator to bear witness to it, and unless
made in his last sickness. Such a will must be put in writing
within ten days or it cannot be proved after six months.

TEXAS.—All persons must be twenty-one years of age in order
to make a will. Wills must be in writing, signed by the testator.
There must be two subscribing witnesses. Nuncupative wills
cannot dispose of over $30, unless made during the last sickness
of the testator, and three witnesses testify that he requested them
to bear witness to his will. Such a will must be put in writing
within six days, or it cannot be proved after six months.

UTAH.—All persons over eighteen years of age, including married women, are competent to make wills of all their property,
real and personal. Wills must be in writing subscribed by the
testator, and attested by two or more witnesses in the presence of
the testator and of each other.

VERMONT.—Wills must be signed by the testator in the presence
of three witnesses, who must sign their names as such in his presence and in the presence of each other. Wills are recorded in the
Probate Court.

VIRGINIA.—Any person over twenty-one may make a will of real
estate; any one over eighteen a will of personal property. Wills
must be in writing signed by the testator, or by some one in his
presence by his direction. If the will is wholly in the handwriting
of the testator no witnesses are necessary. Other wills must be
signed, or the will acknowledged in the presence of at least two
witnesses present at the same time. These witnesses must subscribe the will in the presence of the testator.

WASHINGTON TERRITORY.—Any male person over twenty-one
and any female over eighteen may make a will. Wills must be
signed by the testator or by some person under his direction. A
will must be attested by two or more witnesses, who must subscribe their names in the presence of the testator. A nuncupative
will of more than $200 in value can only be made in testator's last

sickness, and must be proved by two or more witnesses. Such wills must be proved within six months.

WEST VIRGINIA.—Any person over twenty-one may make a will. A will must be in writing signed by the testator, or by some person in his presence and by his direction. If wholly written by the testator no witnesses are necessary. Other wills must be signed and the will acknowledged by the testator in the presence of two or more witnesses present at the same time. The witnesses must subscribe the will in the presence of the testator.

WISCONSIN.—All wills must be in writing signed by the testator, or by some person in his presence by his direction. They must be attested and subscribed in the presence of the testator by two or more witnesses.

WYOMING.—Same as in Wisconsin.

SHORT FORM OF WILL.

I, A. B., being of sound mind and memory, do give, devise and bequeath all my property, both real and personal, to C. D., hereby revoking all former wills by me made.

In witness whereof, I, A. B., have to this, my last will and testament, subscribed my name this 10th day of July, 1884, at the City of New York.

(Signature) A. B.

Subscribed by the testator in the presence of each of us, and at the same time declared by him to us to be his last will and testament, and thereupon we, at the request of the testator and in his presence, sign our names hereto as witnesses, this 10th day of July, 1884, at the City of New York,

(Signatures and addresses of witnesses.)

ANOTHER FORM.

In the name of God, amen. I, John Brown, being in sound health of body, and of disposing mind and memory, do make and publish this, my last will and testament, hereby revoking all former wills, by me at any time made.

I. I direct that all my just debts, including funeral expenses and the expenses of administration, be paid by my executors.

II. I bequeath to my beloved wife, Mary, one thousand dollars annually, in equal quarterly payments, in advance, reckoning from the first day of January in each year, as the means of supporting herself and family, so long as she remains my widow, the first payment, for the current quarter, to be made within one month after my decease. I also give and devise to my said wife the use of my farm-house in Clinton, free of rent, during the term of her natural life, to be occupied by herself, or her tenants.

III. I devise and bequeath all the residue and remainder of my estate, both real and personal, to my children who shall survive me, and to the legal issue of any deceased child or children, by way of representation of such child or children forever in equal parts.

IV. If none of my children shall survive me, and there shall, at my decease, remain no issue of any of my deceased children, then I devise and bequeath all such residue of my estate to such persons as may be my lawful heirs and distributees, at that time, to be distributed according to the statutes then in force; or to such charitable and religious societies, as are hereafter named, in proportion to the several sums attached to the names of such societies respectively. And I hereby appoint A. B. the executor of this my last will. In witness whereof, I have hereunder set my hand, this 16th day of August, 1875.   JOHN BROWN.

Signed by the said testator, John Brown, as and for his last will and testament, in the presence of us, who, at his request, in his presence and in the presence of each other, have subscribed our names as attesting witnesses.

[Signatures and addresses of witnesses.]

CODICIL.

This is a codicil to my last will and testament, dated March 3d, 1872.

Whereas, by my said will, I have given my wife one-third part of all my real and personal estate, I now declare that it is my will, that, instead of that provision, she shall have the use of one-half of all my estate, real and personal, during her natural life: and so much of the principal as may be necessary or convenient for her support during the term of her natural life.

And I hereby revoke the appointment of A. B. to be one of my executors, and I appoint C. D. to take that office, with all the powers and duties in my said will declared.

In witness whereof I have hereunto set my hand this 25th day of May, 1877. [Signature.]

[Attestation clause and signatures of witnesses.]

CHAPTER XXIII.

EXECUTORS AND ADMINISTRATORS.

Duties of—Bonds—Executors not Obliged to Give— Who can be an Executor— Who is Entitled to be an Administrator—Probate of Will—Appraisement and Inventory— Payment of Debts—Order of Payment—Payment of Legacies—Powers of—Should not Sign Notes—Commissions.

An executor is a person appointed by the testator in his will to take charge of the property of the testator on his decease, and to carry into effect the provisions and directions of the will.

An administrator is a person selected by the court having jurisdiction to take charge of the estate of a deceased person who has left no will, and to distribute it among the persons entitled to it under the law.

Duties of. The duties of executors and administrators are substantially the same. There are some points of difference. An administrator only has possession and control of the personal property of the decedent. The real estate goes to the heirs at once. An executor, generally, is entitled to the possession of all the property of the testator.

Bonds. Administrators must always give bonds

for the faithful performance of their duties. The bond is in the amount of double the value of the estate. There must be sureties, two or more, who must qualify as such by swearing that they are each of them worth at least the amount of the bond. They must also, as a rule, be freeholders or householders, owners or lessees of real estate. The administrator cannot act until the bond is given and the sureties have qualified. The bond is given, usually, " to the people of the State," and is kept in the office of the Clerk of the Court. If the administrator is guilty of fraud or dishonesty, the sureties are liable.

Executors not Obliged to Give. Executors sometimes give bonds, but not generally. Wherever the will states that they shall do so, they cannot act until they have done so. If the will is silent on the subject, the executor is not obliged to give bonds, unless it is shown by some one interested in the will that he is an irresponsible person, liable to waste or misapply the property. Very often, if this is shown, the court will remove the executor and appoint some one in his place. In Connecticut, an executor must always give bonds, unless he is expressly excused from doing so by the terms of the will.

The reason why an executor is not under the same obligations as an administrator is that the testator is regarded as reposing a personal trust and confidence in the person whom he names as executor.

Who can be an Executor. In order to be qualified to become an executor a person must be of full age and in the possession of all his faculties. No person incapable of making a contract can be an executor. A person under twenty-one years of age, or a citizen of another country, not residing in this country, or one who has ever been convicted of an infamous crime, such as murder or theft, or any one who is guilty of habitual drunkenness, or dishonesty, or improvidence, or who is wanting in mental capacity, is incompetent to serve as executor. If any such person is named as executor in the will, he will not be allowed to qualify or take possession of the estate.

Married women in New York may act as executrices, but they must have their husband's consent in writing. This consent is filed in the Clerk's office, and the husband is jointly responsible with his wife for her acts as such executrix. In some States a married woman cannot act as executrix at all

If none of the persons appointed executors by the will are competent or willing to serve, the court appoints an administrator to carry out the will. He is known as an " administrator with the will annexed."

Who May be Administrators. The same qualifications are necessary for administrators as in the case of executors. Certain persons are entitled to administer on the property of the decedent in preference to all other persons; and they must be appointed unless some valid objection can be urged against them.

The persons entitled are: 1st, the widow; 2d, the children; 3d, the father; 4th, the mother; 5th, the brothers; 6th, the sisters; 7th, the grandchildren; 8th, the next of kin; 9th, the creditors.

Probate of Will. The first duty of the executor is to present the will to the proper court for probate. Courts having such jurisdiction are variously named Surrogate's Courts, Orphan's Courts, Courts of Probate, etc. They are held at the county seat. The executor applies for and obtains a writ known as a citation, a paper in the nature of a subpœna. This citation demands the presence of the legatees and next of kin in court on a particular day. Copies are served on all persons interested in the will.

The executor subpœnaes the witnesses to the will to appear, and testify as to its execution. If they are dead, witnesses who are familiar with their handwriting, must appear and testify as to its genuineness.

If no objections are made to the authenticity of the will, it is admitted by the Judge or Surrogate to probate, and is transcribed upon the records of the court. The original will is returned to the executor. The executor must then qualify by accepting the trust and taking the oath to faithfully carry out the trust. Letters testamentary, as they are called, are then issued by the court to the executor.

Appraisement and Inventory. On application of the executor, appraisers are appointed to estimate the value of the estate. Notice must be given to all the interested parties.

An inventory of all the personal property is then

drawn up. Property exempt from execution is included in this inventory, though it is not liable for the testator's debts.   All debts due the estate, bonds, mortgages, notes, accounts, money, etc., must be specifically mentioned and described.   The inventory is signed by the appraisers and returned to the office of the court.

The course to be followed is the same in the case of administrators.

Payment of Debts.   The executor or administrator should then give notice, by publication in the newspapers, for all creditors to present their claims against the estate of the deceased in writing.   In addition to this, copies of the notice should be sent by mail to all known creditors.

The creditors must obey this notice within the time limited in the notice, or they cannot complain in case the executor or administrator has paid over all the assets of the estate to those who have presented their claims.

Order of Payment.   The funeral expenses of the deceased are to be paid first.   Then all taxes due to the United States, and debts which have a preference by the laws of the United States.   Then, taxes due to the State.   Then, judgments in the order of their priority.   Then, bonds, sealed instruments, notes, bills and all ordinary debts, in full, if the assets are sufficient, otherwise in proportion.

Payment of Legacies.   Legacies are payable usually one year after the death of the testator,

Specific legacies are paid or the article delivered, whatever may be the condition of the estate after the debts are paid. General legacies are paid last of all, and must abate proportionately if the assets are not enough to pay them all in full.

Legacies to minor children, if very small, may be paid to the father, but in case of large amounts, security is required, or a guardian may be appointed to take care of the legacy; the guardian must give bonds.

Powers of Executors and Administrators. If there is not enough money to pay the debts and legacies the executor may sell sufficient personal property to raise the money to do so. The real estate must be sold if necessary.

The sale must generally be public—at auction. The will, however, frequently confers the right of private sale on the executor.

An executor or administrator has no right to carry on the business of the testator. If he does, he is personably liable for the debts contracted in the business.

Should Not Sign Notes. Negotiable paper should not be issued by an executor or administrator in the name of the estate. He is personally liable on such paper if the assets of the estate are not sufficient to meet it. To relieve himself of this liability he may add to the note, the words "if the assets are sufficient." He is then not liable, but such a note is not negotiable.

Commissions. Executors and administrators are entitled to compensation for their services. This is usually in the form of a commission on all moneys received and paid out. In New York the rates of commission are five per cent. for receiving and paying out sums under $1,000; two and one-half per cent. for sums over $1,000 and under $10,000; one per cent. on sums over $10,000.

CHAPTER XXIV.

DESCENT AND DISTRIBUTION OF PROPERTY.

WHEN a person dies leaving property, without having made a will in his life-time, the law prescribes what persons are entitled to such property. The persons who get the real estate are called the heirs; they take by descent. Those who get the personal property are called the personal representatives, or the next of kin. Distribution is the word applied to the division of the personal property among those entitled to it. The heir and the personal representative are often, but not always, the same person.

The following is a statement of the provisions of the laws in the various States, as to the descent and distribution of real and personal property:

ALABAMA.—Real and personal property descends; 1st, to the children of the intestate, or their descendants *per stirpes* in equal parts; if there is no child, or one child, the widow takes one-half the personal property; if more than one and not more than four children, she takes a child's part; if more than four children, she takes a fifth; 2d, if there are no children or their children, the estate descends to the brothers and sisters and their descendants in equal parts; 3d, if there are no children, or brothers or sisters, etc., the estate goes to the father if living; if not, then to the mother. If there are none of these, then to the next of kin in equal degree in equal parts. If there are no next of kin, the whole estate goes to the husband or wife.

ARKANSAS.—Real and personal property descend: 1st, to children and their descendants in equal parts; 2d, if no children, then to father, then to mother; if no mother, then to brothers and sisters and descendants; 3d, if none of these are living, then to grandfather, grandmother, uncles, aunts and their descendants in equal parts.

CALIFORNIA.—Estate descends as follows: If deceased leaves husband or wife and only one child, in equal shares to each; if more than one child, one-third to husband or wife, and remainder to children in equal shares. If there are no children, the surviving husband or wife takes one-half, and the other half goes to decedent's father; if no father living, then to brothers and sisters and mothers in equal shares. Children of deceased brothers and sisters come in for their parent's share. If there is no husband, wife or children or children's children, the whole estate goes to decedent's father; if no father living, then to brothers, sisters and mothers in equal shares; if no sisters or brothers, the mother takes it all to the exclusion of the children of brothers and sisters. If there is a husband or wife surviving and no children, father, mother, brother or sister, the whole estate goes to the surviving husband or wife. If none of these persons are left surviving, the estate goes to the next of kin in equal degrees. If no kindred, the estate escheats to the school-fund of the State.

COLORADO.—Estate descends to the surviving wife or husband, provided there are no children or children's children. If there are children or their descendants, the surviving husband or wife takes one-half the estate, and the other half goes to the children in equal shares, the children of deceased children taking the share of their parent. 1st, If there is no husband or wife the children take all the estate in equal shares; 2d, if there are no children or descendants, then to father; if no father, to mother; if no mother, then to brothers and sisters and descendants of brothers and sisters; 3d, if none of these living, then to grandfather, grandmother, uncles, aunts and their descendants in equal parts; 4th, if none of these living, then to nearest lineal ancestor and their descendants.

CONNECTICUT.—Estate descends as follows: One-third of the personal property goes to the widow absolutely; one-third of the real estate goes to her for life as dower. The remainder of the estate, real and personal, goes to the children in equal shares, the the child of a deceased child taking his parent's share.

If there are no children or their descendants, one-half of the personal estate goes to widow absolutely, and one-third of real estate for life, and the residue of the estate equally among the brothers and sisters; if no such, then to parent or parents; if no parents, then to brothers and sisters of the half blood; if no such, then to next of kin of equal degree in equal shares.

DAKOTA.—Estate of deceased goes as follows: If there is a surviving husband or wife, and only one child, in equal shares to each; if more than one child, one-third to husband or wife, and remainder to children in equal shares. If no children, the surviving husband or wife takes one-half; the other half goes to decedent's father; if no father living, then in equal shares to the brothers and sisters and mother. If no children, or husband, or wife, the whole estate goes to father; if no father, to the persons aforesaid. If there are no brothers or sisters, the mother takes it all. If there is a surviving husband or wife, and no children, father, mother, brother, or sister, the whole estate goes to such husband or wife. If none of these, then to the next of kin.

DELAWARE.—Real estate descends: 1st, in equal shares to the children; 2d, if none, then to brothers and sisters; 3d, if none, then to father; 4th, if no father, then to mother; 5th, if no mother, then to next of kin. Real estate, however, is subject to the dower of the widow, one-third to her for life if there are any children; one-half for life if there are no children. Also subject to curtesy of the husband, that is, whole for life; even if no child was born, the husband is entitled to one-half for life.

Personal property goes: 1st, to children of intestate; 2d, if none, then to brothers and sisters in equal shares; 3d, if none, then to brothers and sisters of the half blood; 4th, if none, then to father; 5th, if none, then to mother; 6th, if none, then to next of kin. *Provided* that if intestate be a married woman, her husband shall have all. If intestate leave a widow, she is entitled to one-third absolutely if there be children, or, if none, to one-half absolutely; if no kin, to whole personal estate.

DISTRICT OF COLUMBIA.—Lands descend: 1st, to children equally; 2d, if no child, and the estate came from father, to the father; 3d, if not living, then to brothers and sisters; 4th, if no paternal ancestor or descendants, then to mother. If the estate was derived by purchase, and there are no children, it goes to the brothers and sisters of the whole blood; if none, to the brothers and sisters of the half blood; if none, then to father; if no father, then to mother; if none living, then to grandfather on father's side or his descendants; then to grandfather on mother's side or his descendants.

Personal property goes as follows: Where intestate leaves a widow, but no child, parent, grandchild, brother or sister, widow is entitled to whole. If there are no children, the widow is entitled to one-half; if children, to one-third. Residue goes to children in equal shares; if no children, then to father; if no father, the mother, brothers and sisters take equally; if no brothers or sisters, mother takes the whole.

FLORIDA.—Real estate descends: first, to his children or descendants; if none, to father; if no father, then to mother, brothers and sisters, or descendants; if no brothers or sisters, the real estate is divided into equal parts, one of which shall go to the paternal kindred and the other to the maternal kindred; first to the grandfather; if none, then to grandmother, uncles and aunts.

Personal property goes the same way. If a married woman leaves a husband and children, the husband shares the whole estate, real and personal, equally with the children; if no children, the husband takes all. If a husband dies intestate, without children, the widow takes the whole estate.

GEORGIA.—If a wife leaves a husband and no children, the husband takes all the estate; if there are children, he takes an equal share with them. If a husband leaves a widow and no children the wife takes all the estate; if there are children, the wife takes an equal share, unless there are more than five, in which case she takes one-fifth. The children share the balance equally, the descendants of deceased children taking their parent's share. If there is no widow, or surviving husband, or child, the father, brothers and sisters of the decedent take equally. If there is no father, but a mother, she inherits in place of father, if she is a widow. First cousins, uncles and aunts inherit equally in case there are none of these persons.

IDAHO.—Estate descends as follows: If there be a widow or surviving husband and one child, in equal shares to each; if more than one child, one-third to the surviving husband or widow, and residue to children in equal shares. If no children, the estate goes in equal shares to the surviving husband or widow, and decedent's father; if no child, or husband, or wife, the father takes the whole estate; if no father, to the mother, brothers and sisters of decedent, in equal shares; if no brothers or sisters, to the mother. If there is left no child, father, mother, brother or sister, the widow or surviving husband takes the whole estate. In default of any of these persons, to the next of kin; if no kindred, to the school-fund of the Territory.

ILLINOIS.—Estate descends: 1st, to the children and their descendants, in equal parts; 2d, if no child or descendant, and no widow or surviving husband, then to the parents, brothers and sisters, in equal parts, each of the parents taking a child's part, and if one of them be dead, the other receiving a double portion; 3d, when there is a widow or surviving husband, and no child or descendant of a child, one half of the real estate, and the whole of the personal estate goes to such widow or surviving husband; 4th, if there are also children, the widow or surviving husband takes one-third of the personal estate; 5th, if there is no child, parent, brother, sister or descendants, the estate descends to next of kin; if no kindred, the widow or surviving husband takes the whole estate.

INDIANA.—Owing to the peculiar statutes on this subject it is impossible to give any concise synopsis.

Iowa.—Estate descends to children in equal shares, subject to right of dower on the part of widow. The heirs of a deceased child take their parent's share.   If there are no children, one-half goes to the parents, and the other half to the wife; if no wife, the whole estate goes to the parents or the survivor of them.   If both parents are dead, their portion will be distributed among next of kin.

Kansas.—Estate descends as follows: One-half of the real estate goes to the widow in fee-simple.   The residue to the children in equal shares: if no children, the whole goes to the widow; if no wife or child, the estate goes to the parents.   A surviving husband takes his deceased wife's property in the same way.

Kentucky.—Real estate descends: 1st, to children, to father and mother, one-half to each; but if father be dead, his half shall descend to brothers and sisters; if no brother or sister, mother takes the whole estate; if mother is dead, whole estate goes to the father; if no father or mother, then to brothers and sisters and descendants; if none, one-half of the estate goes to the paternal, and the other to the maternal kindred, as follows: 1st, to grandfather and grandmother, equally; if either dead, to survivor; if neither living, to uncles and aunts, etc.   If no kindred, the whole goes to the husband or wife.

Personal property goes the same way as real estate, except that the husband takes the whole personal estate of his deceased wife; and the wife takes one-half of her deceased husband's personal property, if there are no children; if children, she takes one-third.

Louisiana.—Estate goes as follows: If one leaves no descendants, but a father and mother, and brothers and sisters, the estate is divided into two equal portions, one going to the parents, and the other to the brothers and sisters; if either father or mother is dead, his or her share goes to the brothers and sisters.   Children inherit equally.

Maine.—Real estate descends· in equal shares to children or their descendants; if no child or descendant, to father; if no father, to mother, sisters and brothers; if no brother or sister, to mother; if none of these, to next of kin.   The wife has her dower one-third of the real estate, for her life.

Personal estate descends in the same way, except that the widow takes one-third of the personal property absolutely if there are any children; if none, one-half; if no kindred, she takes the whole. The same is true of the husband.

MARYLAND.—Real estate vested by purchase descends: to the children in equal shares; if none, then to brothers and sisters of the whole blood; or if none, to those of the half blood; if none of these living, then to father; if no father, then to mother; if no mother, then to grandfather on the part of father; if none, then to such grandfather's descendants; if none, to grandfather on the part of mother, etc. If there are no kindred the whole estate goes to the husband or wife. Estates coming to the intestate on the part of his father go to his father, or the paternal relatives if there are no children—those on the part of the mother, go to the mother, etc., in the same way, the widow has one-third of the real estate for life.

Personal property goes as follows: If intestate leaves a widow, and no child, parent, grandchild, brother or sister, or the child of such, the widow takes the whole personal estate; if there be a child or children, the widow takes one-third; if there be no child, but a father or mother, or brother or sister, or a child of such, the widow takes one-half; the other half goes to the father; if no father, to the mother, brothers and sisters of the half and whole blood equally; if no brother or sister, the mother takes all; if none of these, to grandfathers equally.

MASSACHUSETTS.—Real estate descends to the children in equal shares; if no child, to father and mother in equal shares; if either is dead, the whole to the survivor; if none of these are living, then to the brothers and sisters, or their issue, in equal shares; if there are none of these, to the next of kin; if no kindred, the widow or surviving husband takes the whole estate.

Personal property goes the same way as real estate, except that the husband takes the whole of his wife's personal estate, and the widow, if there are children, takes one-third of her deceased husband's personality; if there are no children, she takes the whole up to $5,000, and one-half of the excess above $10,000.

MICHIGAN.—Lands descend as follows: first, to his children, or their issue, in equal shares; if no children, the land goes to wife for her life, and after her decease to his father; if there is no widow, land goes to his father; if no father living, to mother, brothers and sisters in equal shares; if no brother or sister, then the whole estate to the mother; if none of these, the land goes to next of kin; if no kindred, the whole estate goes to widow; if no widow, it escheats to the State for the school-fund.

Personal property goes, one-third to the widow, and the residue to the children; if there is only one child, the widow and the child share equally; if there is no child, the widow takes it all, if less than $1,000; if more the property is divided equally between the widow and the father of the deceased; if no father, his half goes to the mother, brothers and sisters in equal shares; if there are none of these, the widow takes the whole. In any other case, it goes as real estate.

MINNESOTA.—The husband or wife may hold one-third of the lands owned by the other before decease, free from any disposition by will or otherwise, liable, however, for its just proportion of the debts. The residue of the real estate, or if there be no widow or surviving husband, the whole thereof descends; 1st, to the children; if no child, then to father; if no father, one equal one-third to the mother, and the residue to the brothers and sisters; if no brother or sister is living, the mother takes the whole; if there are none of these, the estate goes to the next of kin; if no kindred, the whole estate goes to the surviving husband or wife.

Personal property goes in the same way.

MISSISSIPPI.—Real estate descends, subject to the wife's dower or the husband's curtesy, as follows: To the children; if none, to the brothers and sisters; if none, to the father and mother, or the survivor of either; if none of these living, to the next of kin. When there are no surviving children, or descendants of children, the surviving wife or husband takes the whole estate; if there are children, the surviving parent takes an equal share with them.

Personal property descends in the same way.

MISSOURI.—All the property descends: 1st, to the children

and their descendants; if none, then to father, mother, brothers and sisters equally; if none of these are living, then to husband and wife; if neither of these, then to grandparents, uncles and aunts and their descendants in equal shares. If there are no children, the widow takes one-half of the estate. If a child or children, she takes an equal share with them. She is entitled to one-third of realty for life.

MONTANA.—Same as California.

NEBRASKA.—Lands descend to children and issue of deceased children; if no children or descendants, to widow for life; then to father; if no father, then to mother, and brothers and sisters equally; if no brother or sister, the mother takes the whole estate; if none of these, then to next of kin. The widow takes one-third of the real estate for her life as dower, and a husband may have curtesy in his wife's land.

Personal property goes the same way as real estate, except that the widow takes the same share as a child.

NEVADA.—Estate descends as follows: 1st, to surviving husband or wife, and one child equally; if more than one child, one-third to surviving husband or wife, and remainder equally among the children; if no children, the estate goes half to surviving husband or wife and half to father; if no husband or wife surviving, the whole estate to father; if no father, to mother, brothers and sisters in equal shares; if no brother or sister, the mother takes it all; if there is no mother, etc., but a surviving husband or wife, the whole estate goes to such survivor; if none of these persons are living, to next of kin.

NEW HAMPSHIRE.—Real property descends subject to dower and curtesy, as follows: 1st, to the children; if none, to the father; if none, to the mother, and brothers and sisters; if none of these, to the next of kin. The widow is entitled to dower of one-third of the real estate for life.

Personal property goes to the widow in the share assigned by law. The residue goes to the same persons as the real estate.

NEW JERSEY.—Real estate descends, first, to children and their descendants; if none, then to brothers and sisters of the whole blood and their issue; if none, to the father; if no father, to the mother for life; if no mother, to the brothers and sisters of the half blood or their issue. The widow has dower, and the husband curtesy.

Personal property goes: one-third to the widow, if there are children, and the residue to the children in equal shares; if no widow, the children take all; if no children, the widow takes one-half, and the other half goes to next of kin; first, the father; if the father be dead, to the mother, brothers and sisters equally.

NEW YORK.—Real estate descends: first, to children, and their descendants; if none, then to father; if no father, to mother; if no mother, to collateral relatives.

Personal property goes: one-third to the widow, and the residue to the children or their issue; if no children, one-half to widow, and the other half to next of kin; if there is no descendant, parent, brother, sister, nephew, or niece, the widow takes the whole estate; if there is no widow and no children, the estate goes to next of kin. The husband takes the same interest in his wife's property as she in his. The widow is entitled to dower, and the husband to curtesy.

NORTH CAROLINA.—Real estate descends to children and their descendants, then to brothers and sisters or their issue; if no brother or sister, then to father; if no father, to mother; then to next of kin. The widow is entitled to dower.

Personal property goes as follows: If there are not more than two children, one-third part to the widow; if more than two, the widow shares equally with all the children; if there is no widow, the children takes it all in equal shares, the children of a deceased child taking their parent's share; if there are no children, the widow takes one-half, the other half going to next of kin, first to father; if none, to mother, brothers and sisters in equal shares.

OHIO.—Real estate descends: to children or their descendants; if none, then to husband and wife for his or her life; if none, then to brothers and sisters of the blood of the ancestor from whom the estate came; if none, then to the ancestor; if dead, then to children of the ancestor; if none, then to husband or wife of such ancestor, if a parent of decedent for life, then to rest in the brothers and sisters of such ancestors; if none, then to the brothers and sisters of the half blood of the decedent; if none, to next of kin. If the estate was acquired by purchase and not by inheritance, it goes, first to the children; if none, to husband or wife; if none, then to brothers and sisters of the whole blood; if none, then to brothers and sisters of the half blood; if none of these, then to father; if none, to mother; if none, then to next of kin.

Personal property goes the same way as real estate by purchase, except that when the intestate leaves no child, the widow is entitled to all the personal estate; if there be a child or children, she takes one half of any sum of $400 or less, and one-third of the residue. The widow is entitled to dower in the real estate.

OREGON.—Real property descends: first, to the children in equal shares, children of deceased child taking parent's shares; if no lineal descendants, then to wife; if no wife, to father; if none of these, then in equal shares to brothers and sisters the issue of deceased brother or sister, and mother in equal shares; if none of these are living except the mother, she takes all to exclusion of issue of brothers and sisters; if none of these, then to next of kin. Widow has dower.

Personal property goes all to husband, if any; if intestate leaves a wife, she takes all the personal property, unless there are children; in this case, she takes one-half, and the child or children the other half.

PENNSYLVANIA.—Real estate descends as follows: The widow takes one-third for life; if no children, she takes one-half for life; if there are no known heirs, she takes it all absolutely. The husband takes his deceased wife's land for his life. Subject to this, the real estate goes to the children and issue of deceased children in equal shares; if none, to father and mother jointly, and to the survivor for life; if both are dead, then to brothers and sisters, and children and grandchildren of a deceased brother or sister in equal shares; if there are none of these last, the estate rests absolutely in father and mother, or the survivor of them; after these, to next of kin.

Personal property goes: one-third to the widow; if no children, one-half. The surviving husband takes an equal share with children; if no children, he takes all. The children take equal shares. Subject to these rules, the personal estate goes to the father and mother equally or the survivor of them; if no children, husband, father or mother, then to brothers and sisters.

RHODE ISLAND.—Real estate descends in following order on failure of persons in previous classes: 1st, to children or their descendants; 2d, to father; 3d, to mother, brothers and sisters, and their descendants; 4th, to grandfather, one-half to paternal and other half to maternal kindred; 5th, to grandmother, uncles and aunts, or their descendants; 6th, to great-grandfathers; 7th, to great-grandmothers and brothers and sisters of grandfathers and grandmothers, and their descendants. The wife has dower and the husband curtesy.

Personal estate goes one-half to widow if there are no children; one-third to widow when there are children; the remainder the same way as real estate.

SOUTH CAROLINA.—Entire estate, real and personal, descends as follows: If there is a widow and a child or children, one-third to the wife in fee, remainder to children equally. By taking this share, the widow waives her dower. If there is a widow and no child, she takes one-half in fee, the residue going to the father (or the mother), and the brothers and sisters equally. If no brothers or sisters, the father (or the mother if father is dead) takes the residue; if no parent, or brothers and sisters of the whole blood are living, widow takes one-half, and the other half goes to the brothers and sisters of the half blood; if there are none of these relatives, the widow takes two-thirds, and the residue goes to next of kin; if no next of kin, the husband or wife surviving takes the whole. If there is no widow the property goes according to rules above stated.

TENNESSEE.—Land descends as follows: To the children equally; if none, to brothers and sisters of the whole and half blood equally; if none, then to father and mother jointly; if both are dead, one-half to the heirs of the father, and other half to the heirs of the mother; if there are no heirs-at-law, the surviving husband or wife takes it in fee. The wife has dower.

Personal property goes to the widow and children in equal shares, the issue of a deceased child taking parent's share; if no children or issue of children, widow takes it all; if no widow, it goes to the children and issue, etc., in equal shares; if no children or widow, to the father; if no father, to the mother, brothers and sisters, in equal shares; if no brothers or sisters, then to mother; if none of these to next of kin.

TEXAS.—Whole estate, real and personal, descends as follows: If there is no husband or wife surviving, first, to children and descendants; if none, then to father and mother, in equal portions; if only one of them survives, survivor takes one-half and the other half goes to brothers and sisters; but if none, the surviving parent takes whole estate; if there is no parent, to the brothers and sisters of intestate; if none of these are living, the estate is divided into halves, one-half going to paternal, and the other half to maternal kindred, as follows: to the grandfather and grandmother equally; or if only one be surviving, one-half to survivor and the other half to descendants of the one deceased; if no descendants, the whole estate goes to survivor.

Where there is a surviving husband or wife, estate goes as follows: If there be a child or children, or descendants of deceased child, the surviving husband or wife takes one-third of the personal estate, the residue going to the children in equal shares; he or she also takes one-third of the real estate for life. If there are no children, the surviving husband or wife is entitled to all the personal estate, and to one-half the lands absolutely in fee, the other half going according to above rules, except that if there be neither father, nor mother, nor brothers or sisters, or their descendants, the surviving husband or wife takes the whole estate, real and personal.

UTAH.—The whole estate, real and personal, descends as follows: If decedent leaves a husband or wife, and only one child or the issue of one child, the estate goes one-third to surviving husband or wife for life, with remainder and other two-thirds to child; if there are more than one child or issue, etc., one-fourth to surviving husband or wife for life, with remainder, and the other three-fourths to the children equally; if no children, the surviving husband or wife takes one-half of the estate, and the other half goes to the mother, unless the estate came from the father, when the other half goes to him; if there is no mother, it goes to the father, brothers and sisters equally. If there are no children, or husband, or wife, the whole estate goes to the mother; if there are no children, father, mother, brother or sister, the whole estate goes to the surviving husband or wife. There is no dower.

VERMONT.—Estate descends as follows: The widow has one-third of the real estate as dower; if there are no children, she is entitled to the whole estate, if it does not exceed $2,000. If it exceeds that sum, she is entitled to $2,000, and one-half of the remainder, the other half descending in the same way as if there were no widow. Husband inherits from his wife in the same way. If there are no children or widow, the whole estate goes to the father; if no father, to mother, brothers and sisters in equal shares; if none of these, then to next of kin.

VIRGINIA.—Real estate descends as follows: first, to children and descendants; if none, then to father; if none, then to mother, brothers and sisters and descendants; if none of these, one-half the estate goes to the paternal, and the other half to the maternal kindred, as follows: first, to the grandfather; if none, to grandmother, uncles, and aunts and descendants, etc. If there is no kindred, the whole estate goes to the husband or wife of intestate.

Personal estate goes to same persons as real estate, except that husband is entitled to his deceased wife's whole personal estate; the widow is entitled to one-third of her husband's personal property; if there are no children, to one-half.

WASHINGTON TERRITORY.—Real estate descends as follows: If there is a husband or wife surviving and only one child, in equal shares to each; if more than one child, one-third to surviving consort, and residue to children equally; if there are no children, the surviving consort takes one-half, the other half going to the decedent's father and mother; if none, then to brothers and sisters; if no children, father, mother, brother or sister, the whole estate goes to surviving consort; if none of these, to next of kin. No dower.

Personal property goes the same way as real estate, except that if the intestate leaves a husband or wife and issue, the husband or wife takes half; if no children, the surviving consort takes the whole.

WEST VIRGINIA.—Real estate descends as follows: first, to children and descendants; if there is no child, etc., to father; if no father, then to mother, brothers and sisters, and descendants; if none of these, one-half to the paternal and the other half to maternal kindred, as in Virginia. The widow has dower.

Personal property goes the same way, except that a husband, if there are children, takes one-third; if no children, he takes the whole; if there is a widow and children, she gets one-third; if no children, she is entitled to the whole.

WISCONSIN.—Real property descends, subject to dower and curtesy, first, to children; if none, to surviving husband or wife; if none, to parents or the survivor of them; if none, then to brothers and sisters equally; if none of these, then to next of kin.

Personal property goes the same way as real estate, except that the widow takes an equal share with child.

WYOMING.—Dower and curtesy have been abolished. The surviving husband or wife is entitled to the entire estate of the deceased, real and personal, provided it does not exceed $10,000.

CHAPTER XXV.

HOMESTEADS AND PROPERTY EXEMPT FROM EXECUTION.

Homesteads—Owner Must be Head of Family—Record of Notice of Homestead Claim—Consent of Wife to Sale—Personal Property Exempt—Tools of Trade—Wages—Exemption in Money Value—Debt for Purchase Money—Taxes—Family of Deceased Debtor May Claim—Insurance.

A CERTAIN amount of property is now, by the provisions of the statutes of the various States, exempt from liability for the debts of the owner, and cannot be taken by the Sheriff on execution. The amount varies greatly, some States being much more liberal than others.

Homesteads. If such property consists of real estate, it is called a "homestead." The value of a homestead is usually limited to a certain amount, as $1,000, for the purposes of exemption. If the land is worth more, it is sold by the Sheriff; $1,000, or whatever the amount limited by law may be, is paid to the debtor, and the surplus goes to the creditor.

Owner Must be Head of Family. In order to be entitled to claim a homestead in land, the debtor, in most States, must be a resident householder and the head of a family. An unmarried person with no family depending on him for support is obliged to give up all his land for the payment of his debts, and cannot, as a rule, keep as much personal property exempt as the head of a family.

Record of Notice of Homestead Claim. It is generally necessary to file a notice or deed, or paper of some kind, claiming the land as a homestead, in the office of the county where the records of deeds are kept. The word "homestead" entered on the margin of the record of the deed is sometimes sufficient. If this is not done, the debtor is supposed to have waived his right to claim the exemption. Such a notice is not necessary as to personal property.

Consent of Wife to Sale. After the homestead is so claimed or "designated," it cannot be sold or mortgaged by the owner, if married, without the written consent of the wife. She must sign the deed or mortgage with him. In States where the law requires it, her formal acknowledgment must be taken separate and apart from her husband, and she must say that she executes the paper without any fear or compulsion on his part.

Personal Property Exempt. Besides the homestead, if the debtor owns one, there is certain personal property which cannot be taken away from him by his creditors in payment of his debts. This consists generally of wearing apparel, household furniture, family books and pictures, a certain number of domestic animals, and provisions or food for the family, which has been actually purchased.

Tools of Trade. The tools, instruments and implements of trade, by which a person earns his living are usually exempt, as to take them away from him would be to deprive him of the means of a livelihood, or from earning any money with which to pay his debts in the future. The libraries of ministers, lawyers and physicians are exempt for this same reason.

Wages. The wages of laboring men, earned by them within a certain period prior to the levy by the Sheriff, usually sixty days, whether paid to them or still in the hands of the employer, cannot be taken by the creditor.

Exemption in Money Value. In some States instead of certain specific articles being exempt, or sometimes in lieu of such articles, the debtor is allowed to choose or select from out of his personal property, such articles as he pleases, up to a certain amount or value. These he is allowed to keep. Some statutes require the debtor to deliver to the Sheriff, at the time of the levy, a list of the articles he claims or selects. The value is often fixed by appraisers appointed by the court.

Debt for Purchase Money. A homestead or any article of personal property, otherwise exempt, can always be taken on execution when the debt is for the purchase money of the land or article.

Taxes. All kinds of property, real and personal, including homesteads and exempt property, can always be seized and sold for the non-payment of taxes, assessments, or any claim of the State or the United States.

Family of Deceased Debtor May Claim. If any debtor dies, leaving a wife or children, or both, these persons may claim the same exemption of homestead and personal property as that to which the debtor was entitled. A policy of insurance on the life of the debtor in favor of the wife or children, cannot be claimed by the creditors, but the insurance money must be paid to the wife or children only, and is free from all debts.

Insurance. Insurance on homesteads and exempt property is for the benefit of the debtor alone, and in case of loss the money must be paid to him, and he can hold it exempt from execution.

HOMESTEAD AND EXEMPTION LAWS.

The following is a statement of the homestead and exemptions allowed by the laws of the various States:

ALABAMA.—The personal property of a resident to the value of $1,000, to be selected by himself.

The homestead of every resident, not exceeding 160 acres of land, or $2,000 in value; or a lot in a city, town or village with dwelling, not to exceed $2,000. The wages of laborers are exempt to the amount of twenty-five dollars a month. If the owner dies, leaving a wife or child, the exemption is the same in favor of such survivor. Lots in cemeteries, all necessary and proper wearing apparel for each member of the family, all family portraits and books used in the family are also exempt.

ARIZONA.—A homestead with the dwelling, etc., shall be exempt up to $5.000 in value. It cannot be sold or mortgaged without the consent and signature of the wife to the deed or mortgage, and a separate acknowledgment by her.

Property exempt is: all spinning-wheels, weaving-looms, with the apparatus, and stoves put up and kept for use in any dwelling-house; pews in churches; lots in cemeteries; arms kept for use; all wearing apparel of every person or family; the library and school-books of every person or family not exceeding $150 in value; all family pictures; to each householder ten goats or sheep with their fleeces, and the yarn or cloth manufactured from the same; two cows, five swine, and provisions and fuel for the comfortable subsistence of each householder and family for six months; to each householder all household goods, furniture and utensils, not exceeding the value of $600; the tools, implements, materials, stock, apparatus, team, vehicle, horse, harness, or other things to enable any person to carry on his profession, trade, occupation, or business, not exceeding $600 in value; one sewing-machine and one musical instrument; a sufficient quantity of hay, grain, feed and roots for properly keeping for three months the animals exempted.

Any chattel mortgage or bill of sale of these articles shall be void unless signed by the wife of the owner, if he has one, except tools of trade, etc.

ARKANSAS.—The personal property of a resident of the State, if unmarried or not the head of a family, to the value of $200 (the articles to be selected by himself), or if married, or the head of a family, to the value of $500 as before, in addition to wearing apparel, is exempt.

A homestead outside a city, town or village, owned and occupied as a residence by a married man, or the head of a family, is exempt up to 160 acres, not to exceed in value $2,500. This homestead can in no case be reduced to less than eighty acres without regard to value. If the homestead is in a city, town or village it shall not exceed one acre of land in extent, or $2,500 in value. It cannot be reduced to less than one quarter of an acre without regard to value.

CALIFORNIA.—A homestead not exceeding $5,000 in value, selected by husband or wife is exempt. The homestead of an unmarried person, not exceeding $1,000 in value, is also exempt.

The following personal property is exempt: Chairs, tables, desks and books to the value of $200; necessary household table and kitchen furniture, including one sewing-machine, stoves, stove-pipes and stove furniture, wearing apparel, beds, bedding, bedsteads, hanging pictures, oil-paintings or drawings by any member of the family, family portraits and their frames; provisions actually provided for the family sufficient for three months; three cows with their sucking calves; four hogs with their sucking pigs; and their food for one month; farming utensils; two oxen, or two horses, or two mules, and their harness; one cart or wagon; and food for such animals for one month; also seed-grain or vegetables, reserved or on hand for planting within six months, not exceeding $200 in value; seventy-five bee-hives, and one horse and vehicle belonging to a person maimed or crippled and necessary for his business. Tools or implements of a mechanic or artisan; notary's seal; office furniture and records; instruments and books, etc., of surgeon, physician, music-teacher, surveyor or dentist; professional libraries and furniture of attorneys and judges, and libraries of ministers, editors and school and music-teachers; a miner's cabin, not over $500 in value, with his tools, etc., necessary for his business and not over $500 in value, and two mules, horses, or oxen, and the miner's derrick, not over the value of $1,000. Two oxen, horses or mules and their harness and food for one month, and one cart, wagon, dray, truck, coupe, hack or carriage for one or two horses, by the use of which, a cartman, drayman, truckman, huckster, peddler, hackman, teamster, or other laborer earns his living; and one horse, vehicle, and harness, used by surgeon, physician, constable or minister of the Gospel. Poultry worth not more than $25. Earnings for last thirty days, where necessary for support of family; nautical instruments and apparel of sailors; life insurance policies with annual premium of not more than $500; fire-arms required to be kept by law, and one gun; cemeteries.

CONNECTICUT.—No homestead laws.

Personal property exempted as follows: Necessary apparel, beds and bedding; household furniture; arms; implements of trade; one oyster boat of value not over $200; one cow of value not over $150; ten sheep of same value; two swine; poultry, not over $25 in value; twenty-five bushels of charcoal, two tons of coal, 200 pounds of flour, two cords of wood, two tons of hay, 200 pounds of beef, five bushels of potatoes or turnips, 200 pounds of fish, ten bushels of corn or rye, twenty pounds of wool or flax; one stove; the horse, buggy, harness, saddle, and bridle of a physician with value of the horse, not over $200; the library of any person, to value of $500; one sewing-machine; burial-lots; pew in church; accrued wages of person having family to support, up to $25; pension-moneys, on allowances from benefit societies.

COLORADO.—The homestead may be of value not exceeding $2,000.

Personal property of the head of a family is exempt, as follows: Household furniture, not exceeding $100; provisions for six months; tools, implements, or stock-in-trade, not over $200; library and implements of professional man, not over $300; working animals to the value of $200; one cow and one calf, ten sheep and necessary food for them for six months; farm wagon, cart, or dray; one plow, one harrow, and other farm implements, including harness and tackle for team, not over $50 in value.

DAKOTA.—A homestead, if in a town plat, must not exceed one acre in extent, and if not in a town plat, it must not contain more than 160 acres, without limitation as to value.

Personal property exempt is as follows: All family pictures; a pew in church; a lot in burial-ground; the family Bible, and all school-books used by the family, and the family library, to the value of $100; all wearing apparel; provisions and fuel for one year. In addition to this the debtor can select from his other personal property, any goods, chattels, money, etc., which he pleases, to the amount of $1 500, which property is also exempt. Instead of this $1,500, there is an enumeration of articles he may take in its place.

DELAWARE.—Family Bible; school-books and family library;

pictures; pew in church; lot in burial-ground; wearing apparel; tools, implements, and fixtures, necessary to carry on a trade, up to the amount of $75 in New Castle and Sussex Counties, and $50 in Kent County.   Household goods of a head of a family, up to $200 in value, in New Castle County, and $100 in Kent and Sussex Counties, are exempt.   No homestead laws.

DISTRICT OF COLUMBIA.—Wearing apparel; beds; bedding; household furniture; stoves; utensils, etc., not exceeding $300 in value; provisions for three month's support; fuel for three months; tools and implements of trade, up to $200 in value; stock up to $200, for carrying on business; library and implements of a professional man or artist, to value of $300; one horse, one mule, or yoke of oxen; one cart, wagon or dray, and harness; farming utensils and farming tools, up to $100 in value; family pictures and library, up to $400 in value; one cow, one swine, six sheep, the earnings of married residents who provide for support of a family, for two months, not to exceed $100 each month.

FLORIDA.—A homestead to the extent of 160 acres, or of one-half an acre, if within an incorporated city or town, owned by the head of a family, is exempt.   It cannot be sold by the owner without his wife's consent.

Personal property to be selected by the owner to the amount of $1,000 is also exempt.

GEORGIA.—The property, real or personal, or both, of the head of a family, or a guardian of minor children, or of infirm or aged person, or of a person having the care and support of a dependent female, is exempt up to the aggregate amount of $1,600.   If this exemption is not claimed, there are other exemptions of specific articles allowed.

IDAHO.—The law of this Territory is substantially the same as in California.

ILLINOIS.—A householder with a family may claim a homestead in land, up to the value of $1,000.

Personal property is exempt as follows: Wearing apparel; Bibles; school-books; family pictures; other property to be selected to the value of $100.   In addition to this, the head of a family may claim, as exempt, other property of the value of $300. Where the exemption is claimed, the debtor must deliver to the officer a schedule under oath of the exempt property, and all his other personal property.

INDIANA.—The property of a resident householder, either real or personal, is exempt to the amount of $600. The debtor claiming the exemption must give a sworn schedule of his property to the officer.

IOWA.—A homestead, if within a town plat, must not exceed one-half an acre; if without, not more than forty acres, without limitation in either case as to value.

The personal property of a person not the head of a family is not exempt, except his ordinary wearing apparel and trunk. If he is the head of a family, his property is exempt as follows: Wearing apparel, and trunks; one musket, or rifle, and shot-gun; all private libraries, family Bible, portraits, pictures, musical instruments, and paintings not kept for sale; a pew in church; a lot in a burying-ground, not to exceed one acre; two cows and a calf, one horse, fifty sheep, six stands of bees, five hogs, and all pigs under five months; necessary food for these animals for six months; flax raised on less than one acre; one bedstead and necessary bedding for every two in the family; household and kitchen furniture of $200 in value; all spinning-wheels and looms; one sewing-machine, and other instruments of domestic labor; tools, instruments or books, of a farmer, mechanic, surveyor, clergyman, lawyer, physician, teacher or professor; the horse or two horses, or mules, or yoke of cattle and the wagon and harness of a physician, public officer, farmer, teamster or laborer, earning his living by their use; a printer's press and type and material of the value of $1,200; earnings of debtor within ninety days.

KANSAS.—A homestead to the extent of 160 acres of farming land, or one acre within an incorporated town or city is exempt.

The personal property of a resident, who is not the head of a family, is only exempt as to the following: wearing apparel; a church pew; a burial-lot; necessary tools or implements of trade;

stock-in-trade not exceeding $400 in value; the library, imple-ments, and office furniture of a professional man.

The property of the head of a family is exempt as follows:

Family books; musical instruments; church pew; burial-lot; all wearing apparel, bedsteads, bedding, stoves, cooking utensils; one sewing-machine; all implements of industry; $500 worth of other household furniture; two cows, ten hogs, one yoke of oxen, one horse or mule, or span of horses or mules, twenty sheep and their wool; the necessary food for these animals; one wagon, cart, or dray; two plows, one drag, and other farming utensils, to value of $300; provisions and fuel for the family for one year; tools and implements of mechanics, etc.; stock in trade to amount of $400; the library, implements, and office furniture of a profes-sional man.

KENTUCKY.—The property of a resident housekeeper with a family is exempt as follows: two work-beasts, or one and yoke of oxen, two cows and calves, five sheep, wearing apparel, and the usual household and kitchen furniture to value of $100; one sew-ing-machine, one two-horse wagon, or ox-cart, one set of gear, washing apparatus worth $50, carpeting for one room, all school-books, a prayer-book, hymn-book, one bureau, one wardrobe, one wash-stand, one clock, six cups and saucers, six plates, six knives and forks; the libraries of preachers, professional libraries of law-yers, physicians and surgeons, and their instruments, to the amount of $500; one horse and cart, or dray, for a laboring man; tools of a mechanic with a family to the value of $100, the wages of employes, etc., not exceeding $50 unless the debt was contract-ed for food, raiment, or house-rent.

Land, including the dwelling-house of the debtor, to the value of $1,000 is also exempt as a homestead.

LOUISIANA.—The homestead of the debtor owned and occupied by him is exempt; if the head of a family there is also exempt: one work-horse, one wagon or cart, one yoke of oxen, two cows and calves, twenty-five head of hogs, 1,000 pounds of bacon or equivalent in pork, necessary corn and fodder for a year on a farm, and necessary farming implements; wearing apparel, beds and bedding; arms; tools, instruments and books necessary for the exercise of trade or profession, money due for the salary of an officer, laborers' wages, cooking stove and utensils, dining articles, wash-tubs, family portraits, and musical instruments used by the family. The property exempt cannot exceed $2,000. The widow or minor children of a deceased debtor in want, are entitled to claim $1,000 before any debts are paid.

MAINE.—Personal property is exempt as follows: wearing apparel; household furniture to the value of $50, one bedstead, bed, and bedding for each two members, family portraits, Bibles, school-books, copy of State statutes, library worth $150, pew in use, one cooking and all warming stoves, charcoal, twelve cords of wood, five tons anthracite and fifty bushels of bituminous coal, ten dollars' worth of lumber, wood, or bark, all produce until harvested, one barrel of flour, thirty bushels of corn, grain and potatoes, half an acre of flax and manufactures therefrom, tools of trade, sewing-machine worth $100, one pair working cattle, or one pair of mules or horses worth $300, and hay to keep them through the winter, one harness worth $20, for each horse or mule, a horse-sled or ox-sled, two swine, one cow and a heifer under three years, or two cows, ten sheep with their wool and lambs until one year old, hay to keep them through winter, $50 worth of domestic fowls, one plow, one cart or truck wagon, one harrow, one yoke with bows, ring and staple, two chains, one ox-sled, one mowing-machine, fishing-boat of two tons, life insurance policies, except excess of annual cash premiums of $250.

Real estate worth $500. The owner must file a certificate with the Register of Deeds.

MARYLAND.—Wearing apparel; books, and mechanic's tools and $100 worth of other property, to be selected by the debtor, are exempt.

MASSACHUSETTS.—Wearing apparel; one bed, etc.; one iron stove for warming the dwelling-house, fuel not exceeding $20 in value; one sewing-machine to the value of $100; necessary household furniture to value of $300; Bibles, school-books and library to value of $50; one cow, six sheep, one swine, and two tons of hay; tools of trade and fixtures to value of $100; stock in trade to amount of $100; shares in co-operative associations to the value of $20; necessary provisions worth $50; pew in church; boat, fishing-tackle, and nets of fishermen, used by them in their business to the value of $100; uniform of officer or soldier, in militia, and his arms, etc.; tombs in use for burial of the dead.

A homestead, not exceeding $800 in value, owned by a householder with a family, is also exempt, provided a homestead claim is recorded.

MICHIGAN.—The following personal property is exempt: Pew in church; cemeteries, etc.; arms and accouterments; wearing apparel; the library and school-books to the value of $150; all family pictures. If a householder: Ten sheep and their fleeces, two cows, five swine; provisions and fuel for six months; all household goods, furniture and utensils, not exceeding $250 in value. The tools, implements, material, stock, apparatus, team (one pair of horses or one yoke of oxen), vehicle, harness, necessary for debtor's trade or occupation to the value of $250, and necessary food for the animals for six months.

A homestead of a householder, not exceeding forty acres of land, and the house thereon in the country, or, if in a city or village, a house and lot to the value of $1,500, are exempt. The owner cannot sell or convey such property without the written consent of his wife, if he have one.

MINNESOTA.— Personal property is exempt as follows: Family Bible, pictures, school-books, library, musical instruments; pew in church; lot in burial ground; wearing apparel, and bedding; stoves and appendages; cooking utensils; other household furniture not exceeding $500 in value; three cows, ten swine, one yoke of oxen and a horse (or a span of horses or mules), twenty sheep and their wool, necessary food for stock for one year; one wagon, cart or dray, one sleigh, two plows, one drag; other farming utensils to the value of $300; one sewing-machine; grain for one year's seed, not exceeding fifty bushels of wheat, fifty bushels of oats, thirty bushels of barley, fifteen bushels of potatoes, and three bushels of corn; provisions and fuel for debtor's family for one year; tools of mechanics, etc.; stock-in-trade not exceeding $400; library and implements of a professional man; the wages of laborers not exceeding $20 for work done within ninety days; all presses, stones, type, cases and other tools in use by any partnership or printer, to value of $2,000, together with stock-in-trade to value of $400.

A homestead not exceeding forty acres, and the dwelling thereon; or a lot in an incorporated village, city or town having over five thousand inhabitants, or one-half an acre in a village, city or town of less than that number, is exempt.

MISSISSIPPI.—Two horses or mules, or one yoke of oxen; two cows and calves, five head of stock-hogs, five sheep, 150 bushels of corn, 300 bundles of fodder, ten bushels of wheat or rice, 200 pounds of meat; one cart or wagon worth $100; one sewing-machine; household and kitchen furniture worth $100; crops while growing are exempt. For persons living in a city, town or village, personal property to the value of $250 is exempt, and may be selected by the debtor. Wages of laborer to the amount of $100 are exempt. Tools of a mechanic; implements of a farmer necessary for two male laborers; books of a student; wearing apparel; the libraries of attorneys, physicians and ministers; the instruments of surgeons and dentists worth $250; arms and accouterments of a militiaman; globes, books and maps used by teachers; the amount of life insurance policy not exceeding $10,000.

A homestead of a householder with a family, not to exceed $2,000 in value, or a farm of eighty acres in the country, is exempt.

MISSOURI.—Wearing apparel, tools and implements of mechanic are exempt. Also, if debtor is the head of a family; ten hogs, ten sheep and their wool, two cows and calves; two plows, one ax, one hoe, one set of plow gears, necessary farm implements for one man; working animals to the value of $150; spinning-wheel and cards; one loom and apparatus; spun yarn, thread and cloth; hemp, flax and wool, not exceeding twenty-five pounds each; four beds and bedding; furniture worth $100; arms, etc.; provisions worth $100; Bibles and other books in use, grave-stones and a pew; tools of mechanic; lawyers, ministers and physicians may select books and medicines in the place of other property, which is exempt. The head of a family may select and keep in place of the live-stock and implements exempt, any other property worth $300.

A homestead worth $3,000 in a city of over 40,000 inhabitants, not larger than eighteen square rods of ground, is exempt. In the country and in cities, the homestead cannot exceed $1,500 in value; nor thirty square rods in extent in cities; or 160 acres in the country. A homestead may be sold or mortgaged without the consent of the wife, unless she has filed a claim in the Recorder's office. .

MONTANA.—Clothing, chairs, tables, desks and books, to value of $100; household furniture; provisions and fuel for two months; one sewing-machine, worth $100; one horse, two cows and calves, two swine, fifty domestic fowls. A farmer may keep his farming utensils, not exceeding $600 in value; two oxen, or one horse or mule and their harness, two cows, one cart or wagon, food for such stock for three months; $200 worth of seeds, grain or vegetables for planting; the tools of mechanics; the instruments and books of physicians, dentists, lawyers and clergymen. To a miner, his dwelling, not exceeding $500 in value, and all his tools and machinery, worth $500, one horse, mule, or two oxen, and their harness, and their food for three months. One horse, mule or two oxen, vehicle and harness of a physician or clergyman, and food for such stock for three months; arms, etc.; wages for last thirty days, if necessary, for family.

A homestead, not exceeding in value $2,500. If a farm, not more than 160 acres; if in a town, city or village, not more than one quarter of an acre.

NEBRASKA.—A homestead is exempt to the value of $2,000. If in a city or town, it must not exceed half an acre; if in the country, not more than 160 acres.

In case the debtor has no land, he may claim and keep $500 worth of personal property as exempt. Besides this, the following personal property is exempt: clothing of the family; family supplies for six months; supplies for domestic animals for three months; furniture; family Bible and picture-books; cooking utensils, domestic animals, tools and implements of trade; sixty days' wages to laboring men, clerks, etc.

NEVADA.—Personal property is exempt as follows: chairs, tables, desks and books, to the value of $100; household furniture; provisions and fuel for one month; farming utensils and seed for next six months, to the value of $200; two horses, two oxen or two mules, and two cows, and food for one month; one cart and wagon; tools of mechanic; instruments and libraries of surgeon, physician, surveyor or dentist; the professional libraries of attorneys and counsellors, or ministers of the gospel; the dwelling of a miner, worth $500; his tools, worth $500, and two horses, two oxen, or two mules and harness; one cart or wagon, used by teamster or laborer to earn his living with the horses, etc.; one horse, harness and vehicle of a physician, or surgeon, or minister, and food for the animal for one month; one sewing-machine, worth not more than $150; all fire-engines and property of fire-companies; arms, etc.

A homestead, to be selected by the husband or wife, or head of a family, not exceeding in value $5,000, is exempt. A homestead must be recorded. It cannot be alienated, except by consent of both parties, in writing, as in a joint deed or mortgage.

NEW HAMPSHIRE.—Following personal property is exempt: wearing apparel; household furniture, worth $100; necessary beds and bedding; one cooking stove and furniture; one sewing-machine; Bibles and school-books; library, to value of $200; one cow, six sheep and their fleeces; one hog, one pig and slaughtered pork; four tons of hay; provisions and fuel, to the value of $50; tools of trade, worth $100; a yoke of oxen or a horse; uniform, arms, etc., of militiaman; pew in church; lot in cemetery.

A homestead of the value of $500 is exempt.

NEW JERSEY.—All wearing apparel of the debtor and his family, and other personal property to the amount of $200 is exempt. A homestead, including lot and building, occupied as a residence by a debtor with a family, to the value of $1,000, is exempt.

NEW MEXICO.—Personal property is exempt as follows: clothing, beds, etc.; fuel for thirty days; Bibles, hymn-books, testaments, school-books, family and religious pictures; provisions to the amount of $25; kitchen furniture, to the amount of $10; all tools and implements of trade, not to exceed $20 in value.

A homestead to the value of $1,000, belonging to a head of a family, is exempt.

NEW YORK —Personal property, owned by a householder, is exempt as follows: All spinning-wheels, weaving-looms, and stoves, in dwelling-house; one sewing-machine and appurtenances; family Bible, family pictures, school-books; other books not exceeding in value $50 used in the family; pew in church; ten sheep with their fleeces, yarn or cloth manufactured therefrom; one cow, two swine; necessary food for such animals; all necessary meat, fish, flour and vegetables ; necessary fuel, oil, and candles for the use of the family for sixty days; wearing apparel, bed, bedsteads, and bedding; six chairs, six knives, six forks, six spoons, six plates, six teacups, six saucers; one sugar dish, one milk pot, one teapot, one crane and appendages, one pair of andirons, one coal-scuttle, one shovel, one pair of tongs, one lamp, and one candle-stick; tools and implements of mechanics worth $25; necessary household furniture, working tools, and team, professional instruments, furniture and library worth $250; necessary food for the team for ninety days; earnings for sixty days. A woman is entitled to these exemptions in every case, even if not a householder. A lot in a burying-ground, already actually used for that purpose, and not exceeding one-quarter of an an acre is exempt.

A homestead owned by a householder with a family is exempt to the value of $1,000. There must be a notice filed in the Register's or County Clerk's office.

NORTH CAROLINA.—Personal property to be selected by the debtor is exempt to the amount of $500.

A homestead to the value of $1,000 is exempt.

OHIO.—Personal property of a person with a family is exempt as follows: Wearing apparel, necessary beds, etc.; two stoves and fuel for sixty days; certain domestic animals and their food for sixty days; or, household furniture of equal value to the amount of $65; family books and pictures; provisions to the amount of $50, and other necessary household furniture to same amount; one sewing-machine, one knitting-machine; tools and implements of trade to the value of $100; personal earnings of debtor and his minor child for three months. A drayman can keep one horse, harness and dray. A farmer, one horse, or one yoke of cattle, with necessary gearing, and one wagon. A physician, one horse, one saddle and bridle, and professional books, medicines and implements worth $100. An unmarried woman can hold exempt; wearing apparel worth $100; one sewing-machine; Bible, etc., and other books worth $25.

A homestead owned by the head of a family is exempt to the value of $1,000.

Any resident with a family may, if he owns no homestead, hold other personal property beside that expressly exempt, to the amount of $500.

OREGON.—Books, pictures and musical instruments to value of $75; necessary wearing apparel to value of $100, and if debtor has family, to value of $50 for each member of the family; tools, implements, apparatus, teams, vehicle, harness, of library necessary f r trade of profession, to value of $400; food for team for sixty days. Beside this, a householder may hold exempt: ten sheep and one year's fleece, two cows and five swine; household goods, furniture and utensils to value of $300; food for such animals for three months, provisions for family use for six months; pew in church; all property of the State, county, city, town, etc.

PENNSYLVANIA.—Wearing apparel, Bibles, and school-books and other property, real or personal, to the amount of $300 is exempt. The privilege may be waived. All sewing-machines belonging to seamstresses are exempt. There is no homestead exemption.

RHODE ISLAND.—The following property is exempt: the necessary wearing apparel of a debtor and his family; necessary working tools not exceeding $200 in value; household furniture and family stores worth $300; Bible, school and other books in use in the family; one cow, one and a half tons of hay; one hog, one pig, and the pork of same, of a housekeeper; arms, etc., of militiaman; pew in church; a burial-lot; mariner's wages until after voyage; ten dollars due as wages of labor.

SOUTH CAROLINA.—Personal property of the head of a family is exempt as follows: household furniture; beds and bedding; family library; arms, carts, wagons, farming implements, tools, neat cattle, work animals, swine, goats and sheep, not to exceed in value $500.

The family homestead of the head of a family is exempt to the value of $1,000.

TENNESSEE.—Personal property exempt is as follows: To the head of a family, necessary clothing, household and kitchen furniture, one cooking stove and utensils; necessary plate; Bible, hymn-book and school-books; two cows and calves, two horses or two mules, or one horse and mule and one yoke of oxen, one ox-cart, yoke, staple, etc., one wagon not worth more than $75; one man's and one woman's saddle and bridle; large quantities of food and fuel; fifty head of sheep and their fleece; twenty-five stands of bees; farming implements; to a mechanic, one set of tools; if he is the head of a family, $200 worth of lumber or material, or products of his labor; wages of labor to amount of $30.

A homestead belonging to the head of a family to the value of $1,000 is exempt.

TEXAS.—Personal property exempted to every family: All household and kitchen furniture; lots in cemetery; all implements of husbandry; tools and apparatus of trade or profession, and all books belonging to private or public libraries; family portraits and pictures; five milch cows and calves, two yoke of work oxen; two horses and one wagon; one carriage or buggy; one gun; twenty hogs; twenty head of sheep; all provisions on hand for family; necessary bridles, harness and saddles. To every citizen not the head of a family is exempted: one horse, bridle and saddle; all wearing apparel; lot in cemetery; tools, apparatus and books of trade and profession; or private library; wages.

The homestead of a family not to exceed 200 acres is exempt. If it is in a city, town, or village, it can exceed $5,000 in value.

UTAH.—Personal property is exempt as follows: chairs, tables, desks and books of the value of $100: household furniture, wearing apparel, one bedstead, etc., for every two persons, provisions and fuel for sixty days; farming implements, two oxen, horses or mules, and harness; cow and calf; one cart or wagon; food for animals for six y days; seed-grain and vegetables worth $100; tools and implements of a mechanic or artisan, surgeon, physician, surveyor, and dentist, with their libraries; the law library of an attorney; the library of a minister; tent or cabin of a miner, with table, camp-stools, bed, necessary tools not exceeding $400 in value, and provisions for thirty days; two oxen or horses or mules, and harness, and cart or wagon by which a cartman or laborer habitually earns his living, and food for animals for sixty days; horse, harness, and vehicle of physician, surgeon or minister; one sewing-machine, worth $100. If debtor is head of family, there is also exempt: five sheep and wool for every person in the family, two hogs, three pigs, and necessary food for sixty days; all flax and clothes; all spinning-wheels and looms; earnings for sixty days. Fire-apparatus, arms and public buildings are also exempt.

A homestead may be claimed by the head of a family in land to the value of $1,000; and the further sum of $250 for each member of the family.

VERMONT.—Personal property is exempt as follows: Suitable apparel, bedding, tools, arms and necessary household furniture; one sewing-machine, one cow, the best swine, or the meat of one swine, ten sheep; one year's products from wool of ten sheep; forage for animals for one winter; ten cords of fire-wood, or five tons of coal, twenty bushels of potatoes; arms, etc.; all growing crops, ten bushels of grain, one barrel of flour, three swarms of bees with hives and honey, two hundred pounds of sugar; grave-stones; Bibles and family books; pew in church; live poultry worth $10; professional books or instruments of physicians, clergymen and lawyers, to the value of $200; one yoke of oxen or steers, two horses in lieu of oxen or steers, but not worth more than $200; forage for these animals through the winter; arms; two-horse wagon, or ox-cart. with hames, etc.; one sled; two harnesses, two halters, two chains, one plow, and one ox-yoke, which, with the animals, shall not exceed $250 in value.

A homestead to the value of $500 is exempt.

VIRGINIA.—Personal property is exempt as follows: Family Bible; family pictures; school-books, and library for use of family, not exceeding $100 in value; pew in church; lot in burial-ground; wearing apparel, beds, stoves; one cow, one horse; six chairs, other household utensils; provisions and forage in small quantities; cooking-stove; sewing-machine; mechanic's tools to value of $100. A farmer may also keep a yoke of oxen, a pair of horses or mules, with two plows and other implements.

The homestead exemption permits the debtor to keep property either real or personal to the value of $2,000.

WASHINGTON TERRITORY.—Personal property is exempt as follows: To a householder, all wearing apparel; private libraries; family pictures and keepsakes; beds necessary; other household goods to value of $150; two cows with their calves, five swine; two stands of bees, twenty-five domestic fowls; provision and fuel for six months. A farmer may keep one span of horses and harness, or two yokes of oxen, one wagon; farming utensils worth $200. Mechanic's tools of trade are exempt to value of $500; a physician's library, horse and carriage, instruments and medicines; the libraries of attorneys and clergymen to value of $500; fire-arms; small boat not worth more than $50; team of drayman. To a person engaged in logging, three yokes of work oxen and implements to the value of $300.

The homestead of a householder with a family is exempt to the value of $1,000. The word " homestead" must be entered in the margin of the record of title.

WEST VIRGINIA.—A husband or parent may select and keep personal property from seizure for debt to the amount of $200. Any resident mechanic or laborer may keep the working tools of his trade up to the value of $200.

A homestead worth $1,000, belonging to a husband or parent, is exempt.   It must be recorded as a homestead in the public land records of the county.

WISCONSIN.—Personal property is exempt as follows: family Bible; family pictures and school-books; the debtor's library; all wearing apparel, beds, stoves and cooking utensils; other household furniture, to amount of $200 in value; one gun, rifle, or firearm, worth not more than $50; two cows, ten swine, one yoke of oxen, one horse or mule, or two horses or two mules, ten sheep and wool; necessary food for this stock for one year; one wagon, cart, or dray, one sleigh, one plow, one drag; other farming utensils, worth $50; provisions for one year's support; tools and implements or stock-in-trade of mechanic, miner, etc., to value of $200; library and implements of any professional man, not exceeding $200; one sewing-machine; all inventions; sixty days' earnings of married persons, etc.; money arising from insurance of exempt property; money arising from life insurance, made in favor of wife; printing material, and press or presses, to the value of $1,500; books, maps, plates and papers, used for making abstracts of title; pew in church; lot in burial-ground.

A homestead not exceeding forty acres in the country, or one-fourth of an acre if in a city, town or village.

WYOMING.—Personal property is exempt as follows: wearing apparel of every person; to the head of a family, the family Bible, pictures and school-books; lot in cemetery; furniture, bedding, provisions, and other articles to be selected by the debtor to the amount of $500.

The tools, team and implements, or stock-in-trade of a mechanic, miner, or other person, is exempt to value of $300; also the library, instruments or implements of a professional man, not to exceed $300.

The homestead of the head of a family, not to exceed $1,500 in value, is exempt.   It may consist of a house and lot in a city or town, or a farm of not more than 160 acres.

EXEMPTION FROM JURY DUTY.

THE following is a statement of the law of New York as to the persons who are exempt from jury duty. It will be found that the provisions of the other States on this subject are substantially the same.

In order to be qualified to serve as a juror in any trial, a person must be a male citizen of the United States, and a resident of the county, He must be not less than twenty-one, nor more than sixty years of age. It is necessary that he should be the owner of, and assessed for, personal property, belonging to him in his own right, to the amount of $250; or the owner of a freehold estate in real property, situated in the county, belonging to him in his own right, to the value of $150; or the husband of a woman who is the owner of a like freehold estate, belonging to her in her own right.

A person to be a juror must also be in the possession of his natural faculties, and not infirm or decrepit. He must be free from all legal exceptions, of fair character, of approved integrity, of sound judgment and well-informed.

Who are Absolutely Disqualified. The following persons are absolutely disqualified to serve as trial jurors: The Governor; the Lieutenant-governor, the Governor's Private Secretary; the Secretary of State; the Comptroller; the State Treasurer; the Attorney-General; the State Engineer and Surveyor; a Canal Commissioner; an Inspector of State Prisons;

a Canal Appraiser; the Superintendent of Public Instruction; the Superintendent of the Bank Department; the Superintendent of the Insurance Department; and the Deputy of each of these officers.

A member of the Legislature, during the session of the House of which he is a member, a Judge of a Court of Record, a Surrogate, a Sheriff, Undersheriff, Deputy Sheriff, the Clerk and Deputy Clerk of a Court of Record, are also disqualified.

Who May Claim Exemption. The following persons, although qualified, may claim exemption from jury service. If they do not choose to make the claim, however, they are entitled to serve.

A clergyman, or a minister of religion, officiating as such, and not following any other calling.

A resident officer of, or an attendant, assistant, teacher, or other person, actually employed in a State asylum for lunatics, idiots, or habitual drunkards.

The agent or warden of a State prison.

The keeper of a county jail; or, a person actually employed in a State prison or county jail.

A practicing physician or surgeon, having patients requiring his daily professional attention.

An attorney or counsellor-at-law regularly employed in the practice of the law as a means of livelihood.

A professor or teacher in a college or academy.

A person actually employed in a glass, cotton, linen, woolen, or iron manufacturing company, by the year, month, or season.

A superintendent, engineer, or collector, on a canal, authorized by the laws of the State which is actually constructed and navigated.

A master, engineer, assistant-engineer, or fireman, actually employed upon a steam vessel, making regular trips.

A superintendent, conductor, or engineer, employed by a railroad company, other than a street-railroad company; or an operator or assistant operator, employed by a telegraph company; who is actually doing duty in an office, or along the railroad or telegraph line of the company by which he is employed.

An officer, non-commissioned officer, musician, or private of the National Guard of the State, performing military duty; or a person who has been honorably discharged from the National Guard, after five years' service, in either capacity.

A member of a fire-company, or fire department, duly organized according to the laws of the State, and performing his duties therein; or a person who, after faithfully serving five successive years in such a fire-company, or fire department, has been honorably discharged therefrom.

A duly licensed engineer of steam boilers, actually employed as such.

Besides these exceptions a person may be excused from serving in the following cases:

When he is a Justice of the Peace, or executes any other civil office, the duties of which are at the time inconsistent with his attendance as a juror.

When he is a teacher in a school, actually employed and serving as such.

When for any other reason, the interests of the public, or of the juror, will be materially injured by his attendance; or his own health, or the health of a member of his family, requires his absence; or he is temporarily incapacitated for any reason from properly discharging the duties of a juror.

CHAPTER XXVI.

A BRIEF DICTIONARY OF LEGAL WORDS AND PHRASES.

A MENSA ET THORO. Divorce from bed and board; partial divorce.

A VINCULA MATRIMONII. Divorce from the bonds of matrimony; absolute divorce.

AB INITIO. From the beginning.

ABANDONMENT. The act of husband in deserting his wife, or wife in deserting her husband. *Shipping:* The relinquishment of property to marine insurers.

ABATEMENT. Suspension of a suit. *Wills:* The reducing of a legacy in amount.

ABDUCTION. The taking away of a child, or wife, or servant by force.

ACCEPTOR. One who accepts a bill of exchange by writing the word " accepted " across the face and signing his name.

ACCEPTOR SUPRA PROTEST. One who accepts a bill which has been protested.

ACCOMMODATION PAPER. Promissory notes or bills of exchange without any consideration, made or drawn for the accommodation of another person.

ACKNOWLEDGMENT. The declaration of one who has executed a deed or other instrument, before a

Notary Public or some competent official to the effect that he acknowledges the execution.

ACT OF GOD. An occurrence which is caused by some natural agency without the interference of man.

ACTION. A suit in a court of justice.

AD LITEM. For the suit.

ADJUSTMENT. (Insurance.) The determining of the amount of a loss.

ADMINISTRATION. The management of the estate of a deceased person who has left no will, or where there is no executor.

ADMINISTRATOR. One appointed to administer on the estate of an intestate.

ADVANCEMENT. A gift before death by a parent to a child to establish him in life

ADVOCATE. A lawyer who pleads in the courts.

AFFIDAVIT. A statement in writing sworn to before a Notary Public or other official authorized to take an oath.

AGENCY. The relation by which one persons acts for another.

AGENT. One who acts for another.

AGREEMENT. A meeting of the minds, or assent of two or more parties to a contract.

ALIBI. Presence in another place.

ALIEN. A foreigner; a citizen of another country.

ALIMONY. The allowance which a husband is obliged to pay his divorced wife for her maintenance.

ALIENATION. The transfer of real estate.

AMBIGUITY. Uncertainty of meaning.

APPORTIONMENT. The division of anything, such as rent, into proportionate parts.

APPRAISEMENT. A valuation of property.

APPROPRIATION OF PAYMENTS. The application of a payment made by debtor, to one of several debts owed by him.

APPURTENANCES. Things or rights incidental to another thing, and which go with it.

ARBITRATION. The hearing and determination of a controversy by persons selected by the parties.

ARSON. The malicious burning of a building.

ARTICLES. A written document which is divided into various topics; contract of partnership.

ASSETS. All the property of a debtor.

ASSIGN. To transfer to another.

ASSIGNOR. One who assigns.

ASSIGNEE. One to whom property is assigned.

ASSIGNMENT. A transfer of property; as by insolvent debtor.

ASSIZE. A session of court.

ASSUMPSIT. A promise to perform a verbal contract; a form of action to recover damages.

ATTACHMENT. A writ by which the property or the person is taken possession of by the sheriff to await the order of court.

ATTESTATION. The act of witnessing an instrument in writing and signing the name as witness. There is an "attestation clause" at the end of a will.

ATTORNEY. An agent in fact. One who has a power of attorney; an attorney-at-law, a lawyer

AVERAGE. (See general average.)

AVERMENT. A mere statement of facts.

AWARD. The judgment of arbitrators.

BAIL. Persons who become sureties for the appearance of another person in court.

BAILMENT. The delivery of personal property by one person to another to be returned at some future time.

BANKRUPT. One who cannot pay his debts.

BARGAIN AND SALE. A form of deed of land.

BENCH WARRANT. An order of a judge issued from the bench.

BEQUEST. A gift of personal property by will.

BETTERMENTS. Improvements made on an estate.

BIGAMY. The crime of contracting a second marriage when a husband or wife is known to be living.

BILL. A complaint in a Court of Equity or Chancery.

BILL OF EXCHANGE. An order in writing by one person on another to pay a third person a sum of money.

BILL OF LADING. A receipt for goods received for transportation.

BILL OF SALE. An instrument under seal by which one person transfers his personal property to another.

BOND. An obligation under seal, usually to pay a debt.

BOTTOMRY. A peculiar kind of mortgage, made only on ships.

BRIEF. A paper containing the leading points of a lawyer's argument.

BROKER. One who negotiates contracts for others.

BY-BIDDING. Bidding at an auction sale at the request or order of the seller of the goods, for the purpose of obtaining a higher price.

CANCELLATION. The act of crossing out a writing.

CAPIAS AD SATISFACIENDUM (CA. SA.). A writ by which a Sheriff is directed to arrest a judgment debtor for the debt.

CASE. The facts on which an action is based.

CAUSE OF ACTION. Matter for which an action may be brought; the case.

CAVEAT. A notice not to issue a patent of a particular kind, filed by an inventor.

CAVEAT EMPTOR. "Let the purchaser look out for his own interests." The seller is not liable for defects in the article sold unless he has expressly warranted it.

CERTIFIED CHECK. A check which has been presented at the bank; and received the approval of the proper officer, as drawn against existing deposits. The bank is liable on the check after certification.

CERTIORARI. A writ from a superior to an inferior Court, directing the removal of an action from the latter to the former.

CESTUI QUE TRUST. The person for whose benefit the trustee holds the property; the beneficiary.

CHALLENGE. An exception to a juror.

CHAMPERTY. An agreement with a party to an

action, for a portion of what may be recovered in consideration of paying the expenses of the suit.

CHARGE. A burden upon an estate; the address of a judge to a jury.

CHARTER-PARTY. A written contract for the hiring of a ship.

CHATTEL. Any article of personal property.

CHECK. An order upon a bank or bankers by a person having deposits with it or them to pay a third party a sum of money.

CHOSE IN ACTION. A right to recover a debt.

CITATION. A writ in the nature of a summons, issued from Probate or Surrogate's Court.

CODE. A body of statute law, prescribed by the Legislature.

CODICIL. An added clause to a will.

COLLATERAL SECURITY. A separate obligation attached to another contract as security.

COMMISSIONS. Compensation allowed to agents, executors, assignees, etc.

COMMITTEE. One or more persons appointed to take charge of the person or estate of a lunatic.

COMMON CARRIER. One who carries goods for hire for the public generally.

COMMON LAW. The unwritten law derived from England, and deduced from the decisions of judges.

COMPLAINT. The document in which the plaintiff in an action states his case.

COMPOUNDING A FELONY. Agreeing not to prosecute one guilty of felony for a valuable consideration.

CONDONATION. Forgiveness by husband or wife of a matrimonial offense.

CONFIRMATION. Ratification of the unauthorized acts of an agent; a deed making a voidable deed or contract valid.

CONSIDERATION. That for which the promise in a contract is given; the price.

CONSIGNOR. One who ships goods.

CONSIGNEE. One to whom goods are shipped.

CONTEMPT. Willful disregard of the order of court; disorder in court.

CONTINGENT REMAINDER. An interest in an estate which may or may not come to a person, depending upon an uncertain event.

CONVERSION. The appropriation of the personal property of another to one's own use.

CONVEYANCE. The transfer of title of land from one person to another; a deed.

COPYRIGHT. The exclusive privilege of printing and selling copies of books and drawings.

CORPUS DELICTI. The body of the offense; the essence of the crime.

COSTS. The expenses of the parties in an action at law. Do not include counsel fees.

COUNSELLOR. A lawyer who advises on matters of law

COVENANT. A separate agreement in a deed or instrument under seal.

COVERTURE. The legal condition of a married woman.

CREDITOR. One to whom a debt is due.

CRIM CON. Criminal conversation, or adultery with a married woman.

CROSS-EXAMINATION. The examination of a witness by the party opposed to the side which called him.

CUL DE SAC. A street open at one end only.

CURTESY. The life estate of a husband in the land of his wife, to which he is entitled if a child is born during the marriage.

DAMAGES. The compensation recovered by a person who has suffered injury of any kind from another.

DAYS OF GRACE, Three days allowed to the maker of a note or the acceptor of a bill of exchange in which to pay it after the time is up.

DE JURE. Of right; lawfully; by law.

DE LUNATICO INQUIRENDO. A writ to ascertain whether a certain person is a lunatic or not.

DE NOVO. Anew; all over again.

DE SON TORT. Of his own wrong. An executor *de son tort* is one who assumes to act as executor without authority.

DEAD-FREIGHT. Money paid for space in a vessel which is not occupied.

DEBTOR. One who owes a debt.

DECEDENT. A deceased person.

DECLARATION. The statement of the plaintiff's case or cause of action; the complaint.

DECLARATION OF TRUST. An acknowledgement that property held by the trustee belongs to another. A deed or will creating a trust.

DECREE. The judgment of a Court of Equity.

DEDICATION. A donation of land to some public use by a private individual.

DEED. A written instrument under seal, transferring the title of the property from one person to another.

DEED POLL. A deed made by one party only.

DEFAMATION. Slander of a person.

DEFEASANCE. An instrument or clause in an instrument which defeats or changes the operation of a deed.

DEFENSE. Any reasons which may be alleged to defend the persons sued from the claim of the plaintiff.

DEFENDANT. The party sued in an action.

DEL CREDERE COMMISSION. A large commission to an agent who insures the principal a certain price.

DELECTUS PERSONARUM. The choice of persons. The right of any partner to object to the introduction of any new member in the firm.

DEMAND. A legal claim or obligation.

DEMISE. A conveyance of land absolutely, or on lease.

DEMONSTRATIVE LEGACY. A pecuniary legacy, with direction that it be paid from a particular fund.

DEMURRAGE. The payment for the delay of a vessel by the freighter beyond the time allowed.

DEMURRER. An allegation by the defendant that the facts stated by the plaintiff, even if true, do not give him any right to recover

DEPONENT. One who makes an affidavit.

DEPOSITION. The testimony of a witness put in writing.

DERELICT. Abandoned property.

DESCENT. Hereditary succession.

DETAINER. The act of detention of property, or the person of another against his will.

DEVIATION. Any variation by a ship from its course, or the risks insured against. It avoids the policy.

DEVISE. A gift of real property by a person's last will and testament.

DEVISEE. One to whom a devise is made. .

DEVISOR. One who makes a devise.

DICTUM. A mere opinion of the judge who pronounces judgment.

DIES NON. Days when courts do not transact any business.

DIGEST. A systematic collection of cases.

DISBAR. To expel an attorney-at-law from the bar.

DISCHARGE. The setting free of a prisoner; the cancellation of a mortgage.

DISCLAIMER. A renunciation by a holder of a patent of part of his claim.

DISCOUNT. The interest retained by a bank when it lends money on a note.

DISHONOR. The failure to pay negotiable paper when it falls due.

DISSEIZIN. A taking possession of real estate belonging to another.

DISSOLUTION. The annulling of the binding force of a contract. The winding up of the affairs of a partnership.

DISTRIBUTION. The division of personal property of an intestate among those entitled to it.

DIVIDEND. The percentage of profits divided among stockholders.

DIVORCE. The dissolution of the marriage relation.

DOCKET. The book in which judgments and decrees are recorded.

DOMICIL. The permanent home of any person,

DONATIO. A gift of personal property.

DONOR. The giver.

DONEE. One who receives a gift.

DORMANT. Sleeping; a partner who is not known.

DOUBLE INSURANCE. More than one insurance upon the same property against the same risks.

DOWER. The interest of a widow in the real estate of her deceased husband. She is entitled to a life-estate in one-third of such property.

DRAWEE. A person to whom a bill of exchange is addressed, and who is requested to pay the money.

DRAWER. The party who makes a bill of exchange.

DUE-BILL. An acknowledgment in writing that a debt is owed.

DURESS. The acts or threats of one person leading to fear of personal injury on the part of another.

EARNEST. The payment of something to bind the bargain.

EASEMENT.   A right owned by one man in the land of another.

EFFECTS.   Property.

EJECTMENT.   A form of action by which the title or ownership of real estate is determined.

ELECTION.   Choice; selection.

EMANCIPATION.   The freeing of minor children from parental control, especially from any right of the parent to their earnings.

EMBEZZLEMENT.   The fraudulent appropriation of personal property to one's own use.

EMBLEMENTS.   The crops upon the land of a tenant which are on the land when his lease expires.

EMINENT DOMAIN.   The power of the State to take private property for public purposes on making compensation.

ENJOIN.   To command; to forbid by injunction.

ENTAIL.   Real estate settled on a line of descent or certain classes of issue.

EQUITABLE MORTGAGE.   A lien upon real estate as a security for the payment of a debt, not executed in legal form.

EQUITY.   A branch of remedial justice as distinguished from law.

EQUITY OF REDEMPTION.   The right of the mortgagor of land to redeem it by paying the amount of the debt and the interest; the mortgagor's interest in the land.

ESCHEAT.   The reversion of land to the State in default of heirs.

ESCROW. A deed delivered by the grantor to a person to be delivered to the grantee on the happening of a certain event.

ESTATE. The interest a man has in real property; the property itself.

ESTATE IN COMMON. An estate owned jointly by two or more persons.

ESTATE OF INHERITANCE. An estate which descends to heirs; an estate longer than life.

ESTATE AT SUFFERANCE. The interest of a tenant who has possession of land by permission of the owner and continues to hold over after the permission has expired.

ESTATE AT WILL. A variety of lease by which the tenant is holding possession at the will of the owner without a lease.

ESTATE FOR YEARS. An interest in land under contract or lease for a definite period.

ESTOPPEL. The stopping of one from alleging a fact in excuse in cases where his previous conduct has led the person injured to believe otherwise.

ESTOVERS. The right of a tenant to furnish himself with wood from the leased premises sufficient for fuel.

ESTRAYS. Cattle whose owner is unknown.

EVICTION. Ejecting a person from the possession of land; turning out a tenant for non-payment of rent.

EVIDENCE. That which goes to prove a fact.

EVIDENCE, CIRCUMSTANTIAL. Evidence inferred from circumstances.

EVIDENCE, DIRECT. The direct testimony of an eye-witness.

EX OFFICIO. By virtue of his office.

EX PARTE. On the one part; by one side.

EX POST FACTO. After the act; a law passed after the offense is committed increasing the punishment.

EXCEPTION. Objection to the decision of a court during a trial.

EXCUSABLE HOMICIDE. The killing of a human being in self-defense.

EXECUTED CONTRACT. One that is completely carried out.

EXECUTOR. One who is appointed by a testator to carry out his will.

EXECUTORY CONTRACT. A contract where something remains to be done.

EXECUTRIX. A woman appointed to execute a will.

EXEMPTION. The right of a debtor to retain certain property from the payment of his debts

EXHIBIT. A paper or article offered as part of the evidence at a trial.

EXPERT. One who possesses special skill or knowledge in any art or science.

EXPRESS CONTRACT. A contract openly and specially made.

FACTOR. A commission merchant.

FAILURE OF ISSUE. A want of issue or children to take or devise after a life estate.

FALSE IMPRISONMENT. An unlawful restraint of the liberty of a man.

FALSE PRETENSES. False statements or representations, with a design to obtain property or credit.

FEE-SIMPLE. An estate of inheritance; absolute ownership of real estate.

FIDUCIARY. In trust; a trust relation.

FIERI FACIAS. A writ to the sheriff to make the amount of the debt from the chattels of the judgment debtor.

FILIUS NULLIUS. The son of no one; a bastard.

FILUM AQUÆ. The middle line of a stream.

FINAL JUDGMENT. A judgment which puts an end to the action.

FIREBOTE. Wood which a tenant may cut from the leased land for fuel for house.

FIRM. The persons composing a partnership; the partnership itself.

FIXTURES. Personal chattels affixed to land, and which may be removed by the person who affixed them against the will of the owner of the land.

FORECLOSURE. A proceeding in equity by a mortgagee to recover his debt, and cut off the mortgagor's equity of redemption.

FRANCHISE. A special and exclusive privilege conferred by the government on individuals, or a corporation.

FREEHOLDER. The owner of land in fee or of a life-estate.

FREIGHT. The price agreed upon for the carrying of goods.

FRUCTUS INDUSTRIALES. The products of the soil obtained by cultivation.

FURTHER ASSURANCE. A peculiar covenant in a deed.

GARNISHMENT. The attachment of or notice to a third person to hold property of the debtor, which he has in his possession.

GENERAL ISSUE. An issue of fact raised by a general denial of the plaintiff's charges.

GOOD WILL. The benefit of the custom or trade of a business.

GOODS AND CHATTELS. Personal property, including choses in action.

GRAND JURY. A jury consisting of not less than twelve and not more than twenty-four men, before whom indictments are preferred,

GRAND LARCENY. The stealing of above a certain sum, usually twenty dollars.

GRANT. Any conveyance of real estate.

GROUND RENT. Rent paid for the privilege of building on another man's land.

GUARANTY. A promise to answer for another's debt or liability, if he does not.

GUARANTOR. One who makes a guaranty.

GUARDIAN. One who has possession of the person or property of a child.

GUARDIAN AD LITUM. Guardian for the purposes of an action.

HABEAS CORPUS. A writ directed to a person detaining another, and ordering him to deliver the body at a particular time and place, usually in court.

HABENDUM. A clause in a deed; "to have."

HALF BLOOD. The relationship between persons who only have one parent in common.

HEARSAY EVIDENCE. Evidence which the witness gives on the authority of others. It is not admissible.

HEIR-APPARENT. One who is entitled to the inheritance if he outlives the ancestor.

HEREDITAMENTS. Things capable of being inherited.

HIGH SEAS. The ocean.

HIGH TREASON. Treason against the government.

HOLDING OVER. The act of a tenant in remaining in possession of the premises without the consent of the landlord.

HOLOGRAPH. That which is written in one's own hand.

HOMICIDE. The killing of any human being.

HOTCH-POT. The bringing together of all advancements made by the deceased to his children with the property left by him, in order to determine the share of each child.

HOUSEHOLDER. The head of a family; one who keeps house.

HYPOTHECATION. A pledge of property to secure a debt, which property the creditor may sell if the debt is not paid.

IDEM SONANS. Sounding the same.

IGNORANCE OF LAW EXCUSES NO ONE. Every one is

bound to know the law and cannot plead ignorance as an excuse.

IMPANEL. To write the names of jurors on a panel or schedule. To summon jurors to attend court.

IMPEACHMENT. An accusation by a legislative body against an officer of the government.

IMPLICATION. An inference of something arising from what is expressed.

IMPRIMIS. In the first place.

IN BLANK. Without restriction.

IN ESSE. In being

IN EXTREMIS. In the last moments.

IN FORMA PAUPERIS. In the character of a poor man.

IN FORO CONSCIENTIÆ. Before the tribunal of conscience.

IN INVITUM. Unwillingly.

IN NUBIBUS. In the clouds.

IN PARI DELICTO. In equal fault.

IN PERSOMAM. Against the person.

IN PRÆSENTI. In the present.

IN PROPRIA PERSONA. In his own person.

IN RE. In the matter.

IN REM. Against the thing or the property.

IN RERUM NATURA. In the nature of things.

IN SOLIDO. For the whole. Each partner is liable for firm debts *in solido.*

IN SPECIE. In the same form. In kind.

IN STATU QUO. In the same condition as.

IN TOTO. In the whole.

INCEPTION. The commencement

INCHOATE. That which is not yet completed.

INCORPOREAL HEREDITAMENTS Any property which is inheritable, but not tangible, such as an easement.

INCUMBRANCE. Any lien or burden on land.

INDEFEASIBLE. That which cannot be defeated.

INDEMNITY. That which is given to prevent damage or loss.

INDENTURE. A formal instrument executed by two or more parties with different interests.

INDICTMENT. A written accusation against a person of a crime or misdemeanor.

INDORSEMENT. That which is written on the back of an instrument in writing and having reference to it.

INDORSER. One who indorses.

INDORSEE. One to whom a paper is transferred by indorsement.

INFANT. One under twenty-one years of age.

INFRINGEMENT. Trespassing upon the patent right of another.

INJUNCTION. A writ of a court of equity forbidding the parties enjoined from doing a particular thing.

INQUEST. A judicial inquiry about any matter, as a coroner's inquest.

INSOLVENCY. The condition of being unable to pay one's debts.

INSTALLMENT. A part of a debt due by contract,

and payable at a different time from the other part or parts.

INSTRUMENT. A writing containing an agreement.

INSURABLE INTEREST. Any interest in property which will entitle a person to insure it, even if not the owner.

INSURANCE. A contract for indemnity for loss.

INTER VIVOS. Between the living; gifts *inter vivos* are gifts from one living person to another.

INTERESSE TERMINI. The interest of a lessee in a lease before it goes into effect.

INTEREST. Money paid for the use of money.

INTERFERENCE. The covering of the same ground by two patents or applications for patents.

INTERIM. In the meantime.

INTERLINEATION. Writing between the lines.

INTERLOCUTORY. Something done between the commencement and the end of a suit.

INTERPLEADER. A proceeding in which rival claimants of property held by a third party, decide the question of title.

INTESTATE. One who dies without having made a will.

INVENTION. The discovery of some new contrivance or process.

INVENTORY. A list in writing of the property of any person.

JAIL. A place of confinement.

JAIL LIBERTIES. The limits of the jail outside of which a prisoner cannot go, even if on bail.

JEOPARDY. Peril or danger.

JETTISON. Throwing part of cargo overboard.

JOINT. United.

JOINT STOCK COMPANY. A sort of partnership with some of the privileges of a corporation. The firm capital is divided into shares.

JOINTURE. A joint estate of husband and wife.

JUDGMENT. The decision of a court.

JUDGMENT DEBTOR. The one against whom a judgment to pay money is rendered.

JURAT. A part of an affidavit.

JURISDICTION. The authority of a court or of an officer.

JURY. A body of men to decide the facts of a case.

JUS AD REM. A right to the thing.

JUSTIFIABLE HOMICIDE. The killing of a man in discharge of official duty.

KINDRED. Relatives by blood.

LACHES. Negligence.

LANDLORD. The proprietor of leased land.

LAPSED LEGACIES. A legacy to a person who dies before the testator.

LARCENY. Stealing.

LAW. A rule of action prescribed by the State.

LAW-MERCHANT. Business law.

LAY-DAYS. The time allowed to load and unload a ship.

LEADING QUESTION. A question which suggests the answer desired.

LEASE. A contract for the rental of land.

LEGACY.   A gift of personal property by will.

LEGAL TENDER.   Money which may be tendered legally for the payment of debts.

LEGITIMACY.   The state of being born in wedlock.

LESSEE.   One to whom a lease is made.

LESSOR.   One who makes a lease.

LET.   A hindrance or obstacle.

LETTER OF CREDIT.   A letter from one person to another requesting him to furnish a certain person with goods or money up to a certain amount, on the strength of the writer's credit.

LETTERS OF MARQUE AND REPRISAL.   A commission granted by government to a private individual to take or capture the goods or ships of an enemy.

LETTERS PATENT.   The instrument by which the government grants a patent right.

LETTERS TESTAMENTARY.   An instrument granted by the Surrogate or Probate Judge to an executor.

LEVY.   A seizure of property by the Sheriff on attachment or execution.

LEX LOCI.   The law of the place.

LEX REI SITÆ.   The law of the place where the thing is situated.

LEX TALIONIS.   The law of retaliation.

LIBEL.   A written defamation of one person by another.

LICENSE.   A permission.

LIEN.   A claim upon the property of another, as a security for a debt.

LIMITATION. The period within which an action must be brought before it is barred.

LIQUIDATED DAMAGES. Damages whose amount has been determined by agreement between the parties.

LIS PENDENS. A pending suit; a notice.

LITIGATION. Contest in a court of justice.

LOCUS SIGILLI. The place of the seal.

MAJORITY. Full age.

MALA FIDES. Bad faith.

MALA PROHIBITA. Things prohibited by law.

MALA IN SE. Things wrong in themselves.

MALICIOUS PROSECUTION. A baseless prosecution without probable cause and with malice.

MANDAMUS. A writ directing some person or body or court to do a particular thing.

MANDATE. A judicial order or command.

MANIFEST. A document containing an account of the cargo of a ship.

MANSLAUGHTER. The unlawful killing of another without malice or intention.

MARINE INSURANCE. Insurance on property at sea or about to go to sea.

MARRIAGE SETTLEMENT. An agreement made by the parties in writing in contemplation of marriage.

MASTER IN CHANCERY. An officer of a Court of Chancery who acts as an assistant to the Chancellor.

MASTER OF A SHIP. The captain or first officer.

MATERIAL MEN. Men who furnish materials for ships, houses, etc.

MAXIM. An established principle.

MAYHEM. Unlawfully depriving another of the use of the members of his body by which he can defend himself

MEASURE OF DAMAGES. The rule by which the amount of damages to be given is estimated.

MERGER. The absorption of one thing into another.

METES AND BOUNDS. The boundary points and lines of land.

MINOR. One under age.

MISDEMEANOR Any offense against the law which is not felony.

MISNOMER. The use of a wrong name.

MISTRIAL. An erroneous trial.

MOIETY. A half.

MORAL OBLIGATION. A duty which one owes, and which he ought to perform, but which he is not legally bound to do.

MORE OR LESS. Words used in describing land in a conveyance to denote that there may be some difference in quantity.

MORTGAGE. The conveyance of property by way of security for a debt,

MORTGAGE. One to whom a mortgage is made and who holds it.

MORTGAGOR. One who makes a mortgage.

MORTMAIN. (Dead hand.) The possession of land by a corporation.

Motion. An application in court by a party to a suit for an order.

Municipal corporation. One created for the purpose of government, such as a city.

Mutatis mutandis. The necessary changes being made.

Mutuality. Acting in return.

Naturalization. The process by which an alien is made a citizen.

Ne exeat. A writ forbidding a person to leave the State without consent of cou

Necessaries. Those things necessary for life and comfort, such as food, clothing, medicine, shelter, etc.

Negotiable paper. Instruments in writing capable of being transferred by indorsement and delivery; promissory notes, bills of exchange, checks, etc.

New trial A re-hearing of the case before another jury

Next of kin. The nearest relative of a deceased person.

Nolle prosequi. An entry on the record by the District Attorney, declaring that he will proced no further; that he is " unwilling to prosecute."

Nominal damages. A trifling sum awarded to the plaintiff, as six cents.

Non compos mentis. Of unsound mind; a lunatic, idiot, imbecile or insane person.

Non constat. "It does not appear."

NON EST FACTUM. It is not my deed; a denial by defendant to a suit on a bond.

NON EST INVENTUS. He is not to be found; or, "I have not found him."

NON-FEASANCE. The non-performance of some act

NON-SUIT. A judgment against the plaintiff dismissing his suit

NOT GUILTY. A plea by the accused to a criminal charge.

NOTARY PUBLIC. An officer appointed by the governor to take affidavits, acknowledgments, to protest bills and notes, etc.

NOTE OF HAND. A promissory note.

NOTICE OF DISHONOR. A notice given to the drawer and indorser of the non-acceptance of a bill, or to indorsers of the non-payment of a note.

NOTICE OF PROTEST. A notice given to a drawer or indorser of a bill, or to the indorser of a note, that the paper has been protested.

NUDUM PACTUM. A contract without consideration.

NUISANCE. Anything which causes annoyance, inconvenience, hurt, or damage.

NULL. Void; without effect.

NUNC PRO TUNC. Now for then.

NUNCUPATIVE WILL. An oral or verbal will made before witnesses by the testator in his last moments, and afterward reduced to writing.

OATH. A form of attestation by which a person

signifies that he feels himself under a special obligation to tell the truth.

OBLIGATION. Duty; a duty imposed by a bond.

OLOGRAPH. An instrument wholly in the handwriting of one person.

ONUS PROBANDI. Burden of proof.

OPEN ACCOUNT. An unsettled account.

OPEN POLICY. A policy in which the amount of
the insurance is not fixed.

ORDER. A mandate of a judge or court.

OUSTER. The turning out of possession of any person entitled to it.

OVERDUE. A bill, bond, note, or other contract
for the payment of money at a particular day, when
not paid on that day, is overdue.

OVER. Open.

OWELTY OF PETITION. Equality; the sum of money necessary to equalize the amount due to each
coparcener.

OYEZ. Hear ye!

PANEL. A list of jurors.

PARAPHERNALIA. The apparel and ornaments of a
wife or widow.

PARCEL. Portion of an estate.

PAROL. Verbal; oral.

PAROL LEASE. A lease not in writing.

PARTITION. The division made between severa.
persons of real estate owned by them all jointly or in
common.

PARTNER. A member of a firm.

PARTY-WALL. A wall erected on the line between two adjoining estates, belonging to different persons, for the use of both estates.

PATENT. A grant of some privilege by the government.

PAWN. A pledge.

PAWNEE. He who receives a pawn; a pawnbroker.

PAWNOR. One who pawns his property.

PAYEE. The person in whose favor a note or bill of exchange or check is made payable.

PENDENTO LITE. During the continuance of the suit.

PER CAPITA. By head.

PER CURIAM. By the court.

PER STIRPES. By the race or family.

PEREMPTORY CHALLENGE. A challenge to a juror by prisoner's counsel without assigning cause.

PERILS OF THE SEA. A phrase in a bill of lading and marine insurance policies.

PERJURY. A false oath in a judicial proceeding on a matter material to the point in question.

PERPETUITY. A limitation of an estate so as to suspend the final ownership for a longer period than is allowed by law, ususally two lives in being and twenty-one years.

PERSONAL ACTION. An action in which one person sues another in regard to personal rights or personal property.

PERSONAL PROPERTY. All movable property; every kind of property not real estate.

PETTY JURY. The ordinary jury of twelve in distinction from the grand jury.

PETTY LARCENY. Stealing of less than a certain sum, usually twenty dollars.

PETITION. An instrument in writing, containing a prayer from the petitioner for some privilege, grant, or redress.

PLAINTIFF. The party who complains or sues.

PLEA. An answer in equity to a complaint.

POLICY. An instrument containing the contract of insurance.

POLL-TAX. A capitation tax; a tax on every head or person.

POSSE COMITATUS. The power of the county; the escort of the Sheriff.

POST-DIEM. After the day.

POST-MORTEM. After the death.

POST-NUPTIAL. After the marriage.

POSTHUMOUS CHILD. One born after the death of its father.

POWER OF ATTORNEY. An instrument authorizing a person to act as agent.

PRAYER. The request in a petition or a bill in equity.

PRECEPT. A writ directed to the sheriff, directing him to do something.

PRE-EMPTION RIGHT. The right given to settlers

upon the public lands of the United States to pur-chase them at a lower price in preference to others.

PREFERENCE. A provision in an assignment by which one or more creditors receive payment in full, or a larger proportion than the other creditors.

PREMISES. That which is put before; land.

PREMIUM. The money payable to an insurance company for insuring.

PRESCRIPTION. Acquisition of rights by long use.

PRESUMPTION. An inference of a disputed fact in accordance with the probabilities.

PRICE. The consideration in money given for the purchase of anything.

PRIMA FACIE. At first sight.

PRIMAGE. A commission due to the master and sailors of a ship.

PRIMOGENITURE. The condition of being the first-born child.

PRINCIPAL. The sum on which interest runs; the employer of an agent.

PRIORITY. Precedence. Having the first right.

PRIVILEGED COMMUNICATION. A statement by one person to another, which is protected by law; which neither party is obliged to divulge in a court of justice, and which is not actionable as slander or libel.

PROBATE OF WILL. The proof of the execution of a will before a Surrogate or Probate Judge.

PROCESS. The writs employed to compel a defend-ant to appear in court.

PROMISSORY NOTE. A written promise to pay a sum of money to another person, without condition.

PROSECUTION. The proceedings to bring one accused of crime to justice and punishment.

PROTEST. Act of a notary made for non-payment of a note or bill.

PROXY. A person appointed to represent and vote for another.

PUTATIVE FATHER. The reputed or supposed father of an illegitimate child.

QUANTUM MERUIT. "As much as he has deserve or earned."

QUIET ENJOYMENT. A covenant in a deed or lease.

QUITCLAIM. A deed granting all the interest of the grantor in the property without any warranty that he has any interest.

QUO WARRANTO. A writ by which the government ascertains by what warrant a corporation acts.

RATIFICATION. An agreement to adopt an unauthorized act of an agent.

REAL ESTATE. Lands, tenements, and hereditaments.

RECEIPT. A written acknowledgment of money paid.

RECEIVER. A person appointed by a court of equity to receive the rents and profits of land or of a business, to wind up the affairs of a partnership or corporation.

RECISION OF A CONTRACT. The annulling of a contract.

RECOGNIZANCE. A bond of record entered into before a court, with a condition to do some act, as to appear in court.

RECORD. A written account of something done or written or said.

RECRIMINATION. A counter-charge made by a person accused against his accuser of having committed the same or another offense.

REDEMPTION. The purchase back by the seller from the buyer

REFERENCE. The sending of a suit for a hearing before a referee.

RE-INSURANCE. The insurance by an insurer of risks taken by him in another company and usually at a smaller premium.

RELEASE. The giving up a claim against a person.

REMAINDER. The estate which finally rests in some person after previous interests, such as life-estates.

RENT. A return for the use of land.

RENUNCIATION. The giving up of a right.

REPLEVIN. A form of action to recover the possession of personal property wrongfully withheld.

REPUBLICATION OF WILL. The re-execution of a will which has been revoked by the testator.

RES JUDICATA. A legal question decided by a court, so as to settle the law.

RESIDUARY LEGATEE. One to whom the remainder of an estate is bequeathed after the payment of debts and legacies.

RESPONDENTIA. A loan of money at high rates of interest on the cargo of a ship as security.

RETAINER. The act of a person in engaging a lawyer to manage a case; the fee paid to the latter at that time.

RETURN-DAY. Day when writs must be returned to the court from which they are issued.

REVERSION. The coming of an estate to the grantor, or his heirs, after being enjoyed by others.

REVERSAL. The decision of a Superior or Appellate Court, overturning the judgment of an inferior court.

REVOCATION. The recall of the authority given to an agent; the destruction or change of a will.

ROBBERY. Stealing from the person.

RULES OF PRACTICE. Order made by courts for the purpose of regulating court business.

SALVAGE. Compensation given to those who save property at sea.

SATISFACTION. Payment of a debt; the cancelling of a mortgage.

SCILICET. That is to say.

SEAL. An impression on wax; something affixed to a paper by an adhesive substance.

SEARCH-WARRANT. A warrant directing an officer to search a house for stolen property, of the person of a fugitive from justice.

SEIZIN. Possession of land with the right of ownership.

SEMPER PARATUS. Always ready.

SEPARATE ESTATE. The estate which belongs to a married woman and over which her husband has no control

SEPARATION. Living apart of husband and wife; partial divorce.

SET OFF. A demand made by the defendant against the plaintiff to reduce the amount of his recovery.

SHIP'S HUSBAND. An agent of the owner of the ship who attends to repairs and general equipment of the ship.

SHIPPING ARTICLES. An agreement in writing between the master of a ship and the seamen, as to the voyage, wages, etc.

SINE DIE. Without date.

SLANDER. Words spoken tending to injure the character of another, and which are untrue.

SPECIAL PLEADING. A plea not denying the truth of the plaintiff's statements, but which sets forth other reasons why he should not recover.

SPECIFIC LEGACY. A bequest of a particular thing,

SPECIFIC PERFORMANCE. The actual performance of the contract compelled by the court.

SPECIFICATION. The detailed description of an invention.

STARE DECISIS. To stand by decided cases.

STATUS. The condition, station, or position of persons.

STATUTE. A law established by act of the Legislature.

STOCK. Goods and merchandise; the capital of a corporation.

STOPPAGE IN TRANSITU. The right of a seller to stop the delivery of goods in transit to the buyer, in case the latter becomes insolvent before the goods reach him.

SUBAGENT. An agent appointed by an agent to do something for him in a matter connected with the agency.

SUBMISSION. The agreement to submit a controversy to the decision of arbitrators.

SUBORNATION OF PERJURY. Inducing a person to perjure himself by money or otherwise.

SUBPŒNA. A process or writ ordering a person to appear before a court and testify.

SUI JURIS. Of his own right.

SUIT. An action at law.

SUMMONS. A writ ordering a defendant to answer the complaint against him.

SUPPRESSION VERI. Concealment of truth.

SURETY. One who promises to pay the debt of another if he does not.

SURRENDER. Yielding up possession of leased premises to the landlord.

SURROGATE. A judge who has jurisdiction of wills and estates of intestates.

TENANT. One who hires land of another for a definite period.

TENDER. Offer to deliver something.

TENEMENT. House, building, land; anything that can be held.

TERM. The period for which a lease is to run.

TESTATOR. One who makes a will

TESTATRIX. A woman who makes a will.

TESTIMONY. The sworn statements of witnesses.

TITLE. The ownership of property.

TORT. A wrong done to an individual.

TRADE-MARK. A symbol or mark placed by a tradesman or manufacturer on his goods.

TRAVERSE. To deny.

TRESPASS. An unlawful entry on the real estate of another; any wrongful act done to the person, property or rights of another.

TRIAL. The examination of the facts of a case before a court.

TROVER. A form of action to recover damages against one who has appropriated the property of another to his own use.

TRUST. A right of property held by one person for the benefit of another.

TRUSTEE. One who holds such property.

ULTRA VIRES. Acts done by corporation in excess of their powers.

USE AND OCCUPATION. Where no rent was agreed upon, the owner of land, the landlord, is entitled to a reasonable amount for use and occupation.

USURY. Taking of more than legal interest for the use of money.

VALUABLE CONSIDERATION. An equivalent in money or something having value.

VALUE RECEIVED. Phrase used in notes and bills.

VALUED POLICY. An insurance policy where the goods have been valued and the amount of risk is stated.

VENDEE. The purchaser.

VENDOR. The seller.

VENDOR'S LIEN. The lien or claim of the seller upon the article sold for as much of the price as is unpaid.

VENUE. Neighborhood.

VERDICT. Unanimous decision of a jury on the facts of a case.

VERSUS. Against.

VI ET ARMIS. With force and arms.

VIS MAJOR. Superior force; inevitable accident.

VIVA VOCE. Verbally.

VOLUNTARY CONVEYANCE. Deed of an estate without adequate consideration.

VOUCHERS. Receipts, etc.

WAIVER. The giving up of a right.

WARD. Infant in charge of guardian.

WARRANT. A writ issued by a judge.

WARRANTY. An agreement to make good all defects in an article sold; a stipulation in an insurance policy.

WASTE. Injury done to real estate by a tenant to the prejudice of the owner.

WILL.   A disposition of property in writing by the owner, to take effect after his death.

WITNESS.   One who testifies as to a matter of knowledge.

WRIT.   An order of court.

INDEX.

www.ingramcontent.com/pod-product-compliance
Lightning Source LLC
Chambersburg PA
CBHW032313280326
41932CB00009B/801